Fiscal policy

Trends in taxation, monetary control and public debt spread throughout the developed world. The UK has been at the forefront of some of these changes and in turn has been influenced by other countries' policies.

Graham Hockley provides the reader with a comprehensive introduction to fiscal policy, concentrating on recent developments. Encompassing both financial issues and 'real' problems of inflation, unemployment, housing and poverty, it uses up-to-date material from the USA, Australia and Japan, and focuses particularly on current changes in Europe.

Fiscal policy looks initially at the role of the state, public choice, government expenditure, taxation and debt. It then goes on to analyse in greater depth the aims and principles of public finance, covering the various ways the budget impacts on the economy, ability to pay, wealth, poverty and social security. Micro- and macro-economic policy is examined and the problems associated with multi-level government is considered in depth. The book concludes with an assessment of the European Monetary System and Community Budget.

By offering a variety of approaches to the key topics, Graham Hockley provides a stimulating analysis of the essentials of fiscal policy.

Fiscal policy

An Introduction

Graham C. Hockley

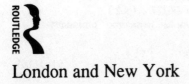

London and New York

First published 1992
by Routledge
11 New Fetter Lane, London EC4P 4EE

Simultaneously published in the USA and Canada
by Routledge
a division of Routledge, Chapman and Hall, Inc.
29 West 35th Street, New York, NY 10001

© 1992 Graham C. Hockley

Typeset in Times by LaserScript, Mitcham, Surrey
Printed and bound in Great Britain by Mackays of Chatham PLC, Chatham,
Kent

British Library Cataloguing in Publication Data

0–415–06276–4 Hb
0–415–06277–2 Pb

A catalogue entry for this book is available from the British Library.

Library of Congress Cataloging in Publication Data

Hockley, Graham C.
    Fiscal policy : an introduction / Graham C. Hockley.
        p.   cm.
    Includes bibliographical references and index.
    ISBN 0–415–06276–4. — ISBN 0–415–06277–2 (pbk.)
    1. Fiscal policy.   2. Fiscal policy–European Economic Community
countries. I. Title.
HJ192.H63 1992   1055134 4
336.3–dc20
                                                        91–31161
                                                          CIP

22/10/92

To Irene, Andrew, Corinne and Steve

Contents

Figures

Tables

Preface

Fiscal policy has now come, when widely interpreted, to encompass the corpus of what used to be called 'public finance'. The latter term is out of favour as it carries the implication that the subject is confined to financial issues whereas 'real' problems of economic incentives, and aggregate management of the economy, inflation and employment levels are also very much its concern.

This book is intended as an introduction text for university courses and for students studying for professional examinations. Also, it should be intelligible, and of interest, to the general reader.

The author's earlier volume on Public Finance carried considerable detail about the UK system; this volume makes a conscious effort to put fiscal policy in a wider context. Ideas, perhaps fashions is not an inappropriate word, in both taxation and the role of the state now spread quickly in the developed world and this volume traces the changes that have been made in recent years. While most emphasis is placed on the European Community, the wider grouping of countries in the Organization for Economic Co-operation and Development and other developed economies are included as appropriate.

Part I of this volume, 'The public sector', starts in Chapter 1 by raising old, but still unresolved and important, issues about the correct role of the state, its size and efficiency. These have been made even more topical by global pollution problems and by events in the East, where Communist regimes have failed to deliver adequate living standards to their populations. Chapter 2 examines government expenditures; the difficulties of defining what this is, due, for example, to the high level of 'tax expenditures' and of making comparisons over time and between countries. It examines the factors influencing the level of expenditures. This chapter contains a section on public choice: the possible motivation of politicians, bureaucrats and voters who together

determine budget decisions. Chapter 3 is about the nature of tax changes
in the 1980s and differences in countries' tax regimes. Tax changes,
rather than overall tax reductions, characterized this period. In most
countries tax burdens continued to rise but there was a switch from
income taxation to indirect tax on the grounds that this would achieve
greater neutrality and more allocative efficiency. As part of this process
there was a reduction in the marginal rates of income tax and the number
of tax bands. Income tax rates were lowered and top rates reduced
relative to standard rates, by a combination of broadening the base of
income tax and switching taxes to consumption. A section looks at
compliance costs. Chapter 4 examines some of the many aspects of
National Debt and the Public Sector Borrowing Requirement. The upward trend in public expenditure when expressed as a proportion of
GNP, experienced in most countries has slowed or showed a slight
reversal in the late 1980s.

Part II, Chapters 5 to 9, deal with the core of public finance. Chapter
5 examines principles of public finance; the allocation, distribution and
stabilization aspects of fiscal policy. The concepts of fiscal neutrality,
optimal taxation, horizontal and vertical equity, and the benefit and
ability to pay principles. Chapter 6 has an extensive discussion of ability
to pay in the context of an expenditure and an income based tax.
Problems common to either base: valuation, inflation, fluctuating income or expenditure and the taxpaying unit are explored. Chapter 7
looks at various concepts of incidence and examines the latest UK
budget studies of the incidence of taxes and benefits. Chapter 8 looks at
various concepts of wealth and the part played by land, other assets
generating economic rent, and housing. The case for and against taxing
wealth is taken up with alternative wealth taxes considered. Chapter 9
examines social security systems and poverty. It reports studies for the
UK showing an increase in inequality and poverty during the 1980s.
Problems caused by the overlap of tax and benefit systems and methods
of extending financial help are given.

Part III, in Chapter 10, examines the effect of taxation on various
choices: personal and corporate saving, investment, prices and output,
and work effort. Chapter 11 takes up the problems associated with
macro-economic management of the economy and whether management is desirable. Supply-side policies and monetary control, features of
the 1980s, are taken up. An Appendix on Chaos Theory shows how this
recent work in mathematics throws doubt on the ability of economic
models to predict the long term behaviour of the economy.

Part IV, in Chapter 12, looks at the difficult and controversial questions surrounding the division of public sector responsibilities between different layers of government, within a country, and how these layers should be financed. The meaning of 'tax effort' and the various types of equalization that can be attempted are given. An Appendix examines The Community Charge, or poll tax, in the UK. Chapter 13 broadens these issues out to embrace wider relations between groups of countries with particular reference to the European Community. Reasons for and against harmonization are given and the substantial benefits that can be expected from the Single European Market of 1992. The difficulties of striking down tax barriers within the community are examined.

Part V, the final section, deals in Chapter 14 with the European Monetary System. A brief account of European monetary co-operation since the War is given and the aims and successes of the European Monetary System set out. The workings of the European Currency Unit and its current uses, together with the exchange rate and intervention mechanism are given. Chapter 15 examines issues of the Community budget after setting out the background details of the European Community. The dominance of agricultural spending is explained and the serious threat to world trade this now poses. The Community institutions concerned with the budget are set out, together with details of how the budget is formulated. Recent changes that have been made to financing and spending in preparation for the single European market of 1992 are noted.

Acknowledgements

I wish to record my great indebtedness to Jean Walters and Arnold Thomas, who read the bulk of the manuscript and made many suggestions for improvement. Caroline Joll, Bob Turner, Sir Bryan Hopkin, and Professor A. Dreyer all helped with selected chapters. I claim for myself any remaining shortcomings.

The author and publisher would also like to thank the following: the Organisation for Economic Co-operation and Development for permission to quote the figures on pages 25, 43 and 68; the Office for Official Publications of the European Communities for permission to quote the table on page 27; the Controller of Her Majesty's Stationery Office for permission to use material from *Economic Trends* on pages 28, 44, 46, 112, 117, 118 and 119, and from the National Accounts on page 171; the Institute of Fiscal Studies for the table on page 135; and George Allen & Unwin for the extract from D.R. Denman, *Origins of Ownership*, 1958.

Abbreviations

BIS	Bank for International Settlements (p.228)
CAP	Common Agricultural Policy (pp.238–43)
CEN	Capital export neutrality (pp.211–12)
CIN	Capital import neutrality (pp.211–12)
EBA	Eco Banking Association (p.228)
EBRD	European Bank for Reconstruction and Development (p.248)
EC	European Community
ECB	European Central Bank see ESCB
Ecofin	European Community Finance Ministers (p.223)
ECSC	European Coal and Steel Community (pp.229, 238, 243, 247)
Ecu	European Currency Unit (pp.225–6)
EDF	European Development Fund (p.246)
EEA	European Economic Area (pp.221–2)
EFTA	European Free Trade Association (pp.221–2)
EIB	European Investment Bank (pp.248–9)
EMCF	European Monetary Cooperation Fund (pp.227, 232)
EMF	European Monetary Fund (p.232)
EMS	European Monetary System (pp.221–35)
EMU	European Monetary Union (p.233)
ESA	European System of Integrated Accounts (p.26)
ESCB or Eurofed	European System of Central Bankers (p.233)
Euratom	European Atomic Energy Committee (p.238)
IMF	International Monetary Fund (p.242)
MTFS	Medium Term Financial Strategy (pp.35, 66, 177)
NATO	North Atlantic Treaty Organisation (pp.221–2, 238)

OECD	Organisation for Economic Co-operation and Development (pp.221–2)
PAYE	Pay-as-you-earn (p.31)
PBC	Public business cycle (pp.35, 38)
PES	Public Expenditure Surveys (p.34)
PSBR	Public Sector Borrowing Requirement (pp.24, 34–5, 66–78, 174–7)
PSDR	Public Sector Debt Repayment (p.66)
PT	Partisan theory
VAT	Value Added Tax

Part I

The public sector

Chapter 1

The role of the state

INTRODUCTION

Discussion about the role of the state is an old one. As Keynes (1926) said:

> We cannot therefore settle on abstract grounds, but must handle on its merits in detail what Burke termed 'one of the finest problems in legislation', namely, to determine what the State ought to take upon itself to direct by the public wisdom, and what it ought to leave, with as little interference as possible, to individual exertion.

The past decade has seen a particularly lively debate about this issue. There has been a world-wide retreat from direct state provision of services, and changes in regulation, particularly in currency and financial markets. The changes have frequently been towards less regulation but sometimes this has been more apparent than real. The form has shifted towards self-regulation which does not always mean less control. In some areas, for example the environment, regulation has increased.

In the 1990s the debate about the role of the state is being re-enacted with particular urgency in the Communist bloc. The failure of the Communist command type economy to deliver satisfactory living standards to its citizens has been a powerful force in the reappraisal they are currently undertaking, old barriers and stereotypes are being re-examined.

In this chapter the role of the state is examined as it operates through revenue and expenditure policies. The economic welfare of an individual is their command over goods and services. This command comes from income from work, income from savings, accumulated wealth, inheritance, gifts, government provision and legislation.

This book is not concerned with the return from work as such. It is sufficient to note that returns from different kinds of work are altered by society in various ways. The beginning of this century saw the start of minimum wage legislation; more recently equal pay legislation has changed the income of women doing similar work to men. The provision of education and training out of general taxation, so that entry to work requiring formal training is no longer confined to those able to afford it, has been of considerable practical importance. Parts I to III of this book show, within the existing framework of income distribution, how the individual, corporation and the economy are influenced by taxation and government provision.

After giving the advantages of a competitive pricing system the necessity, nevertheless, for government intervention and therefore the need for raising revenue or debt is argued on a number of grounds.

ADVANTAGES OF COMPETITIVE MARKET PRICES

The model of a perfectly competitive pricing system has often been held up as an ideal: prices act as a guide to producers as to the goods and services and quantities of these that they should produce with competition ensuring least cost production. High prices obtainable for their output stimulate firms to expand and other firms to enter the market and higher prices force the consumer to consider the relative scarcity of goods. Lower prices stimulate consumption and force firms to reconsider the quantity they produce and possibly leave the market entirely. The interplay of market forces usually results in an equilibrium price being established at which supply and demand are in balance. Assuming certain assumptions are met, output will be optimum. The usefulness of the price mechanism in invisibly, but not costlessly, arranging the immensely complex assortment of goods and services found in a modern developed economy is hard to overstate. Most economies revert to planning in wartime because the aims of society are simplified and channelled into the war effort. Central planning for a peacetime consumer society with a wide variety of goods and services is much more difficult. Inefficiency, lack of incentives and bureaucracy are hard to combat as both the capitalist and more particularly the Communist world have found out to their cost.

IMPERFECTIONS OF COMPETITIVE MARKET PRICES

If the market system is so good why is it not possible to leave everything to market forces? Not even the most ardent supporters of free markets are willing to go to this extreme and it will be seen that it is the imperfections of the pricing system, or market failure, which provide a role for government intervention. The market mechanism, by itself, does not produce the best of all possible worlds, and intervention is needed to correct its deficiencies and supplement its role.

One drawback of a pricing system in allocating goods is that it only takes account of *effective demand*, i.e. demand backed by money. As income and wealth are unevenly spread, deficiencies in allocation will occur. Few people are willing to see others nearby starve (a motive that may not extend to those in other countries) and a developed economy is able to afford to redistribute to these unfortunates who will include many old, young or disabled persons. Similar considerations apply to those who are genuinely unable to find work. 'The invisible hand is blind to even the grossest inequalities of power and wealth within an economy' (Hammond 1990). It can be shown (Coles and Hammond 1986) that perfectly competitive markets are quite capable of producing Pareto efficient markets in which some consumers have insufficient resources to survive. This deficiency in allocation of goods may be relieved by private charity but few believe that private charity is capable of providing more than marginal help. If this is so it provides a powerful reason why people tolerate and indeed welcome some state intervention, either to redistribute income and/or wealth to some extent, or to ensure in other ways some basic standard of living for its citizens. These arguments can be used to support social insurance over private insurance schemes. Those that fail to provide insurance for themselves, such as for illness, unemployment or old age are likely to become an expense on the public purse and therefore on those who have been prudent and made such insurance provision. Compulsory insurance, or meeting these charges out of general taxation, can thus be seen as a way of spreading the fiscal burden in a more equitable way.

Another important modification to the competitive pricing system ideal has long been recognized although the global nature of the problem is only now coming to the fore. It is usually discussed under the heading of *externalities* although the terms spill-outs and spill-ins and neighbourhood effects may be used. Positive externalities draw attention to the fact that some goods, and services confer large benefits not only on the person directly involved but on other people as well. The costs and benefits experienced by the individual are referred to as private costs and benefits, the wider costs and benefits felt by the community as social costs and benefits. Steps the individual takes to keep healthy such as cleanliness and having inoculations against disease can benefit society generally by keeping epidemics down. Education benefits the individual concerned and the wider public. More newsworthy are negative externalities where harm is done to other people, for example, noise, dirt, pollution and possibly global warming.

The free market system does not price these third party consequences so that goods with positive externalities are likely to be under-produced and those with negative externalities are likely to be over-produced. Part of the difficulty is referred to as the 'free-rider' problem. People may hope to benefit from the provision made by other people without providing anything themselves. People who dislike inoculations, or the cost of paying for them if they are subject to a charge, may reason that they are in no danger if everyone else is inoculated and they are not. Of course if many people reason in this way there is a danger of the disease spreading. Provision for sewage disposal and water supply can be left to the individual in a sparsely populated area, but the concentration of populations in towns make it essential to ensure that both are adequate, whether these are provided directly by the state or by private markets under state supervision. It is no accident that many of the diseases of the past have been eliminated from developed countries since the state took up the responsibility of ensuring these basic services.

Governments are therefore seen to have a role in trying to correct for these deficiencies and trying to ensure an optimum supply. They can tackle externalities by regulation, taxes, subsidies or pricing pollution. We leave open the political question of whether the government should itself undertake the provision of the service and, if so, how the cost should be met, or whether the government should supervise, and, if necessary, subsidize the private provision of the service. Either route means that market forces are modified.

In extreme cases any provision of a service means provision for everybody, the goods are indivisible and non-rival in consumption, i.e one person's consumption does not diminish the supply available to others. These services are termed social goods or '*pure public goods*'. Defence against external aggression and police protection are obvious examples. It is a nonsense to think of setting up a defence system only for the county of Surrey, or for enforcing traffic laws only on red headed people. In these cases the pricing system cannot operate and provision of these services if left in private hands is likely to result in zero or very little supply. Defence cannot be packaged and sold in little bits. In other words the pricing system requires 'exclusion' – the ability to exclude those not paying from enjoyment of the product and the ability to price the product. Private consumption is described as rival i.e. consumption by A excludes consumption by B. The meal you have just eaten is not available for anyone else to enjoy.

The essence of public or social goods is that because consumption is non-rival pricing is inappropriate even if it is feasible. Efficient resource use requires that price equals marginal cost and in the case of social goods the cost of an additional user is zero. Social goods then fall in two categories: firstly, those that cannot be priced, or where pricing could be applied but since additional users impose no cost it is inappropriate to do so, and secondly, those where pricing would be prohibitively expensive. The principle is clear but the practice shows little consistency. The issues can be discussed in relation to roads and radio and TV broadcasting.

The cost of providing these services has to be met but direct pricing deters some users from the service and so some social benefit will be lost where the cost of an additional user is zero. The position is, however, complicated if congestion is possible; this can apply to roads but not broadcasting. The social cost of an additional user of a congested road can be high as he further delays the flow of traffic and imposes costs on all other drivers. On the other hand many toll roads are under-utilized as traffic prefers the more congested but free roads. Diverting traffic to the under-utilized toll roads could have substantial social benefits. In Britain at present, apart from a few ancient private charges, tolls are only charged on public roads at a few river crossings such as the Severn, Thames, Humber and Forth. The rationale behind charges in these few places has never been satisfactorily explained (except as an expedient to raise revenue) since many other new river crossings have been established without being subject to tolls. Technology now makes it possible to price all roads by fitting meters to vehicles which are triggered by electrical pulses from cables buried in the road, or placed at intervals along the road. Charges could be set to vary with the time of day, degree of traffic congestion and so on. To offset the cost of meters and cables it is suggested that there would be large savings in infrastructure costs as people would rationalize their vehicle use in line with true cost, rather than at present only having to take their own marginal cost into account. In economic terms the congestion costs, estimated by the Confederation of British Industry at £15 billion per annum in the UK, would be internalized. At the present time, although a number of countries have examined the case for road pricing on these lines, Singapore is the only country that has experimented with it.

Broadcasting is a case where an additional user imposes no cost on the supplier or other users; the radio or TV signals are waiting to be picked up by anyone with suitable equipment. Setting up property rights by allowing companies to scramble their signals and to prosecute those evading their charges is, however, common in many countries. The rationale is presumably that private enterprise will not provide the service unless it has property rights which allows it to sell the product and the state does not deem the service to have sufficient social benefit to merit free (or subsidized) access with the cost met out of general taxation. The alternative, or additional, method of financing is to allow advertising, the revenue from this financing the programme. It seems that this is an example where a monopoly producer is likely to produce a more varied programme than competitive firms (Steiner 1961). In both methods of payment revenue largely depend on the size of the audience for the programme. This is obvious in the case of direct payment by the viewer. The rates broadcasting companies can charge for advertising also depend heavily on audience ratings. Competitive firms are naturally driven to cater for the tastes of the majority. Since the audience for pop music is larger than for classical music the former is likely to drive out the latter. If quiz programmes reach an audience of 5 million people and documentary programmes an audience of 500,000 people, firms in competition with each other are likely to maximize profits by competing for a share of the larger audience, rather than catering for the minority taste. A monopoly producer wishing to maximize the audience will of necessity extend coverage to minority interests once he has catered for the majority.

Another aspect of many services is that they result in 'natural' monopolies. Having many companies laying duplicate services for rail, gas, electricity, water, sewerage and telephones makes little sense. One or a few companies is the likely result and if this is so governments are likely to want to regulate the firms in the public interest. Competition may be introduced by giving one company power as a common carrier, responsible for the track, pipeline, cable or other infrastructure and ensuring regulation of that company so as not to discriminate against users. Unfortunately in Britain little use has been made of this method of introducing competition into industries that have been privatized.

Governments also, rather more controversially, intervene in markets in the case of merit or demerit goods. Merit goods are those deemed by the government in the public interest such as education, health and public open spaces. The majority, it is suggested, support the provision or subsidizing of merit goods because they feel local or national pride and these goods help bind a community together. Demerit goods are those deemed harmful such as alcohol, tobacco and drugs. Government advertising can be used to encourage or discourage the use of these goods while subsidies and taxes are alternative methods. Outright prohibition is resorted to in the case of a few goods such as dangerous drugs. Good intentions are unfortunately not always sufficient to ensure good outcomes. Some commentators charge the prohibition of alcohol in the United States in the 1930s with much of the organized crime that is found there and puts its continuance and expansion down to the prohibition of drugs. Prohibition undoubtedly gives the opportunity for enormous illegal profits to be made and the use of this money in bribes and other illegal activities can corrode the fabric of society. Freeing drug use from illegality and subjecting it, like alcohol, to high taxation and curbs on advertising, seems unthinkable to most people but a number of serious writers have suggested it as the lesser of two evils. A summary discussion of the issues is found in Dialogue No. 3 (1989).

The smooth working of a market system may also be upset by groups exercising some degree of market monopoly power. Such power may be exercised by producers, workers, or more rarely, consumers. Power may be exercised through some legal right, by the large size of the unit in relation to the total market or from collusion between smaller units. Most governments take the view that this is a breach of free markets with the potential to harm the public interest and seek to regulate such activities.

As a final point the market system can fail to establish an equilibrium or achieve society's aims such as growth, price stability and high employment. If left to itself the system appears to be subject to periodic boom and slump. Most governments hope that they can smooth the economy by using a variety of means. The extent to which they succeed in this task is not easy to assess and it is possible to point to occasions where they have made matters worse. For example, attempts to stimulate the economy during a downturn, by the time they take effect, may occur when the economy is experiencing overheating. Most commentators would not rule out action because of faulty diagnosis or prescription but urge better diagnosis and more appropriate measures. The government can use a variety of other measures beside tax and spending policy such as monetary policy, regulation, planning and the encouragement of future or other markets for risk-taking. A controversial aspect of this market failure is the charge that private capital markets may not provide adequate finance for important sectors of the economy such as small risky projects, or providing capital to large firms that may be in temporary difficulty. Markets are charged with 'short-termism' – being interested only in short-term gains. Supplying capital, directly or indirectly, from the state is then seen as a way of compensating for this failure. Most governments have provided finance to help out in this way in exceptional circumstances, e.g. in the UK to British Leyland and Rolls-Royce and in the United States to Chrysler.

IMPERFECTION OF GOVERNMENT INTERVENTION

It has been established that the free market system has drawbacks; it must also be borne in mind that intervention by the government to correct for these deficiencies also has a cost, and if carried too far can be self-defeating. Who produces the goods, the state or the private sector, is not at issue here, the concern is how the state ensures provision of goods and services to consumers (whether produced privately or by the state) when the cost is met in whole or partly out of general taxation, or when the state decides to intervene in a market for some other reason such as to ensure safety or regulatory standards. The cost makes itself felt in the resources of manpower, materials and money that have to be devoted to this intervention but more importantly in the distortions to the economy that can be introduced.

A prime example of harmful intervention is the American system of regulation of certain financial institutions. Poor regulation in the 1980s was compounded by the fact that deposits were insured up to a limit of $100,000. This places the regulator in 'moral hazard'. Depositors have no need to seek out credit worthy institutions – in fact astute investors simply seek out the highest rate knowing they will get their money back even if the institution fails, and, in the meanwhile they benefit from higher than average returns. The cost to the taxpayer, of rescuing the savings and loan associations (S & Ls), equivalent to British building societies, has been put at an enormous $500 billion ($500,000 million). This figure is tentative but not the highest estimate that has been put forward. It is equivalent to $2,000 for every taxpayer in the United States. S & Ls had much of their lending out on low fixed-interest terms and the increased interest rates in the 1980s was reflected in the S & Ls having to pay more for their deposits. Coupled with considerable deregulation in 1982 this initiated a wave of innovative, but more risky, lending outside their traditional business. Given the 100 per cent guarantee on deposits up to $100,000 dollars the way was open for dishonest operators to obtain deposits by offering rates slightly above their competitors, using the proceeds to line their own pockets. The depositors had no need to establish the uses to which their money was being put, only to ensure they placed no more than $100,000 in any one institution.

In Britain more than 40 years of government intervention in the provision of electricity by nuclear power is another example of the cost of government intervention. In the United States nuclear power expansion was halted when researchers were able, under the Freedom of Information Act, to challenge the cost and safety assumptions made by the electricity industry. In the UK nuclear power was promoted by the government and the Central Electricity Generating Board as producing cheaper electricity than that obtained from coal-fired stations. Information to challenge these findings was refused to private researchers. As a result of privatization of the electricity industry in 1990–1, it seems that nuclear power has never produced electricity at an economic price and the consumer is to be saddled with paying £900 million per annum as a subsidy to keep it going. As a final example, government intervention in the housing market in the UK, by means of rent and tenancy controls since the First World War, has resulted in the virtual demise of the private rented sector.

As with so many economic activities there is a trade-off between correcting for deficiencies and the distortion bureaucracy, friction and frustration which this can engender. The optimum position to draw the line is often hard to see. Bhagwati used the phrase *directly unproductive profit-seeking* to cover activities which while rational from an individual's or firm's point of view do not directly contribute to the output of goods and services. Responses to government policy are part of a much wider range of activities which may give rise to such social loss. Thus much of the activity of parliamentary pressure groups to seek protection, alter government spending, change taxation or government regulation falls in the category of directly unproductive profit-seeking. Actions to evade government policy are another example. Resources are devoted to *tax avoidance* or *tax evasion*. The difference is that tax avoidance is using legal means to reduce taxation, tax evasion is using illegal means. Smuggling and bribery are further examples of such distortion.

THE GOVERNMENT SECTOR

The previous account helps to put a discussion of the public sector in perspective. Three questions are frequently posed:

1 How big should the government sector be?
2 How to determine how much to produce when the price system is inoperative, either through necessity, or a deliberate choice to meet

the cost out of general taxation?
3 How to ensure that expenditures are efficiently, not wastefully, applied?

How Big?

On the first question on the optimum size of the government sector the economist has no unique answer, although nonsense figures are put forward from time to time, for example Friedman (1976). For one thing the level of government spending can be made to mean almost anything that the government wants it to. The question implies incorrectly that a level of activity can be specified which will be valid over time, valid under varying conditions, and which admits of a unique solution. 'Public goods', where externalities are large, are not constant over time. The growth, and particularly the concentration of population, means that problems of health and amenities (open spaces, clean air, water supply, sewerage, communications, and so on) have more externalities. If size is measured by the amount of government expenditure, it is worth emphasizing that different decisions on the way to achieve a particular object will involve different levels of government expenditure. For example, a decision to maintain employment in the coal industry can be achieved by subsidies to the industry or to coal users, which will raise expenditure, or by tariffs, which will not. Similarly the government may undertake to redistribute income to a particular sector which will add to government expenditure or to do this by means of a tax expenditure (explained in Chapter 3) which will not show as increased outlay. The conclusion is that the level of government activity at any one time is, in a democracy, essentially decided by political means. The inherent difficulty in determining the right quantity of social goods is the problem of getting people to reveal their true preferences since they are not directly paying for these goods. In a democratic state votes are substituted for money in the decision process.

How Much?

The question of how much to produce, say of defence or public health, where the price system is inoperative, is an important one that admits of no easy solution. The principle of achieving equal marginal benefits from various expenditures needs to be borne in mind; it may avoid crude waste of expenditure. This important point about equal marginal benefit is illustrated in Figure 1.1 for allocating a fixed sum between two different projects. The principle generalizes for any number of projects. On the vertical axis are shown the marginal benefits from two projects and on the horizontal axis the amount of expenditure.

In order to achieve maximum satisfaction from spending a fixed sum, given the marginal benefit curves shown, a sum OA should be spent on A and OB on B where OA and OB sum to the given outlay. At this point marginal benefits are equal and total marginal benefit cannot be increased by reallocating expenditure between the projects. The graph highlights the economic concept of opportunity cost: to spend more on A involves less on B and vice versa. The total sum to be spent by the public sector as opposed to the private sector can in principle be shown to be the same the marginal benefit from each sector should be equal to achieve the highest level of satisfaction.

This reasoning may appear totally abstract but it can be used to counter the understandably emotionally, but wrong, reasoning of the kind: 'if only one life is saved the expenditure (on, say, a road modification, or a particular safety device) is worth while.' If the objective is

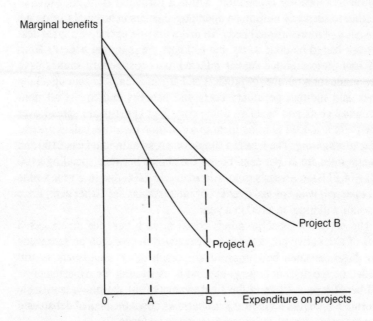

Figure 1.1   Equal marginal benefit

to save life the question that should be considered is 'In what way can this particular sum of money be spent so as to save the most lives?' This idea can be turned round to judge the effectiveness of past decisions. Mooney (1978) quoted estimates that in the UK a change in building regulations, made after a corner of a block of flats collapsed after a gas explosion in Britain, cost over £20 million per life saved. At the other extreme a test on pregnant women to prevent still births was estimated to cost less than £50 per life saved. The former was undertaken the latter was not. The economist is not, it should be stressed in these cases, saying that the value of a person is £25 million or £50 but is simply pointing out that society by its actions has put these implicit values on human life. If the object is to save life, these decisions were extremely callous. Future decisions, say on hospital spending, can be better informed if the information about the cost of saving human life in alternative ways is available.

As a practical guide for day-to-day decision-making, putting this rule into practice is not easy. Knowing whether £1 million spent on hospitals would yield more benefit than £1 million spent on defence or roads is more a matter of judgement than fact. This principle is likely to be more fruitful in allocating expenditure within a particular field, for example whether to spend £1 million on operating-theatres in hospitals, or on the provision of more hospital beds. To make the rule operative a great deal of work has to be done to try and estimate the marginal benefits from different projects. Such studies referred to as cost benefit studies have been made for a number of projects and are an attempt to sum up all the direct and indirect pecuniary costs and benefits and to list all non-pecuniary costs and benefits. Since costs and benefits are spread over time there is a need to bring them to a common measure, called *present value discounting*. The idea is a simple one if an individual has £100 and interest rates are 10 per cent, he has the choice between spending £100 today or £110 in a year's time. Alternatively £100 due in a year's time has a *present value* of just over £90 if interest rates are 10 per cent, since this sum will grow to £100 in a year.

The net sums (benefits minus costs) in each year for the expected lives of alternative projects can be discounted to give their present value and these can then be compared with each other. Judgement is still needed on the discount rate to use and in estimating the expected costs and benefits as well as in the final evaluation of the non-quantifiable information but the method at least narrows down the area of debate and should enable a more informed decision to be made.

A similar set of considerations apply to Cost Effectiveness Analysis.

Here the benefits are taken for granted and a comparison is made between different ways of achieving the same outcome. For example, would commuters to a business centre of a city be served most cheaply by an overhead rail, underground or a surface transport system?

One way out of the difficulty of weighing up expenditure in disparate activities is to set up minimum standards of service, suggested by Drees (1967), say a policeman for every 1,000 of the population, the elimination of serious epidemics, maximum size of school classes of 25, maximum permitted levels of pollution, and so on. Provided these standards are based on the cost and benefits that flow from achieving them, they should aid decision-making. The standards will not be obtainable overnight but quantifying the costs and benefits and listing the non-quantifiable advantages and disadvantages should enable more rational decision-making. On the question of deciding how much of a particular good should be produced in the absence of price guidelines, no economist would claim that, with existing knowledge and techniques, they can do more than assist in decision-making, however the assistance given is a valuable one.

Efficiency

The question of ensuring economy in public affairs, in the sense that after expenditure decisions have been made the money is used efficiently and not wastefully, is important and one that is only touched on here. Examination in detail will be found in Holtham and Perrin (1986).

It may be noted that 'extravagance' may be an indication of too little rather than too much administrative expenditure, in the sense that the misallocation of resources might have been avoided wholly or in part if there had been more, or better-trained, government officials. Each country will have its own examples, in the UK poor government oversight of aircraft and nuclear development since the end of the Second World War seem an apt illustration together with the development and taxation of North Sea oil.

The trend, as Chapter 2 shows, is that in most developed countries the share of government spending increased in the post-war period at least until the mid-1980s. Industrial intervention, the welfare state and redistribution of income were factors pressurizing government spending in the earlier period. The 1980s saw concern beginning to crystalize on the size of Government deficits, increasing debt payments and the fear of crowding out the private sector. Thus government aims shifted to the control of public expenditure. Increasing taxation was not seen as an option as taxes were perceived as already too high and damaging incentives.

Three main strategies emerged:

a Imposing 'top-down limits' whereby the government sets a goal for total spending within which subsequent decisions and cost increases should be accommodated. Virtually all OECD countries now set limits on total spending and most have multi-year projections of the financial consequences of expenditure plans. The extent to which countries set overall limits for individual departments or spending groups varies.

b Ensuring that spending outcomes adhere to plans. Most countries have information systems that enable monitoring of spending. Some have implemented detailed controls. The latter runs the risk that the budget office rather than the spending department is seen as bearing primary responsibility for ensuring budgets are kept. In contrast is the growing practice of the use of block budgets. Detailed allocations and reallocations of funds can then be left to the appropriate spending level.

c Increasing value for money. All countries seek to promote efficiency by a variety of methods. In some the budget is cut each year in line with expected improvements. Some rely on efficiency and effectiveness reviews. Other countries, aware of the dangers of too tight annual budgets and the number of unforeseen circumstances that crop up, allow departments flexibility to shift funds between resources and a few break with the annuality in budgeting and allow carry over of funds.

The drawback of these measures is the realization that budgeting skills are a scarce resource and many local inefficiencies may replace centralized inefficiency. Too often, at least in the short term, if cuts have to be made because say inadequate allowance for inflation has been made in the grant then expediency may decide what is cut and long-term goals suffer. Using the UK health budget as an example, 'getting the patient off my budget' is an understandable response of those under severe financial constraint. So a patient can be shuffled between doctor, hospital and various community services in the interest not of the patient's health but of the finance budget of one of the components of the health service. The more the budgetary process is fragmented the greater the danger that the overall picture is lost.

THE MINIMUM LEVEL OF GOVERNMENT ACTIVITY

The above outline enables us to discuss the minimum level of government activity – the level on which all reasonable people can agree.

Nearly all societies give some help to those who are incapable of helping themselves and have no one on whom they can depend. These will be mainly the young, the old, the sick and the disabled; also, in developed economies, those genuinely unemployed. Public or social goods, such as the administration of justice and defence of the realm, will form part of government activity for the reasons given in this chapter. There may be deep divisions of opinion about the nature and extent of defence, about whether it is necessary at all, but if the need is granted nobody seriously suggests that private armies be formed.

Again, it is generally agreed that where an operation has elements of monopoly in order to be efficient, for example sewerage and the supply of electricity, then the state should either regulate, or itself run, the service at the central or local government level.

General agreement occurs that where there are strong externalities government action is needed. Difficulties occur over those goods which have both a benefit to the individual and externalities: education is an example. Education at least at an elementary level is recognized as having strong externalities: our present society would not be able to function without a certain level of education of the population. Not everybody agrees that higher education has sufficiently strong externalities to justify meeting the cost, for at least some, wholly out of general taxation.

This, then, is the minimum scope of state activity: some form of aid for the unfortunate, the judicial system, defence, the regulation of natural monopolies and of those goods which have strong externalities, and expenditures necessary to regulate the economy. Public opinion in most societies would recognize this as the lowest common denominator of government action. Even at this level disagreements can creep in. If government action is admitted as necessary in a certain area, say education, it leaves open the question of whether the government should itself undertake the provision of the service, or merely supervise its provision, and, if necessary, subsidise the private provision of it.

Government activity, even at this minimum level, involves some redistribution of resources from the 'better off' to the 'worse off'. The questions raised by redistribution will now be tackled.

REDISTRIBUTION

Redistribution in a community can take place by provision of services above the minimum levels just discussed, provided these are met out of taxes paid by the 'better off', or alternatively by direct money transfers from the 'better off' to the 'worse off'.

In discussion about the redistribution of income and/or wealth, three strands of thought are apparent. These will be discussed in turn. The first strand is unavoidable if it is granted that help should be given to the unfortunate. The second strand of thought aims at deliberate redistribution above the level required to supplement the lowest incomes. The third strand is directed at changing the conditions which help create and foster the inequalities. In practice, these ideas may be interwoven, but conceptually much confusion can be avoided if they are kept separate.

If it is granted that a society should assist those who are incapable of helping themselves, then this implies that society has already made a decision that some redistribution of income and/or wealth is desirable. This conclusion is inescapable. In these circumstances the government cannot be neutral in its attitude to the redistribution of income and/or wealth since a decision to help a needy section of the population entails redistribution from a 'better off' to a 'worse off' section.

Leaving to one side humanitarian arguments, the core of the argument for those who advocate government provision, or alternatively argue for some redistribution of income and/or wealth above the minimum level, is that needs are not satisfied equally if income is spread unequally. The case is that economic welfare can be increased by government provision or redistribution. This was well put by Dalton:

> Income consists of the means of economic welfare, and great inequality in incomes in any community implies great inequality in the economic welfare attained by different individuals. But this is not all. For it implies also considerable waste of potential economic welfare. Put broadly, and in the language of common sense, the case against large inequalities of income is that the less urgent needs of the rich are satisfied, while the more urgent needs of the poor are left unsatisfied. The rich are more than amply fed, while the poor go hungry. This is merely an application of the economists' law of diminishing marginal utility, which states that, other things being equal, as the quantity of any commodity or, more generally, of purchasing power, increases, its total utility increases, but its marginal utility diminishes.

> (1959, p. 10)

This quotation contains two ideas. The first is that the economic welfare of different individuals can be compared. However reasonable such an idea may seem, particularly when we compare extreme positions such as giving a loaf of bread to a man who already has plenty with giving a loaf to a man who is hungry, there are those who hold that we have no objective measure by which we can compare needs of different individuals. We need not enter into this controversy because the second idea contained in this quotation is that the community through its voting preferences should judge relative needs. Such judgement will not be to any absolute standard but will change as ethical, political, social, economic and other conditions change in the community. Much of the study of public finance can be taken up with a consideration of how these changes in community standards have affected ideas about government spending and revenue.

The more fundamental problem is to change the conditions of society which create and foster the inequalities and paradoxically this seems to receive less practical attention. It is perhaps inherent in most of us to regard as 'normal and just' whatever framework of society exists at the time. Even Plato carried forward the conditions of slavery into his Republic. An important example of this tendency is to regard as just the current base for a particular tax. Income tax in most countries excludes quite wide streams of income and popular discussion is mostly confined to comment about the rates at which this base is taxed. As we shall see in later chapters, questions about the nature of wealth and income are at least as important in discussing a tax system as the rates which happen to be applied at any particular time.

It should not be thought from the above discussion that redistribution is always and necessarily an act forced on individuals. The existence of charities is a contrary indication that voluntary transfers take place. Redistribution may have a number of aims. It may indeed be a forced redistribution, a reflection of existing political power. It may reflect a social preference for security against drastic income fluctuations, for example a willingness to be taxed now to ensure a right to payments if sick or unemployed in the future. Some redistribution may be welcomed by the rich as a hoped-for protection against disease, riots and civil disorders emanating from the poor. More widely, if individual utility functions are interdependent, it is possible that some redistribution will increase everyone's welfare, in the same sense that a transfer of pocket-money from parents to children can increase the welfare of both. The recognition that man is a social animal that can gain welfare from seeing a transfer to a less fortunate person enables redistribution to be analysed in terms of Pareto optimum, which seeks in this context to establish transfers that can take place with nobody being worse off. People may voluntarily consent to be taxed for these purposes to rule out the 'free-rider' problem, that is people may be willing to be taxed provided they know persons in similar positions will also be taxed. For a seminal article analysing voluntary redistributions, see Hockman and Rodgers (1969).

SUMMARY

By the economic welfare of an individual is meant his command over goods and services. This command comes to the individual from a number of sources. It is derived from work, from wealth, from inheritance and gifts, and from government provision and legislation.

Imperfections in the competitive marketing price system leave a vacuum for the community to fill. These are due to the uneven spread of income and wealth, leading to deficiencies in allocation, the presence of public goods and goods which have strong externalities, the natural bias of the private sector of the economy towards goods for which it is easy to collect payment, monopoly elements and failure of the market system to establish an equilibrium.

Intervention itself has a cost in the resources of manpower, material and money that have to be devoted to achieve this intervention. Directly unproductive profit-seeking is part of a wide-ranging concept which embraces the resources which are used to try and circumvent the rules. The economic distortions caused by trade restrictions, agricultural subsidies, tax evasion, smuggling and bribery can be high. These costs need to be weighed against the expected benefits from the intervention.

It has been suggested that there is no unique solution to the question about what is the correct level of government activity. The level itself is likely to change with time, with changes in population, in the complexity of society and according to political fashion.

In deciding the quantities of goods to be produced, where no pricing system acts as a guide, the economist has a useful, if limited, role to play.

Ensuring efficiency in public spending has no simple solution. Setting overall budgetary targets is common, success in meeting the targets less so. Imposing public spending limits on particular sectors has become widespread but itself has dangers that resources will be less than optimally allocated over time in order to satisfy short term budget constraints.

A budget that takes account of tax expenditures, which are examined in more detail in Chapter 2, is likely to obtain a better allocation of resources than one that ignores the very large sums that are distributed in this way.

Government provision and legislation form the back-drop of a public-finance study. Government provision out of general taxation, or transfer payments such as pensions, are an obvious way of supplementing income deficiencies. Society judges the extent to which redistribution above this level is desirable. The economic justification for such provision is that command over goods and services is spread unevenly. In a democratic society, government in no very exact fashion, judges the relative needs of its members and deems that some minimum needs must be met for all; that is, some redistribution of command over goods and services shall take place.

Chapter 2

Government expenditures

CONCEPTUAL DIFFICULTIES

Government spending and taxation affect every individual. It is not therefore surprising to find that in public finance there are many attempts by sectional interests, including governments themselves, to present biased, incomplete or misleading information. It is not uncommon to find opposite views being asserted; for example, some might claim that public expenditure has gone up, others that it has gone down. Ignoring deliberate attempts to mislead by, for example, choosing a base period when expenditure was particular high or low, or deliberately picking an item which 'proves' the point in question and ignoring all the evidence to the contrary, there are a number of difficulties in trying to present a meaningful picture.

First, figures on money outlays, although useful in showing how expenditures on different sub-categories have changed relative to each other, tell us little about the share of government expenditure in relation to total resources. In order to measure the latter it is necessary to make allowances in some way for changes in the value of money. This can be done by some form of price index which can be used to express the money figures to 'real' terms, i.e. in terms of current purchasing power. An alternative is to express government expenditure as a percentage of Gross Domestic Product (GDP). GDP is a measure of economic activity during a year. It can be calculated by adding up the final value of goods and services produced or, by adding up the income received from producing these. Adding in net income from abroad gives Gross National Product (GNP). Government expenditure as a percentage of GDP therefore looks at the proportion the government uses of domestic current output or of current income; presenting both in nominal terms will not be misleading. Adjusting both sets of figures by the same inflation rate would not change the picture substantially. Expressed in this way meaningful comparisons can be drawn between different countries.

GDP can be valued at 'factor cost' or at 'market prices'. Factor cost measures output in terms of costs of production, whereas market prices calculations adjust for the fact that prices paid by the final consumer will be higher or lower than this if indirect taxes or subsidies are applicable. Factor costs are generally lower than market prices, since most goods are taxed rather than subsidized; so expressing taxes as a percentage of GDP at factor cost will show higher percentages than when they are expressed at market prices. In Britain in 1987 the difference was 6 per cent.

Second, particularly when comparisons are made over long time periods it may be misleading not to adjust for population. For example, doubling the expenditure in real terms does not imply doubling the amount of government activity if population has changed significantly in absolute numbers or composition, or both. Real expenditures per head of population give a better picture. The adjustment for population change is not made here, as the countries concerned do not have rapid population changes over the time period considered, and this will not be seriously misleading.

Third, it is necessary to take account of the nature of government expenditure and draw a clear distinction between transfer payments on the one hand and direct government expenditures on goods and services on the other. Transfer payments are, as the name implies, payments made by the government, such as pensions, child allowances and interest payments on the National Debt.

Transfer payments do not involve the government in direct use of the nation's goods and services. They are taking money from taxpayers and giving money to selected groups. Since all citizens pay taxes of one sort or another it is a complicated task to work out the benefits and costs of these transfers to individuals. Transfers are often in the nature of insurance payments: we may hope never to be unemployed or sick but if the worst happens our previous contributions give us a right to payment. Transfers may be classified in different ways: for example, transfers between persons such as child benefits; transfers over time such as pensions; and transfers to meet contingencies such as sickness or unemployment. The misleading term 'National Insurance Contributions' gives the impression that payments are earmarked for health, pensions, etc. In practice, in Britain and many other countries, current payments are used to pay existing benefits; there may be no actuarial balance between revenue and expenditure. National Insurance (NI) contributions are a straightforward tax whose proceeds may or may not be sufficient to meet NI payments. State pensions, for example, are usually a transfer from taxpayers to the pensionable group. If the NI pension component is sufficient to pay pensions then this will be a distribution from the working population to the retired since retired people do not pay NI contributions. If they are insufficient the shortfall is made up from other taxes paid by all the population including the retired. Therefore NI contributions do not build up a fund for future payments but are in the nature of 'rights'. Current payments build up rights to benefits which it is hoped will be honoured when the time arrives.

As a final illustration of the difficulties of defining government expenditure, a great deal of confusion is caused because different levels of government may be included or excluded from the figures. For example should government spending include spending by local authorities? Should it include spending by nationalized industries? Fortunately, there is no need to seek a non-existing 'right' definition. Sometimes one definition, sometimes another, is useful: what must be avoided is misleading conclusions from figures drawn up on different bases.

In the UK the definition of public spending was narrowed to something like the OECD's 'general government' definition in 1977. The major changes were the substitution of nationalized industries' external finance from all sources taking the place of their capital investment figures; the measurement of GDP at market prices rather than factor cost and the exclusion of debt interest to be met out of trading income.

A contentious issue in the 1980s in the UK was the treatment of the proceeds of asset sales as negative expenditure rather than as a means of financing the Public Sector Borrowing Requirement (PSBR). This practice apparently reduces the level of public spending and the PSBR. Asset sales include receipts from the sale of nationalized industries, public-sector land and buildings and the part sales of assets the proceeds of which are retained by nationalized industries themselves. Since 1989–90 local authority self-financed expenditure has been excluded.

Further details will be found in Heald, as he says:

It is quite possible that . . . in both 1988–89 and 1989–90, the negative PSBRs of, respectively, £14,365 million and £7,911 million will have been more than accounted for by public sector asset sales. The much-trumpeted fiscal surplus is largely illusory.

(Heald 1991)

INTERNATIONAL COMPARISONS OF GOVERNMENT EXPENDITURE

Making international comparisons of government expenditure is fraught with even more difficulty than making a comparison over time for a single country, but is a valuable exercise in sorting out political claims about public expenditure. The squeeze on public spending in the 1980s has sometimes been at the expense of the public infrastructure which has left a legacy which varies between countries of underprovision in environmental services such as water purity, in health, education and other basic provisions. Many transfer payments, in particular pensions, family allowances, education benefits and unemployment pay have been cut or benefits increased at less than the rate of growth in wages and prices in Belgium, Luxembourg, Austria, Germany, Denmark, Spain, Sweden, Ireland and the UK.

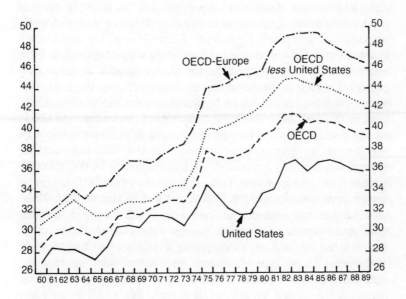

Figure 2.1 Total public expenditure as a percentage of GDP/GNP in OECD countries, 1960–89

Source: OECD, *Historical Statistics* and *OECD* Secretariat estimates 1 Total general government outlays, national accounts basis (i.e. excluding government lending operations).

Fig. 2.1 gives a picture of total public expenditure as a percentage of GNP for OECD countries. This shows that the average share of Government outlays in OECD GNP increased from just under 30 per cent in 1960 to over 40 per cent in the early 1980s. By 1989 this proportion had dropped to just below 40 per cent.

Table 2.1 uses information, adjusted to conform with the European System of Integrated Economic Accounts (ESA), to facilitate comparison between seven EC countries for which information is available. Unfortunately there are gaps in the figures and for the latest year, 1985, many countries returns are not available. However a number of important conclusions can still be drawn.

Table 2.1 shows central and local government expenditure as a percentage of GDP for 1977, 1982 and 1985. For all the countries shown the proportion of government expenditure went up between 1977 and 1982. Germany showed the least increase, other countries a 5 per cent increase or more. Slight decreases from the 1982 levels are experienced by the four countries for which figures are available for 1985, except for Italy, which has an increase of 2.8 per cent. The UK is not, contrary to much public thinking, among the countries in this group with the highest proportion of total public expenditure, but the lowest. The next chapter is able to give figures on taxes and social security contributions for a wider group of countries and the UK shows up as a medium-taxed country. Looking at individual sectors, column 2 gives the proportion spent on defence: the UK has the highest proportion and has consistently been in this position in every year since 1945. In contrast the UK is among the low spenders on education (column 3). These differences may be one of the results of Britain's relative economic decline; alternatively they may be one of the factors accounting for the economic decline. The latter seems more plausibly in view of an EEC 'Report on Social Developments' (1990). This found that Britain in 1986–7 had only 6.0 per cent educated at Third level – the lowest of the nine European countries for which figures were available. The other countries had 9.5 per cent or more, rising to 14.6 per cent for Denmark. In Germany 10 per cent of children leave school with less than the equivalent of O-level qualifications; in Britain the figure is 45 per cent. Britain is also among the low spenders on health, social security and welfare services – columns 4 and 5 respectively.

Social security transfers have been a big and increasing part of government spending. These will be mostly transfer payments, such as pensions, sickness, unemployment and other welfare payments, from taxpayers to social security recipients. They do not involve the

Table 2.1 Selected levels of government expenditure as a percentage of GDP (1977,1982 and 1985)

	1	2	3	4	5	6	7	Total
1977								
Denmark	4.2	2.4	7.5	5.5	18.2	1.7	9.0	48.5
Netherlands	–	3.1	7.4	–	19.6	–	22.3	52.4
France	4.0	3.2	5.9	5.6	17.5	2.8	5.5	44.5
Belgium	2.9	2.8	7.7	5.3	24.7	0.7	12.1	56.2
F.R. Germany	4.8	2.9	5.0	6.3	20.3	1.2	7.0	47.5
UK	3.6	4.8	5.9	4.8	11.3	0.5	12.8	43.7
Italy	4.0	1.8	5.1	5.6	14.8	1.1	10.8	43.1
1982								
Denmark	4.0	2.6	7.8	5.9	23.3	1.2	15.5	60.3
Netherlands	–	3.3	6.7	–	22.7	–	28.2	60.9
France	3.0	3.8	6.0	6.5	20.7	3.0	7.6	50.6
Belgium	2.0	2.9	8.1	8.0	26.6	0.8	18.3	66.7
F.R. Germany	3.0	2.9	5.0	6.3	20.5	1.2	9.5	48.4
UK	1.8	5.3	5.5	5.1	14.7	1.9	12.8	47.0
Italy	3.5	1.8	5.3	5.4	15.3	1.8	15.3	48.4
1985								
Denmark	–	–	–	–	–	–	–	–
Netherlands	–	3.0	5.9	–	20.8	–	29.3	59.0
France	–	–	–	–	–	–	–	–
Belgium	–	–	–	–	–	–	–	–
F.R. Germany	3.0	2.8	4.6	6.4	19.0	1.1	9.5	46.4
UK	1.6	5.2	5.0	5.1	14.8	2.1	12.4	46.1
Italy	4.5	2.1	5.1	5.4	16.2	1.9	16.0	51.2

Source: General Government Accounts and Statistics 1970–86; Eurostat (1989)

1 General public services
2 Defence
3 Education Amenities
4 Health
5 Social security and welfare
6 Housing and community amenities
7 Other

government in direct use of the nation's resources. Attempts to reduce
these expenditures in the 1980s has led as noted above to real reductions
in payments in many countries.

WHAT INFLUENCES THE LEVEL OF GOVERNMENT ACTIVITY?

Using the United Kingdom as an illustration, Figure 2.2 shows the ratio
of government expenditure to Gross Domestic Product (GDP) at market
prices since 1890.

The trend is upward; in this the UK is typical of other countries. The
graph shows general government expenditure, that is the combined
spending of central and local government, including both capital and
current spending, net lending, gross interest on the National Debt and
the finance which public corporations raise directly from the market.
The unbroken line gives general government expenditure, the amount

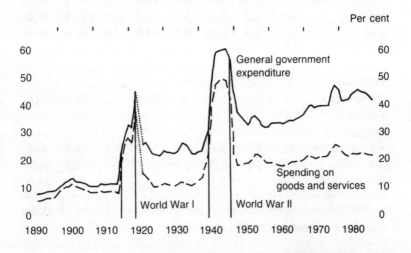

Figure 2.2   UK general government expenditure as a percentage of
GDP at market prices, 1890–1986

Source: *Economic Trends*, 403, October 1987, HMSO

the government has to raise in taxation or to borrow. The broken line shows spending on goods and services, the government's share of the economy. The gap between these lines is a measure of transfer payments. The sharp increase in spending during the First and Second World Wars is clear, with smaller peaks during the Boer War (1899–1902) and the Korean War (1951–2). The post-war periods show higher levels of spending than pre-war and rising levels of spending are apparent in the period of the 1960s and 1970s with a downturn in the 1980s, from some 47 per cent to 43 per cent. More realistically the figure is 44 per cent in 1986–7 when adjusted for asset sales is made. The widening gap between the lines in the post-war period indicates that transfer payments have accounted for much of the rise in level of spending. A more detailed account of public expenditure in the UK for the period 1964–84 can be found in Levitt and Joyce (1987).

What is the explanation for these trends? Pressures on government expenditure are diverse and a single all-embracing theory is unlikely. A number of explanations have been put forward with somewhat different emphasis in each.

Adolph Wagner (1890) was predicting that public expenditure would increase (at least for a time) at a faster rate than national output. We get 'a law of growing public expenditure'. Time has been kinder to Wagner's prediction than to many other forecasts made by economists as a glance at Figure 2.1 indicates. He based his observations on the results of a study of developed Western countries and on the grounds that state activity would need to increase as a result of industrialization, social progress and the need for greater infrastructure.

The extension of the vote to adult men, and subsequently women, is likely to have played a very important, though unquantifiable part in adding to government spending. With adult suffrage Parliament is more likely in its spending and revenue to reflect the needs of the community as a whole, because Members of Parliament depend on the votes of the majority for their seats.

The *growth* of population and in particular the *concentration* of population in towns have led to pressures on public spending. Services which can be safely left to the individual in a sparsely populated area have to be coordinated and provision ensured in a more populated areas. Sewerage and water supply being obvious examples. The growth of the motor car this century has exerted, and is continuing to exert, enormous pressure on the public purse.

Many developed countries are now experiencing an ageing population which adds to government expenditures on state pensions, medical and other services. The OECD estimates demographic changes could raise pension expenditures by about 5 per cent on national income by the year 2020, with social security budgets in Japan, Germany, France, Italy, the Netherlands and Switzerland subject to most pressure.

Technological change in general is difficult to predict and its impact on the public sector dependent on a number of factors. However, in some areas such as health care it seems likely to increase costs, and many of these will fall on the public sector purse. Correction for pollution externalities is beginning to take up increasing amounts of public and private expenditure.

Social reasons for public spending, i.e. the wish to spread benefits to the community at large, have played an important but again hard to quantify part. This is particularly noticeable in the extension of education, health and the social services generally. The desire to spread income and wealth more evenly has also helped to shape the expenditure and the revenue sides of the budget. Since the depression of the 1930s most governments accept that they have a positive role to play in trying to keep the economy in balance avoiding both the extremes of slump and of severe inflation. The form that this stabilization takes may change, the current trend being away from direct intervention. But provision of unemployment benefits, government training initiatives and investment incentives lead to a role for government.

Peacock and Wiseman (1961) in their study of public expenditure place emphasis on the revenue constraints felt by governments. An examination of expenditures over time reveals an uneven pattern. In particular we can single out wars as causing large jumps in government expenditure. By itself this is not surprising. What is interesting is that government expenditure does not go back to its former level after the war. This observation is apparent even when allowance is made for price changes and when war related expenditures are excluded.

Peacock and Wiseman use the term 'displacement effect' to cover this phenomenon. Many strands knit together to cause this effect. They develop the idea that in normal times there is a dichotomy between the desire for public goods and services and the level of taxation considered tolerable. A large-scale disturbance, such as a war or extensive flooding, may create an upward displacement of the level of taxation considered tolerable, so that new levels of public spending can afterwards be maintained.

In time of war new methods of raising revenue or new methods of collecting existing revenue may be accepted. The introduction of purchase tax in the UK, the predecessor of VAT, was an example of the former, pay-as-you-earn (PAYE) is an example of the latter. War also focuses attention on social ills: 'It has taken the catastrophe of war to bring home to those in power that economic progress does not automatically disseminate the benefits of education and health'(Peacock and Wiseman 1961: 93). A time of heightened national interest may also see an acceleration in the reorganization of government accounts, statistical information and in civil service procedures. Thus periods of crises such as war and the severe slump in the earlier 1930s seem to act as catalysts. We do not know what would have happened in the absence of these disasters, but in the light of hindsight they appear to break the 'cake of custom'.

A number of writers have put forward *relative price effects* as a cause of at least part of the increase in government spending. Public services are often labour-intensive and the costs of such services will be driven up if they have less scope for raising productivity and have to keep pace with private sector wage increases. Any sector that falls into this category will face higher costs. The uncertainty is the extent to which the public sector generally fits this case. Changing information and other technology could tip the balance either way.

We have already seen that goods with large positive externalities are likely to be under-produced by the private sector and goods with large negative externalities over-produced. If the government steps in will it get it right? This issue is taken up in the final sections of this chapter, under the Economics of Public Choice.

TAX EXPENDITURES

Tax expenditure is the term given for revenue not collected from a tax because of tax reliefs, concessions and preferences. It can often be a substitute for direct government spending. The amounts involved have been large in most countries in recent years. There is nothing intrinsically wrong with tax expenditures; for example the relief from income tax of low incomes serves a social purpose and saves considerable compliance and administrative costs. However, while government spending comes under considerable scrutiny by both Parliament and the public, tax expenditures tend to be 'hidden'. Once incorporated in a tax system they tend to stick even when the original purpose of the change has faded away. Many tax expenditures will violate both horizontal and vertical equity since the incidence of these expenditures has a marked variation (OECD 1984). The use of tax expenditures to subsidize various forms of economic activity is a major source of distortion and lack of equity.

Almost half of OECD countries now provide for some review of tax expenditures in their budgets. Only in France, Spain and the United States are consolidated tax expenditure statements required by law. A number of countries have considered publishing consolidated accounts, including Germany, the UK and Ireland, and decided against it on varying grounds, for example, that identifying tax expenditures is a subjective matter. Most countries that have attempted to define tax expenditures do so by defining them as a departure from a 'normal', 'bench-mark', 'basic' or 'generally accepted' tax structure. Concessions to particular groups, to particular classes of assets or to particular geographical areas would then be classified as tax expenditures but some tax reliefs may not be so easy to classify and it is these that can give rise to disagreement. As an example should a tax system be based on real or nominal income? If the latter, any ad hoc or partial adjustments for inflation would be treated as tax expenditure whereas if based on real income they would not. A number of other countries, including the UK, which do not integrate tax expenditure with their budgets, provide separate estimates of these sums. A budget that ignores the large measure of resource allocation provided by tax expenditures can only be considered seriously incomplete.

Estimating who benefits from tax expenditures raises the usual incidence problems of tracing out who ultimately benefits a matter that is taken up in Chapter 7. As an illustration of incidence problems most governments issue some securities in tax-exempt form. Various reasons have been given, e.g. to encourage small savers, or the provision of assistance to another level of government. In so far as governments are able to attract buyers at lower than market rates of interest the net cost of such a concession may be low. They avoid the administrative difficulty of paying a higher market rate of tax and then collecting tax on the payment. However, on equity grounds these concessions are objectionable. The tax-exempt status is of most benefit not to small savers, who if their incomes are below the tax threshold may be worse off if they buy these securities, but to higher rate taxpayers. Securities of this type that are held by individuals are therefore mainly held by rich persons.

ESTIMATING TAX EXPENDITURES

There are three principal ways of estimating the costs or value of tax expenditures: revenue forgone, revenue gain and outlay equivalence. All methods are used within the OECD area, further complicating comparisons between countries.

Revenue forgone is an estimate of the amount by which tax revenue is reduced because of the existence of the concessions. The revenue gain method looks at the revenue that would be obtained if the concessions were scrapped. In principle the revenue gain method should look at the behavioural changes likely to be made by taxpayers and how these impinge on tax revenues directly and indirectly. The outlay equivalence method estimates what direct pre-tax expenditure outlays would be required, to achieve the same after tax benefit. Because of the interactions between taxes all approaches to measuring tax expenditures suffer from the drawback that the costs of different tax expenditures cannot be added together to give a total figure. The simultaneous elimination of two tax expenditures is generally not the same as the sum of their individual revenue impacts as individuals modify their behaviour. The reduction of some benefits push taxpayers into a higher tax bracket so increasing the value of remaining benefits.

The United States and particularly Canada have taken consolidation furthest. Most developed countries now provide estimates of the costs of new tax reliefs when they are introduced or modified and a few countries have obliged their governments to provide regular accounting of them. Governments seeking to hold down or cut back government expenditure have naturally increased interest in this area.

Figures in this chapter will exclude tax expenditures from estimates of public spending due to the paucity of comparative information. The argument for consolidating tax expenditures into budget accounts is the hope that policy will be more effective if all the different methods of government intervention are taken into account at the same time. Control over expenditure should be tighter if governments and spending departments find it more difficult to substitute tax expenditures for direct expenditure.

As an example it is difficult to imagine that the UK Parliament in 1989 would have voted a new measure to pay out in excess of £7 billion to help house purchasers. This was the amount automatically received by way of tax expenditures as interest rates rose in the economy. The higher interest rates pushed up mortgage payments and the value of tax relief on the first £30,000 of borrowing was therefore greater.

In Canada spending departments may propose increases in tax expenditures and these come out of the department budget just as proposals for increased expenditures would. Departments are also free to suggest reductions in tax expenditures if they wish to increase direct expenditures.

TAX CAPITALIZATION

Capitalization refers to the way in which capital values adjust to tax or subsidy changes. Consider, as an example, the case of housing mortgage relief. The main beneficiaries of this relief are not those who enter the market for the first time but owners of housing at the time the concession was brought in or increased. This inference is based, on the not unreasonable assumption, that the concession is likely to drive up the price of the asset. Existing owners will benefit from increased values rather than new purchasers. Tax capitalization works in reverse, ending a tax concession or subsidy is likely to result in capital values being lower than they would otherwise be. This explains why governments find it so hard to remove or reduce tax concessions and subsidies once they have been introduced. The abrupt ending of all farm subsidies or all mortgage concessions would leave many, especially recent purchasers, with mortgages in excess of the capital value of their property. Not surprisingly losers are likely to protest vigorously about the change. However economically sensible a system would be without the concessions, achieving a system free from distortion is not easy. Refusing to upgrade the concessions in line with inflation will gradually reduce their value over time. Phasing the concessions out over some years has been done in a few cases but is politically difficult. Consolidation of tax concessions and subsidies in one budget statement should help ensure Parliamentary scrutiny.

BUDGETARY TARGETS

Most countries now set overall annual budgetary targets in quantitative terms, sometimes for several years ahead. The extent to which targets can be met is another matter and will depend in part on how large a component the Government controls. Much expenditure on items such as pensions and social security payments is contractual rather than discretionary. While governments may find it comparatively easy not to upgrade benefits, in line with inflation, in order to keep expenditures down, cutting benefits levels is more difficult. Targets can be formulated in a number of ways. The most frequent is a ratio of spending to GDP or a similar indicator. Also used is a rate of change for expenditure in nominal or real terms, or as an absolute value in nominal terms. Countries usually use more than one measure.

In the UK the government publishes multi-year Public Expenditure Surveys (PES) covering the whole public sector and consistent with the two plans that follow. The medium-term public expenditure plans have been published each year since the late 1960s. The government has also since 1980 published a medium-term financial strategy (MTFS). This last sets out its projections for the growth of money national income which are consistent with a reduction in inflation while permitting sustained economic growth. Targets are set for the growth of monetary aggregates and the path of the PSBR. The targets for expenditure are in money terms which imply a declining ratio of public expenditure to GDP. From what has already been said it is clear that governments have considerable ability to manipulate the various components of these targets.

Alas, the publication of targets does not mean that they are necessarily achieved and the UK, like many countries, has failed year by year, often by wide margins, to meet many of its published targets.

ECONOMICS OF PUBLIC CHOICE

Dissatisfaction with welfare theories of public finance that rely on interpersonal comparisons or invoke a social welfare function has led a number of economists to try to ground a theory in the standard economic ideas of maximization. Public goods often do not enter the market sector so interest is turned to non-market resource allocation mechanisms. See Downs (1957 and 1967), Buchanan and Tullock (1962), Tullock (1965 and 1976), Buchanan (1977), Niskanen (1971), Breton (1974) and Nordhaus (1975). Jackson (1982) provides an overview. This work has been applied to both private- and public-sector organizations; the concern here is with the latter.

These writings explore a number of hypotheses: that democratically elected governments seek to maximize their chances of re-election; voters seek to maximize their net benefit – that is the excess of the benefit received from government expenditure over their tax cost; and bureaucrats their personal utility which may be represented by their pay, status, power of patronage, etc. One method of analysing these various motives is to examine the budgetary process and the part each of these groups play in its formulation. Another is to seek evidence for a 'political business cycle' (PBC) caused by government spending before an election. The assumption that the state, and associated bureaucracy, always act in the public interest is thus open to question by examining other possible behavioural motives of the suppliers and users of public services. The term bureaucrat can typically be thought of as a civil servant, although it covers a wider range such as managers of large enterprises, bureaucracy is the structure within which the bureaucrat works.

Budget determination

In small groups decisions may be reached by direct negotiation and bargaining. More usually individual preferences are expressed at one remove; the individual votes for a party and the party makes a political decision on the budget.

The allocation of votes will clearly influence the outcome. Most democratic countries have scrapped property, sex, race or other qualifications as prerequisites for giving their citizens the right to vote; they now adhere to one vote per adult person. Clearly who is given a vote can affect the outcome, as does the choice of voting rule. The most common rule is that of simple majority – an option that secures more than half of the votes cast is adopted. Voting by qualified majority, often two-thirds, is not uncommon and is so required to change the US constitution or parts of the European Economic Community agreements. Occasionally unanimity is required for decisions. Plurality voting is where each voter ranks his choices in order of preference. Point voting is where each voter has a number of points to allocate among the choices in anyway they wish. A transferable voting system allows votes, for the option with the least votes, to be allocated among the remaining choices according to voters expressed second choices.

The public finance literature has made a distinct contribution in pointing out that the voting rule adopted may alter the outcome. With simple majority voting, where voters have to select among more than two choices, the order in which the pairs are selected can influence the final outcome.

A simple illustration will make the voting paradox clear. Imagine three voters, Albert, Betty and Cath, selecting among three alternative ways of allocating a given sum of money: say on health, education or roads which are labelled respectively policies H, E and R. If the choices of each voter in order of preference are:

Albert: H then E then R
Betty: R then H then E
Cath: E then R then H

Then there are three cases depending on the order in which the pairing takes place.

Case 1 voting between H and E followed by choice between the winner and R.

Choice	Voter	Option	Winner
H or E	Albert	H	
	Betty	H	H So Health wins the first vote.
	Cath	E	
H and R	Albert	H	
	Betty	R	R So Roads wins the final vote.
	Cath	R	

Case 2 voting between E and R followed by choice between the winner and H. In this case the winner is Education in the first round and Housing in the second.

Case 3 voting between H and R followed by choice between the winner and E. In this case the winner is Roads in the first round and Education in the second.

In this example the policy adopted depends on the order in which the choices are paired. Had the preference order of Betty been R then E then H, there would be no contradiction E would have been successful however the voting was paired.

More complicated voting patterns, with different tax packages to pay for the increase in expenditure, are explored in the literature. Voting strategies, whereby voters try and take into account the believed preferences of other voters, are also examined. This voting paradox has been known since the eighteenth century and explored more recently by Arrow (1963) and Buchanan and Tullock (1962).

Another aspect of the budget process explored in the literature comes to the not very surprising conclusion that most budgets proceed incrementally. Most resources have to be allocated to the maintenance of the existing system of road, schools, hospitals and other infrastructure and in the salaries of those concerned. Most budget decisions are incremental, that is about the size of the increase or decrease of the budget from the previous year. The danger in incrementalism is that fundamental reappraisals of services do not get undertaken, slack creeps into some areas while others are overstretched. For this reason many governments have review committees, or other procedures, which from time to time overhaul the work being done in particular areas. Incrementalism is normally also associated with sequential decision making, each decision area makes its own choices taking little account of the impact of its choices on other budget areas. Normally separate

budgets are grouped and submitted to The Treasury, or other department, co-ordination should take place at this stage if it has not been
implemented previously.

Motivation of politicians

Evidence that the politicians forming a government may be primarily
motivated by the desire to be re-elected is suggested by the political
business cycle that has been noted at times in Britain and elsewhere. See
Nordhaus (1975), MacRae (1977), Frey (1978) and Alesina (1989).
However, it is by no means a universal rule and contra behaviour has at
other times also been noted. A political business cycle can be created when
governments engineer a pre-election boom by, for example, cutting taxes or
increasing government expenditure some time before they seek re-election.
More dramatic results can be achieved if they depress demand soon after
they are elected in order to make the latter boom seem even more
spectacular. Electorates are commonly supposed to have short memories, a
supposition at odds with a 'rational expectations' view of behaviour, and in
gratitude for a booming economy are further supposed to be willing to
re-elect the government concerned. The political party in power may also
enact legislation that favours particular groups in the hope that political
donations to their party will increase enabling more to be spent advertising
their cause, or in more corrupt regimes, the legislation may be passed in
return for personal favours to the politicians or bureaucrats concerned. A
variant of the PBC has been suggested by Hibbs (1977) termed the 'partisan
theory' (PT) he claimed to find left wing governments tend to have higher
inflation and lower unemployment than right-wing governments, who are
more concerned with inflation and less concerned about unemployment.
Empirical work suggests that the PT is a short-lived effect that occurs
primarily after a change in government.

Subscribing base motives to politicians and bureaucrats may be a
popular pastime that accords with reality at some times, and in some
places, but does not have to be the whole truth. Both can also act in what
they perceive as the common good and try and lead and direct voters
rather than follow them. These theories suppose that governments are
able to fine tune the economy in such a way that the timing of their
actions coincides with an election. The theories are also simplistic in
supposing that there are always policies which can be implemented that
will appeal to the majority of voters. Most practical policies have
gainers and losers and it is rare for these to be aligned in any simple way
to the interests of one political party.

Cynics suggest that government behaviour may better be described by a 'cock-up' theory – if governments can get it wrong they will. Such sweeping generalizations are unwarranted although the history of some government actions, such as the poll tax and its proposed replacement by the Council Tax in the UK, detailed in the Appendix to Chapter 12, give one pause for thought.

Motivation of bureaucrats

The size of the bureau's budget may be used as a proxy for the possible motives of bureaucrats, e.g. Niskanen (1971). An increase in budget is seen as a way to raise their salaries or extend their power. This assumption considerably weakens the argument. Bureaucrats may, especially in the current political climate where politicians wish to reduce government expenditure, be rewarded by being able to demonstrate that they have kept their budgets down. The bureaucrat may also have a trade off between budget size and the amount of leisure he has available, opting for a quiet life is not unknown. Depending on the career structure of the bureaucrat they may also aim for promotion to a senior position in the most powerful department. In many structures this will be a Treasury section, which will have prime concern with control over expenditure rather than expansion. See Kogan (1973).

Voters' behaviour

Individual voters may feel powerless to influence decisions of government so pressure groups for particular causes abound. Powerful pressure groups may appoint full time lobby members to represent their case to politicians and to 'vet' proposed legislation to see their interests are, as far as possible, served. Buchanan and Tullock (1962) among others argue that the actions of pressure groups can result in the overexpansion of the size of the public sector. While this is a possibility, not all pressure groups will be arguing for increases in services as the considerable pressure for tax cuts in recent years has shown. In turn politicians may support different groups to try and maintain majority support both among their own elected members and voters. Kay (1985) argues forcibly that the complexity in taxation is not, at least in the UK, primarily due to pressure groups but rather to 'attempts to buttress bits of the system that do not work and probably never could have worked'.

Buchanan and Tullock also put forward the view that publicly provided goods will be over-supplied on the grounds that 51 per cent of the voters can impose their will and the tax cost will be met by all the group. The voters taking into account only their own costs will therefore vote for excess services. But this argument is reciprocal; 51 per cent of voters can block legislation that impose some tax cost on themselves. At any one time expansionists or tax cutters may predominate there is no reason to expect total dominance by one side or the other.

In a similar manner it has been suggested that voters tend to underestimate the cost of taxation. They may underestimate the cost, particularly if an indirect tax is involved, or naively believe that others will bear more of the cost than is in fact the case. Automatic increases in tax revenues due to inflation or growth provide also it is suggested opportunities for greater spending. Again this argument can be turned round. Voters may underestimate the benefits that follow from increased government spending and under-provision of public services may be the result. Automatic revenue gain provide politicians opportunities to cut taxes which may appeal to voters more than increased expenditures. The argument is indecisive and can only be settled by empirical investigation.

Public choice summary

The literature of the economics of bureaucracy thus seeks to enrich the discussion of the public sector by looking at the possible motives of participants: namely the political parties, the bureaucrats, and the public who benefit or lose from the resulting government actions or failure to act. This detailed study is of interest in its own right but has not yielded, and perhaps should not be expected to yield, any grand generalizations about public-sector behaviour. Attempts at empirical investigation of the various theories has yielded little in the way of firm conclusions see Alesina (1989). The mixed motives of the different sectors in the process may at times cancel each other out, at other times the bureaucrats, the politician or the voter may appear to have the upper hand. Undoubtedly the literature has generated a number of contributions by those with extreme political views, whose myopic vision sees all public-sector actions in terms of political vote maximizing, bureaucratic manipulation or pressure groups. Most democracies have a system of checks and balances in them, of a formal or informal kind, which try and ensure that no one sector completely dominates the other. The idea cannot be rejected that the public sector, in a rough and ready way, does, more often than not, seek the public interest rather than the narrow interest of the participants. A more constructive attitude is to regard this literature on non-market resource allocation mechanisms as complementary to the more traditional approach of the economist. The former is more concerned with short-term relationships of the participants the latter is more concerned with allocation, quantities, equilibrium and long-run tendencies.

SUMMARY

Most developed countries showed an increasing trend of government expenditure in the 1970s. The 1980s saw an attempt by many governments to reduce or reverse this trend but most countries only managed to secure some levelling off of the trend. Social security and welfare expenditures form around a fifth of total spending. Factors influencing the level of spending were examined.

Figures on government expenditure often exclude the sums that the revenue fails to collect because of a variety of tax reliefs – termed tax expenditures. The sums involved can be large. Tax expenditures may serve a social purpose but all too often they benefit particular interest groups at the expense of others. Often designed to help the poor they frequently are of most benefit to the rich.

Tax expenditures, like subsidies, are difficult to remove once introduced as the benefit tends to be capitalized into asset values. Many countries have, however, recently reduced a number of these expenditures, as they affect the individual and the company, and used the increased revenue as a way of reducing income tax and company taxation respectively.

As part of the attempt to reduce the levels of government spending many countries have introduced some form of annual overall budgetary targeting. Most governments have failed to have much success in meeting these targets. A final section of the chapter looked at the Economics of Public Choice, dealing with the motivation of politicians, bureaucrats and voters.

Chapter 3

Taxation

The increase in government spending noted in Chapter 2 resulted in corresponding increases in government taxation. The reactions to the second oil price shock in 1979 induced recession, which cut back tax receipts while increasing Government spending on welfare and employment measures. A slight reversal has been seen in most countries since the mid-1980s. This trend is evident from Figure 3.1, showing that in OECD-Europe countries government receipts increased from about 31 per cent of GDP in 1960 to a peak of 45 per cent in 1985. There has been a slight fall-off since to a little over 43 per cent.

INTERNATIONAL COMPARISONS OF TAX

All developed countries rely on a mix of taxes for their revenue. Taxes on personal income, corporate income, social security contributions, value added tax (or other indirect taxation) and taxes on specific goods, provide some 95 per cent of revenue. The definitions of income for both persons and companies – whether, for example, they include capital gains, the treatment of depreciation and the amount of subsidies and tax allowances – show wide variations.

Table 3.1 presents taxes and social security contributions for OECD countries as a percentage of GNP at factor cost for 1977, 1982 and 1987. Social security contributions are called payroll taxes in the United States. Countries are ranked from highest to lowest taxed in the year 1987. Sweden has the highest level of tax and Switzerland and the United States the lowest. The ranking alters a little in previous years for some countries but not significantly so.

Table 3.1 shows that among the OECD countries shown, Sweden and Denmark have the highest proportion of taxes and social security benefits to GNP, with Japan, Switzerland and the United States lowest.

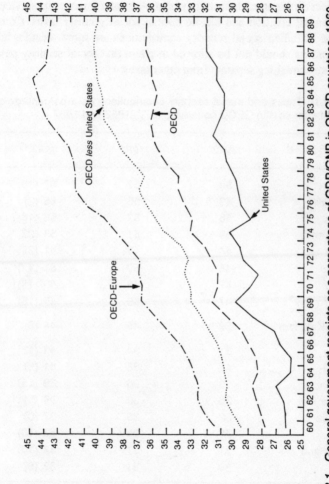

Figure 3.1 General government receipts as a percentage of GDP/GNP in OECD countries, 1960–89

Source: OECD, *Historical Statistics* and OECD Secretariat estimates. 1 Total current receipts, national accounts basis (*i.e.* excluding capital transfers and consumption of fixed capital)

The bulk of countries in 1987 lie between 37 per cent and 56 per cent, with the UK near the middle of this range at 44 per cent. The expressed desire of many governments to cut government expenditure in the 1980s was largely unsuccessful: only the UK and Norway show a drop of a modest 1 per cent.

The figures in brackets for 1987 show the proportion of taxes contributed by social security payments. They do not indicate that Australia has a non-existent social security service and Denmark a very low one but reflect different methods of payment. Australia finances its services from general taxation and has no special social security taxes. Comparisons including social security contributions are more meaningful. Governments should not be allowed to claim that social security payments are something separate from other taxes.

Table 3.1 Taxes and social security contributions as a percentage of GNP at factor cost in OECD countries, 1977, 1982 and 1987

	1977	1982	1987 *
Sweden	58	57	67 (16)
Denmark	49	55	65 (2)
Norway	56	57	56 (16)
Netherlands	49	51	53 (22)
France	44	49	51 (22)
Belgium	46	50	51 (17)
Austria	47	49	50 (15)
FR Germany	47	46	45 (18)
United Kingdom	39	45	44 (8)
Greece	31	34	43 (13)
Finland	42	38	41 (6)
Italy	30	36	39 (13)
Canada	36	38	39 (5)
Australia	32	35	37 (0)
Japan	25	29	33 (10)
Switzerland	31	31	32 (10)
USA	30	31	32 (8)

Source: *Economic Trends* April 1990 No.438 HMSO.

Note: * Figures in brackets refers to the proportion attributed to social security contributions see text.

Table 3.2 shows a breakdown of total taxes and social security contributions into (1) those that fall directly on households, (2) those that fall directly on corporations, (3) those derived from indirect taxes and (4) those derived from social security contributions and capital taxes. Capital taxes are a very small part of the total, less than 0.5 per cent in most cases. Social security contributions are levied on both individuals and firms; there are considerable differences between countries about the proportions. It is generally accepted that the final incidence of contributions levied on firms is likely to be on individuals through increases in prices or wage adjustments.

Table 3.2 exhibits the considerable diversity in tax structures among countries. Those countries which are members of the European Community have a long way to go to achieve their declared aim of tax harmonization.

The United Kingdom is noticeable as one of the countries that shows the most marked movement away from direct taxes, which have fallen from 36 per cent of the total tax take in 1977 to 28 per cent in 1987. In contrast indirect taxes have increased from 38 per cent to 43 per cent in the same period. This change has not been brought about by reduced taxes overall, as Table 3.1 showed the total tax take increased sharply between 1977 and 1982 and was only slightly lower in 1987 than it was in 1982. Higher value added tax has been substituted for lower income tax and this, with a number of other changes, has caused a substantial redistribution of income to the already well off.

THE NATURE OF TAX CHANGES IN THE 1980s

Tax change was the trend across nations in the latter half of the 1980s. Substantial changes have been introduced in the USA, Canada, Japan, Australia, and many of the countries in the OECD.

A common factor was the process that occurred over earlier years for higher income tax rates on a smaller and smaller tax base. The tax base was being eroded through a variety of tax allowances, fringe benefits and by the courts. This process had reached the point of diminishing revenue returns and caused widespread economic distortion, and violation of horizontal equity, as economic agents sought to avoid, or remove themselves from, high tax areas. Most countries were spending a disproportionate amount of time trying to make an equitable income base when that tax formed a diminishing amount of total revenue. Stories of millionaires paying little or no tax were not uncommon.[1]

Table 3.2 Breakdown of total taxes and social security contributions in OECD countries, 1977, 1982 and 1987

	1977				1982				1987			
	(1)	(2)	(3)	(4)	(1)	(2)	(3)	(4)	(1)	(2)	(3)	(4)
Sweden	42	30	3	25	41	29	3	27	38	31	5	26
Denmark	57	41	–	2	57	40	–	3	58	32	–	4
Norway	28	39	6	27	24	35	16	25	25	39	7	29
Netherlands	27	27	7	39	25	25	7	43	21	28	8	43
France	15	57	6	42	15	36	6	43	15	35	6	44
Belgium	34	28	6	32	37	27	6	30	34	26	7	33
Austria	25	43	4	28	28	38	4	30	28	39	4	29
FR Germany	28	30	5	37	25	31	4	40	26	30	4	40
United Kingdom	36	38	7	19	30	43	10	17	28	43	10	19
Greece	11	54	4	29	15	47	4	34	13	52	4	31
Finland	43	36	4	17	41	40	5	14	41	42	3	14
Italy	22	33	5	40	30	28	5	37	*	27	*	35
Canada	36	40	12	12	37	40	11	12	39	38	9	14
Australia	46	41	12	1	45	45	10	–	46	44	10	–
Japan	22	30	18	30	25	28	17	30	24	27	19	30
Switzerland	42	22	6	40	41	22	5	32	39	23	5	33
USA	35	30	13	22	40	29	7	24	37	28	10	25

Source: Economic Trends April 1990 No 438 HMSO.

Notes: Columns (1) to (4) express the percentage of total taxes and social security contributions:

(1) Derived from direct taxes on households
(2) Derived from indirect taxes
(3) Derived from direct taxes on corporate income
(4) Derived from social security contributions and taxes on capital. The latter account for a very small proportion often less than 0.5%.
* Amount 38% not split between household and corporations.

Fringe Benefits

Fringe benefits distort consumer choice but here the concern is with the revenue implications. When fringe benefits are untaxed they reduce tax revenue, impinge on the fairness of the tax system and may influence the international competitiveness of companies. Most countries, faced with a revenue loss from the growing practice of companies paying fringe benefits in partial replacement of wage and salary increases, have taken some action to limit or tax these benefits. The USA, UK, Australia, New Zealand and Belgium have introduced recent legislation on these lines.

There is no universal definition of a fringe benefit. A 1968 OECD report used the following: 'fringe benefits are payments in cash or in kind, current or deferred, which, while arising out of the employment or the employment performance, are not made because of it. They are made because of the occurrence of some other event, e.g. sickness . . . or they may be forms of reward not in a cash form, such as housing. . . .'

The essence of a fringe benefit is that it is a reward over and above monetary salary and wages and not a benefit available to all. Fringe benefits seem limited only by the ingenuity of the employer and cover such things as expenses in excess of those actually incurred, provision of a car, subsidised accommodation, non-contributory pension and sickness schemes, cheap loans, discounted goods and services, and share options.

Tax practices between countries differ; some try to establish a comprehensive code, others use a general provision for taxing these benefits. The borderline between fringe benefits and other benefits is not always easy to draw and countries differ in their practices. Most countries do not tax gifts and gratuities made on special occasions such as retirement or weddings.

The opportunity to use fringe benefits to reduce tax depends on the attitude of governments to them and the tax regime currently in force. Thus if social security contributions are paid on a graduated scale, and if fringe benefits are not included in the tax base, reduced social security contributions are paid as well as a lower rate of income tax.

The former benefits both the employer and employee. For this reason most countries require employers to declare wages and salaries and the fringe benefits they pay. The UK, Ireland and Spain are exceptions in not taking fringe benefits into account when calculating social security contributions. The UK, however, requires an annual return from companies on fringe benefits paid to directors and 'higher paid' employees and has tightened up legislation in recent years to tax some of these benefits. For the first time in 1991 the benefit of company cars was assessed to National Insurance Contributions.

If social security benefits are paid inversely to the level of cash income, the more the employee receives by way of fringe payments instead of direct money wages, the higher the level of entitlement to social security benefit the employee will have. Fringe benefits will not be so acceptable where they reduce an employee's entitlement, e.g. if the state pension is based on monetary income.

Fringe benefits have increased in those countries, and at those times, when an incomes policy has been in force. They have also increased during a time of labour shortage when they may be seen as a way of attracting labour. Some forms of fringe benefit are also seen as a productivity incentive.

Failure to tax fringe benefits reduces the equity of a tax system because highly paid employees are more likely to receive a greater proportion of their remuneration in this form. The UK Royal Commission on the Distribution of Income and Wealth Report No. 8 (1979) found that the cost to the employer of fringe benefits in 1978 for employees at the very highest levels was about 36 per cent of their total remuneration. These recipients have a double benefit as noted, since if the benefits are not taxed, as well as the recipient saving income tax at their highest marginal rate they also escape National Insurance contributions. UK data for 1983–4 indicate that approximately 6 per cent of all employees had a company car and 4 per cent had wholly or partly paid private medical insurance. The public sector is also placed at a disadvantage in recruiting labour as they are limited in their ability to compete with private firms on fringe benefits. They also interfere in the free functioning of the labour market as employees may feel tied to a particular company because of, say, a pension or health benefit. It also makes comparison between different jobs more difficult and therefore can reduce labour mobility.

The revenue loss from fringe benefits is considerable. The government in Australia estimated a gain of A$750 million equivalent to a 2.55 per cent gain in PAYE tax revenue for the year 1986–7 if fringe benefits were fully taxed. New Zealand gained in the tax year ending 31 March 1987 NZ$166 million from tax on employer-provided cars and NZ$33 million from taxing low-interest loans. In the UK an estimate for 1986–7 was a loss of revenue of £2.2 billion, about 4.5 per cent of income tax revenues, as a result of not treating employers' contributions to approved pension schemes as part of the taxable income of the employee. In addition to this loss of revenue for the government there is a loss of welfare for the recipient who may well prefer cash, equal to the value of the fringe benefit, in order to buy a different assortment of goods.

Somewhat paradoxically governments may encourage some fringe benefits by favourable tax treatment. For example, they may seek to encourage private provision of pension, sickness and insurance schemes to relieve public expenditure. More controversially they may encourage employee share ownership schemes in the hope that this will improve the work incentive of the labour force. Such schemes may be welcomed by the employer as a means of tying down his labour force.

Those fringe benefits that are taxed are as a rule taxed as ordinary income of the employee. The exception since 1985 in New Zealand and 1986 in Australia points to an important departure. In these countries most fringe benefits are taxed on the employer who provides the benefits. This is perhaps an idea whose time has come. Administratively it is simpler for both the tax authorities and individual taxpayers. Companies have compliance costs but these should not be too onerous and presumably a good company should know the cost of paying fringe benefits. Tax at a standard rate is imposed on the aggregate of advantages enjoyed by all employees although this still leaves those on higher tax with an advantage. The tax is 48 per cent in New Zealand and 49 per cent in Australia.

In the UK since 1976 a distinction has been made between those whose remuneration including fringe benefits, is £8,500 a year or more, and those below this figure. However, for benefits provided by way of a credit card or voucher the same rules apply regardless of income. For the lower paid a benefit that is not a discharge of an employee's debt and cannot be exchanged for cash is not subject to tax. More stringent rules apply to the higher paid.

Employee share schemes

Employee share schemes may take the form of share issues with or without a time limit on when the shares can be disposed of, or options to buy shares. The schemes may embrace all workers in the concern or only directors or senior management. If, as is normally the case, the issues are on advantageous terms the benefit can be assessed to tax.

The general approach of most countries is to impose income tax on the benefit derived by the employee based on the difference between the market value of the shares over the amount paid. Similarly for options, the benefit on receipt has a market value and may be taxed. Also, if the holder chooses to exercise his right at some time in the future the gain is normally then assessed to tax. In the UK before 1980 the value of the option rights was subject to tax. Since then only the capital gain on realization is taxable. The UK also has important concessions for approved savings-related share option schemes. The scale of these options can be very large, millions of pounds, for a few fortunate individuals.

The black economy

The term black economy refers to work for cash where the income is not declared for tax purposes – for example, the artisan who quotes one price for cash and a higher one for a cheque settlement; or tips that failed to be declared.

Evidence on the black economy is hard to ascertain. Those who have attempted to estimate its magnitude not infrequently come up with a figure around 5 per cent of national income. In Europe only Italy is generally thought to have a black economy substantially higher than the rest. If this is the case the international comparisons of tax made above will not be seriously misleading as, except for Italy, the problem although not negligible is not unduly distorting.

Search for simplicity

Simplicity has long been held as one of the desirable canons of taxation as this is believed to add to public acceptance of tax. Most tax systems are highly complicated. Well publicised cases of multi-millionaires legally paying little or no tax due to tax loopholes, together with the hope of substantial efficiency gains, provided popular support for change. Once started, the process continued as countries feared being out of step internationally and losing a competitive edge. By cutting out many corporate tax incentives that were generally held to have led to undesirable investment distortions, corporation tax reductions were introduced in many countries.

Although sometimes paraded by politicians as tax reductions in general, the changes have not significantly reduced the overall level of taxation nor can this be expected unless the share of government expenditure is reduced. These changes were usually introduced by pledges to limit government expenditure and they were financed in two major ways. The first method was by cutting out a number of tax allowances, the second method was widening the indirect tax base and in some cases increasing the rate of indirect and other taxes.

The UK

The UK has significantly reduced income tax rates s[...]
the basic rate of income tax from 33 per cent to 3[...]
financed mainly by an increase in VAT from 8 per [...]
Rate cutting continued partly by cutting tax expenditures, by a mo[...]
extension of the VAT base in 1984 and 1985 and increases in other
taxes. By 1988 the top rate of income tax had been reduced from 83 per
cent (98 per cent on unearned income) to 40 per cent with no unearned
income surcharge.

In 1984 the UK started significant change in corporate tax by reducing investment tax reliefs enabling corporation tax rates to be cut.
This was part of the philosophy that believed firms knew better where to
invest than governments and that choices should not be distorted by
considerations of tax advantages.

However as the right hand of government was reducing tax expenditures on companies and individuals, such as the removal of relief
for life insurance policies taken out after 1984, the left hand of government has been busily erecting new concessions in the form of business
expansion schemes, pension and savings schemes, share options and
relief for approved medical schemes for the over-60s. These are likely
to involve large tax expenditures in the future and to lead once again to
significant tax distortions.

The UK in the 1980s laid most emphasis on efficiency, paying scant
heed to equity considerations other than suppressing or delaying
government data on the effects on the distribution of income and wealth.
The culmination of this trend was the introduction of a flat rate Community Charge, or poll tax as it is universally known, introduced in
Scotland in 1989 and England and Wales in 1990. The tax was not
intended to raise extra revenue. It had, however, a large regressive
impact, was extremely costly to collect, and roused strong opposition
including some street riots. There is a much wider level of civil diso-
bedience by people refusing to register for the tax or delaying payment.
Its repeal is promised for 1993. The Appendix of Chapter 12 gives
details.

The United States

The United States in 1986 made a significant change in cutting income
tax rates by reducing tax expenditures, a process that has been copied in
many parts of the world see The Treasury Department Report to the

dent (1984). The US system was a tax lawyer's dream where the ...st of deductions, credits, special deferrals, and credits enabled very rich individuals to pay little or no tax. A lot of these were swept away, widening the tax base and enabling substantial reductions in income tax rates. A major step was to include all realized capital gains in taxable income.

Surprisingly to many outsiders the United States is only now studying the feasibility of a system whereby tax returns for the majority would be unnecessary being largely based on returns from employers and financial institutions. The United States is also increasingly out of line with other countries in not having an imputation system for company dividends and a VAT.

The United States is similar to the UK in that the tax reductions of the 1980s mainly benefited the top 5 per cent of income earners. A Congressional Budget Office Study in 1990 found that, if all federal taxation is included, 60 per cent of American families ended the 1980s paying more tax than when the decade began. Their pre-tax income was either less than before in real terms, or about the same. The top 5 per cent had a 45 per cent gain in pre-tax incomes and an effective tax cut of 10 per cent. Proposals by Congress to reduce the budget deficit, which would have resulted in the poorest 10 per cent of US families paying 10 per cent more in tax while the richest 10 per cent paid 1.7 per cent more, resulted in the House of Representatives rejecting the package which triggered a budget crisis in October 1990.[2]

Other countries

Similar measures to those outlined above have been adapted by a large number of countries among them Australia, Canada, France, Germany, the Netherlands and Japan. Many have reduced individual tax rates particularly at the top end and cut the number of tax bands. Similarly, company tax rates have also been reduced by cutting investment tax incentives.

Australia finding it difficult, like most countries, to tax fringe benefits effectively as income of the employee, followed New Zealand and made the decision to tax the employer on the value of non-cash employee fringe benefits, at the corporate tax rate. As expected a number of fringe benefits have been eliminated or reduced, nevertheless the revenue yield from the change greatly exceeded expectations. The Australian government also wanted to introduce a broad based consumption tax but failed to get public approval.

Canada converted personal exemptions and other deductions to tax credits. Denmark limited the value of deductions to the first bracket rate of 50 per cent. Japan sharply cut exemptions for interest on small savings accounts.

The aim of the changes has been to increase economic efficiency, with countries varying in their attitude to equity. The UK, as shown above, laid most stress on efficiency, paying scant heed to equity considerations. The United States, Australia, Canada and Japan have all considered the adoption of VAT. Its regressive nature has however meant reconsideration of its introduction. Administratively one rate on all goods would be ideal but its regressive nature has resulted in zero or low rates for necessities in most countries that have adopted it.

EUROPEAN DIFFERENCES IN TAX

The aim of this section is to provide a very general examination of the tax systems in the European Community with a view to highlighting some of their major differences. As other barriers are struck down, so fiscal distortions become more important in influencing the allocation of labour and in particular the location of firms. Some comparisons are also drawn with other developed countries. No attempt is made to investigate the minutiae of the various systems see Platt (1985) for further details. However, and this is an important point, the complexity and differences are a considerable barrier to free trade in the Community.

European tax systems exhibit various degrees of maturity and the enlargement of the Community has widened the differences. Musgrave (1989) classifies as 'advanced' those countries where the progressive income tax has been in existence a long time, tax administration is efficient and taxpayers, by and large, honest. The opposite case he labelled immature countries. There is a wide spectrum in between, where many countries fall.

Among the original Community members, Italy had the least developed tax system; a truly general and progressive income tax was not introduced until 1974 and its immaturity allows evasion, which has been estimated at 40 per cent of declared incomes. Almost 70 per cent of net income tax is paid by employed workers with low to average incomes. The European Commission found it necessary to apply pressure for change by reducing border refunds connected to Italy's old tax on gross sales before Italy adopted VAT in the early 1970s. The newer members, Spain, Portugal and Greece, also have less developed tax systems.

France has a tax system which is somewhat different from those of other members. Its level of overall taxation, while below those of Scandinavian countries, is among the highest of the rest of the Community. It achieves this not by high income tax – this is the lowest in the Community apart from Greece – but by having the highest level of social security contributions. In the mid-1980s it was estimated that for a worker on an average wage the employer contributions to social security amounted to over 40 per cent of gross wages and employee contributions to nearly 17 per cent.

The Netherlands introduced a major tax reform in 1990. This includes the integration of the general social security contributions with income tax. About 80 per cent of taxpayers are taxed at 40 per cent, a rate that applies up to an income of 50,000 guilders (about £15,000).

The differences in tax maturity of member countries, added to the different tax regimes and detailed country regulations, are making it difficult to achieve tax harmonization.

Income tax

The tax unit

One of the many conflicts in public finance is that it is very difficult to find a simple way to do justice both to single persons and to married persons in different circumstances. For example, to go over completely to a system whereby the individual is the unit of taxation may seem unjust to a single person. Married persons have a considerable advantage in spreading unearned income to their spouses thereby reducing their overall tax payment. Aggregation of *earned income* varies. Aggregation of the income of couples, or of families, will under a progressive tax system mean a higher tax burden for many couples unless special concessions are made. This question is taken up again in Chapter 6.

This lack of a single clear equitable rule for taxing persons in different household circumstances results in a wide diversity of tax treatment between countries. For example, Australia, Canada, Italy, New Zealand, and since 1990 the UK, all have *independent taxation*. Denmark, Japan, the Netherlands and Sweden have *independent taxation of earnings and joint taxation of investment income*. The latter is to reduce the loss of tax revenue caused when couples rearranged investment income between themselves for tax purposes. France, Germany, Ireland, Belgium and the United States use some form of *joint taxation* whereby married couples are taxed as a single unit. France and Germany apply a *split or quotient system*: here the income of the family unit is added together and split between the members. In the case of a family, say, husband, wife and two children, they will have their total income divided by three (if children have a weight of a half). Each family member is then taxed as a single person on his share of income. These quotient systems can be extremely generous to married couples, particularly those with large families. Ireland, where joint taxation is an option, and the United States operate different tax schedules for married couples. Joint taxation involves one spouse knowing the income of the other, is more administratively complex and acts as a disincentive for the other spouse, usually the wife, to take on paid work as all this income will usually be subject to tax as the partner's income will have used up the tax allowances. In the case of high-income earners, couples' aggregation of income will also bring them into higher tax brackets sooner than if their incomes were subject to separate taxation.

As well as differences in rates, differences exist in the income base because of what is included in income and the nature of tax reliefs, aggregation or otherwise of household incomes, and the extent, if any, to which inflation is taken into account and averaging allowed. In OECD countries tax is deducted on income currently earned except in France, where tax is collected on the previous year's earnings, and Switzerland, where tax is payable on average income earned in the two previous years (Platt 1985).

Income base

Attempts as noted are being made in many countries to bring fringe benefits into the tax base. Practices vary widely. Some countries include some imputed income from home ownership although this may be at less than market value and there are considerable variations in the taxation of imputed rent. Exceptions to this can be found in Australia, Austria, Canada, France, Germany, Ireland, Japan, Turkey, UK, and the United States. Income tax relief is granted in most countries, except the United States and the UK, for life insurance premiums. Although in the UK there is relief for policies in force before 1986. Pension premiums get tax relief except in France and Greece. All give some form of mortgage interest relief, or more rarely against capital repayment, but this is restricted in France to two years and to three years in Germany.

Tax reliefs may take the form of allowances available to all who are eligible such as a married persons allowance, or they may be related to actual expenditures. The latter may include relief for interest payments, insurance premiums, contributions to private pension schemes and charitable donations. Tax allowances are deductions from income before tax is applied. Tax credits are offset against tax payable. Usually the credits are a fixed sum but they may be positively or negatively related to tax liability. Non-wastable tax credits are those where the recipient receives cash for any excess of his credit over his tax liability. Other countries apply zero rate brackets, quotient systems apply in France and Luxembourg. Income splitting among family members is practised in Germany and Ireland.

The treatment of capital gains varies, e.g. recent changes in the United States treat all gains as ordinary income, and Greece does not tax personal capital gains at all. In general capital gains receive more favourable treatment than other income. Some countries allow indexation so as to tax only real gains; others make a distinction between short and long term gains. What constitutes a capital gain also varies widely.

The UK has moved from a system that taxed investment income more heavily by way of an investment income surcharge to a system that tends to favour investment income. Separate taxation of husband and wife in 1990 means that non-working spouses can have investment income up to the level of their tax allowance and avoid tax whereas it was formally aggregated with their spouses.

Wealth, estate and gift taxes

All EC countries tax transfers of wealth at death and lifetime gifts with wide variation of actual practice. In some the tax varies with the degree of relationship between the donor and donee.

Denmark, Germany, the Netherlands, Luxembourg and Spain levy annual net wealth taxes. Germany and Luxembourg at a flat rate of 0.5 per cent and Denmark at a flat rate of 2.2 per cent.

Company taxes

Free movement of capital across national boundaries is well under way and can be expected to go where its return is highest. What matters to the firm considering setting up or expanding a business is the after-tax return. So the allocation of resources can be distorted if capital is allocated because of tax reasons. The importance of harmonization in company taxation has therefore been brought forward by the European Commission. Also, because corporation taxes are a relatively small part of total tax revenues – they comprised on average only 7.2 per cent of the total in 1986 – severe disruption to a country's revenue is less likely, if company tax is altered, than with some other taxes.

There are considerable differences at present in almost all aspects of corporation tax. Differences are wide in the definition of what constitutes gross and net profit, the tax rate, the tax base, the treatment of depreciation, investment relief, stock valuation, capital gains, averaging of profits, subsidiaries and small companies, provisions for losses and concessions made to small businesses and new firms. In some countries the 'forfait' system allows small businesses' tax liability to be calculated as a percentage of turnover rather than on the basis of profit. There are major differences in the treatment of partnerships.

Should firms' profits be taxed separately to shareholders? Since ultimately all profits accrue to individuals the first best solution, some argue, would be to attribute all profits to shareholders, as is the case with partnerships, and tax them accordingly. The usual, rather weak, objection to this is that the taxpayer would be liable to tax on income he has not received. A more practical objection would be the compliance costs imposed on firms whose shares had a rapid turnover. It would hardly be practical for a single EC country to tax all firm profits in this way because of the likely distortion to investment flows. A corporation tax on these grounds is then seen, at best, only as a method of approximating individual tax. The counter argument is that corporations are legal entities and as such have a taxable capacity. The fact that such a tax is shifted on to owners, workers or customers weakens this argument but in its favour is the point that company owners benefit extensively from government provision, such as infrastructure and education and should therefore contribute to the cost. Most countries do tax corporations and this in turn can provide governments with an instrument to use against monopolies and for regulating the economy. All EC countries have a separate tax on the income of incorporated firms. There are four systems whereby this can be achieved:

1 The complete separation of corporate and personal tax (the classical system). This brings in the 'double tax' argument whereby profits are taxed and then taxed again if distributed to shareholders. The system is at present in use in Luxembourg, the Netherlands and the United States.
2 Two-rate or split rate system. Companies are taxed less on profits distributed to shareholders. This system is in use in Germany, Japan and Portugal.

3 Tax credit or imputation system. This was designed partially to avoid
   double taxation by imputing part of profits tax to the tax benefit of
   the shareholder. This system is used in the UK and most other EC
   countries.
4 Full integration. Shareholders are taxed as if partners in the company
   under personal taxation.

Most EC countries operate 3, the imputation system, a Commission
draft Directive requires its implementation: shareholders are given a tax
credit against part of the tax paid on distributed profits. Not all member-
states have implemented the Directive and of those who have done so it
is far from harmonized.

As a result of these differences firms with the same pre-tax profit will
pay very different amounts of tax in different countries. Suggestions are
made from time to time that companies should change to a cash-flow
type of tax. In a European context such a change would not merely be a
means of 'achieving a level playing field' but would also have other
advantages.

Cash-flow tax

Under a cash-flow tax no distinction is made between capital expenditure and expenditure on current items such as labour and materials. The
base for tax is simply the difference between income from the sales of
goods and services and the money spent on producing them. Since
capital assets are written off in the year of purchase complicated provisions to allow for inflation become unnecessary. Such a tax also
avoids the problems of defining depreciation and economic profit.
Companies can effectively postpone tax by high investment policies.
Companies undertaking large investment in any particular year might
therefore have no tax to pay in that year, or have tax losses to carry
forward, but in subsequent years their profits would be greater (because
the depreciation would have been used up) and these profits would be
subject to tax. With a 50 per cent tax rate the government is saying in
effect 'we are financing half of your investment in return for half of the
profits'.

Social security contributions

The differences in treatment of social security contributions in various
countries have already been remarked on. Most countries levy on both

the employee and the employer and at very different rates and some differentiate between types of worker. Employer rates are usually higher than employee rates although the final incidence of the tax may not rest with the employer.

Most countries maintain the fiction of separate insurance funds although few benefits are linked directly to contributions. Within the EC only Denmark and the Netherlands have integrated social security contributions with income tax.

Value added tax

In the EC there has been harmonization on VAT as the main source of indirect tax. All members of the EC levy such a tax; however, it is far from being uniform across the Community. The tax is levied on the value added at each stage in the production and distribution process. Since the sum of values added at successive stages is equal to the final price of the product, the amount of tax paid will be the same as if the tax was charged once on this final value. Exports are free of tax and imports taxed at national borders although this will have to change with the advent of 1992 and the breaking down of border restrictions. Because of exceptions, such as banking, most financial services, education, medical services and real estate, about 30 per cent of total consumer expenditure is not subject to VAT. As yet, there are differences in coverage, in the level and variety of rates of VAT, in the way business is allowed to reclaim certain items and in the treatment of small firms. A number of countries have integrated the administration of VAT with that of other business taxes so that a firm need only deal with one office. Compliance costs for firms can vary widely between member countries and some countries offer partial recompense to firms for expenses incurred in collecting VAT.

The aim eventually seems to be to apply the *restricted origin principle* to goods crossing borders in the Community; that is they carry the tax of the producing country (the origin principle) while goods from outside the EC have the destination principle. The restricted origin principle eliminates fiscal barriers between countries in the Community and argues for a common tax between members.

There still remain considerable differences between member-states in the goods subject to tax, the structure of rates and zero rating. The extent to which full harmonization is needed is not clear. The United States allows each of the 50 states, as well as the District of Columbia, to levy sales taxes at different rates and there are no border tax checks between them. The evidence seems to point to tax differences of no more than 5 per cent being sustainable without involving too much border crossing for tax purposes.

The debate with 1992 in mind is protracted. The Commission in July 1987 suggested a plan for VAT approximation by squeezing all VAT rates in the Community within two bands, 4–9 per cent for necessities and 14–19 per cent for other goods and services, and the abolition of zero rating. It accepted that member governments should be able to apply for special treatment for politically sensitive items (such as baby clothes in the UK). It also wanted harmonized rates of excise duty for tobacco, wine, spirits, beer and petrol. Unanimous agreement of the 12 governments is required for the implementation of these suggestions.

Excise taxes

Excise on cigarettes has been partly harmonized since 1978, although wide differences still remain, but measures in other areas have still to be approved. As excise taxes account for more than 25 per cent of total tax receipts in some countries and Denmark taxes alcohol almost 40 times higher than the lowest rate in Italy, the negotiations are difficult. Another difficulty to be overcome is that countries use indirect taxes to discriminate against other countries: soak whisky if you produce wine and not whisky, and vice versa. A number of countries have been taken to the Court of Justice by the Commission for fiscal discrimination and the Commission has generally succeeded in winning its case.

A further dilemma with high indirect taxes, especially those on alcohol and tobacco, is between their regressive impact and the wish to limit the consumption of the individual so to minimize the social harm that is caused by these products. The regressive impact follows since many individuals in poor income families either smoke or drink or do both. A family study in the UK found that the poorest fifth of the population were spending 9 per cent of their disposable income on tobacco tax if that family contained at least one smoker (Fry and Pashardes 1988)

The December 1985 summit of the EC made certain amendments to the Treaty of Rome; one was to Article 99 making necessary a commitment to harmonize indirect taxes to ensure a free internal market.

Proposals for such harmonization were presented by the Commission in July 1987 but these have not yet been adopted. The differences to be bridged are considerable. The Commission proposed uniform rates throughout the Community generally reflecting the average of members' existing rates. On rates in force in the mid-1980s we have, looking at some extremes:

Beer Ecu per litre: Spain 0.03, Ireland 1.13, UK 0.68. The Commission proposes a rate of 0.17.
Wine Ecu per litre: Germany, Greece, Italy, Portugal and Spain zero, Ireland 2.79, UK 1.54. The Commission proposes 0.17.
Spirits Ecu per bottle: Greece 0.14, Denmark 10.50, UK 7.45. The Commission is proposing 3.81.
Cigarettes Ecu per 20 VAT and excise duty: Greece and Spain 0.01, Denmark 1.52, UK 0.96. The Commission is proposing 0.39.
Petrol Ecu per litre: Spain and Luxembourg 0.2, Italy 0.53, UK 0.31. The Commission is proposing 0.34.
Diesel Ecu per litre: Spain 0.03, Ireland 0.29, UK 0.26. The Commission proposes 0.18.

The particular figures given above are only important as an illustration of the wide range of differences between EC member countries. With the rates proposed by the Commission Denmark would experience a fall of some 11 per cent in tax revenue and Ireland a fall of some 5–7 per cent. Spain, Portugal and Greece would get substantial increases because they would be levying more on tobacco and alcohol.

It is clear that these changes would present severe problems to some national budgets. They also would have a substantial impact on individuals, which would be welcome by some – the alcoholic chain smoker in the UK would do very well – but would be abhorrent to others.

The rationale of complete tax harmonization, discussed in Chapter 13, is rather weak in the field of indirect taxes and it is not perhaps surprising that the Commission has in recent years switched much of its attention to the more important harmonization of company taxation.

Failure to agree measures to bring indirect taxes more into line with one another would, with the proposed scrapping of custom posts, presumably be one way of getting nearer to a common tax base and common tax rates, by way of competitive pressures. If we take the 5 per cent difference as being feasible between any two borders there could be a considerable difference between VAT rates in Denmark and Italy or Spain which are separated from each other by other boundaries and long distances.

Local taxation

All EC countries except Denmark and the UK have local taxes on property. Britain has a business property tax but abolished domestic rating, in Scotland in 1989 followed by England and Wales a year later, in favour of a Community Charge or poll tax. A new system, called a 'domestic tax', which will be a tax on property is to replace the Community Charge in 1993. (Details will be found the Appendix of Chapter 12.) Most countries impose local taxes on businesses as well as individuals but there the uniformity ends. In some the capital value of the property is used as a tax base, in others actual or imputed rents, or the value upon acquisition, transfer or appreciation. Belgium, Denmark, Finland, Norway, Sweden and the United States operate a local income tax. Local government also in some countries receives part of the proceeds of centrally raised income tax. Local payroll taxes are paid in a few countries.

Compliance costs

Compliance costs are incurred by the public sector in collecting tax and by the corporation and individual in complying with a given tax system. Most interest is centred on private compliance costs and the term is frequently confined to this meaning, administrative costs being used to refer to the public sector.

A recent study of the effect of taxation on small and medium-sized business in the UK Bannock (1990) makes the point that the burden on businesses has increased. They now collect taxes on expenditure, social security contributions and taxes on employment income, as well as assessing their taxable profits and withholding tax on dividend payments. The tax authorities' role, apart from the self-employed, is largely restricted to the verification of tax returns, the issue of assessments, the receipt of payments and anti-avoidance measures. The study believes the growing isolation of the tax authorities from the administration of the tax has been a contributory factor in the growth of complexity of the tax system and therefore of the growth in compliance costs. By way of example they quote the situation in France, where the treatment of business capital gains depends upon whether the assets have been held for more or less than two years, the type of asset, whether the business is unincorporated or incorporated, whether the firm is taxed on the forfait system, and so on. More generally, most countries do not consolidate tax payments, thus necessitating separate payments, frequently to separate tax offices.

The main compliance costs for firms they see as: understanding the frequently changing tax law; training employees; maintaining records; calculation of taxes due and making tax returns and payment; and issue of special tax invoices, e.g. VAT, dealing with queries from tax authorities, customers, etc. Tax compliance costs are difficult to work out. A number of studies undertaken at different times for different countries indicate that costs could conservatively be in the order of 1–2 per cent of GNP, a significant amount. The studies all show that compliance costs are significantly higher for small and medium sized firms. A recent study by Bannock and Albach in 1987 of German and UK compliance costs found costs for firms in the £15,000 and under turnover range were 2.5 per cent of turnover in the UK and 7.8 per cent in Germany. Costs fell with size until firms with a turnover of £2 million or more had costs which were well below 1 per cent of turnover. Some countries, such as the UK, apply a lower rate of tax to small profits (with the result that large firms experiencing small profits also benefit) which can at best be seen as a rough and ready measure to compensate small firms for these additional costs. Many taxes, particularly on business, are collected in arrears and this can be looked on as an interest-free loan offering partial offset to compliance costs.

A wide ranging study of administrative and compliance costs of individuals as well as firms was published by Sandford et al. (1989). They put an estimate of over £5 billion as the total compliance costs for the UK in 1986–7. This is some 4 per cent of total tax revenue or some 1.5 per cent of GDP at factor cost, a figure in line with other studies; like them it finds business compliance costs concentrated on small firms. For the personal sector the burden appears to fall disproportionately on poorer pensioners, widows and divorced or separated women. These costs may be intangible due, for example, to anxiety in dealing with tax matters, often for the first time. The advent of independent taxation in 1990 will in this respect affect women in particular. The introduction of the Community Charge, or poll tax, in the UK ranks very high on both administrative cost and compliance cost. It is estimated to have increased the costs of collection by local government by some four to five times. A number of persons who are able to pay the tax are, on a matter of principle, willing to suffer the inconvenience of being taken to court rather than pay.

WHICH WAY?

EC countries use the same sort of taxes to raise revenue and the contribution of each tax to total revenue may often be close but as the brief sketch above shows there are chaotic differences in the way each country administers each tax. That countries tax differently is not surprising. Tax regimes are seldom the result of master plans, they are rather the result of piecemeal changes brought about by legislation and legal precedent which are grafted on to systems which have existed for very long periods.

These differences may not matter much in largely independent countries which have relatively isolated economies. In an interdependent world, which has a considerable measure of freedom of trade and of capital movement, these differences are of considerable importance. This is especially so in a Community pledged to close economic ties, as other barriers to trade are swept away fiscal barriers assume increasing importance. The drawbacks of unco-ordinated tax systems in stifling enterprise, holding back growth and creating large compliance costs on firms and individuals become more apparent. A recent survey of tax policy is found in Kay (March 1990).

This is a familiar problem in public finance. The absurdities of the present systems are clear. Spelling out a better system is not difficult, but getting from the present to the better system is a minefield. Although a new system can be presented, were it obtained, as better, benefiting most people, the changes needed to get there will harm many who have based their decisions on current tax procedures. Those taxpayers with vested interests in present systems can be expected to raise vigorous opposition to change.

Under these circumstances it would seem that change is likely to be piecemeal, on the lines of VAT. When the Commission decided on the form of indirect tax, VAT on French lines was preferred over the German cascade system and the British system of purchase tax. The cascade system was a tax levied at each stage of production with no rebate made for tax paid at a earlier stage of production. This system encourage vertical integration of firms who could thereby reduce the amount of tax to be paid on the final commodity. Purchase tax was payable on a narrow range of commodities and levied once at the wholesaling stage. Now all countries operate a VAT system. Directives have since set bands within which rates of tax should be set and harmonization of the VAT base has been proposed. On corporation tax, the Commission favours the imputation system of assessing tax and most countries now conform.

Just as in a single country more radical proposals for reform in Europe are put forward from time to time. Thus an expenditure tax could be implemented in EC countries on a uniform basis to replace existing income, estate/gift, capital gains, and value added taxes. Company taxation could be undertaken on a unitary or formula basis, as noted in Chapter 13.

It might, somewhat paradoxically, be easier to implement a fundamental change on an EC basis than in a single country. If dissatisfaction with the current complexity continues to grow and as the benefits from a more unified system become apparent, pressure on politicians to change will increase. If change is inevitable, then a radical change that overcomes many of the complexities that have been outlined could be presented as the best alternative. Politics and economics would be on the same course.

SUMMARY

The increase in government spending noted in Chapter 2 has resulted in a corresponding increase in taxation including social security contributions. Attempts since 1982 to reverse this trend have largely been unsuccessful. While developed countries rely on similar taxes to raise revenue the tax base, tax rates, and the amount raised by each tax, show marked differences. The countries of the European Community have a long way to go to reach their aim of harmonized taxation.

Common to most of these countries has been a movement in the 1980s away from income tax to indirect taxes, but not a lowering of the overall tax bill. This has caused a substantial redistribution of income to the well-off. Several countries have attempted to overhaul their tax systems by reducing tax allowances and taxing fringe benefits. The black economy has been a problem for tax authorities, particularly in Italy.

The major differences in taxation in European Community countries was given. Evidence points to compliance costs being a considerable burden especially to small businesses. A final section looked at taxation alternatives for EC countries

Chapter 4

National Debt and the Public Sector Borrowing Requirement

MEANING OF THE TERMS NATIONAL DEBT AND PSBR

When a government spends more than it receives this results in the issue of some sort of security, which can include banknotes, to cover the deficiency. In like manner a surplus results in a reduction of securities. Roughly speaking, the aggregate of securities over time, less redemptions, is called the National Debt. In practice, factors such as currency flows from abroad mean that changes in the National Debt are not exactly identical with the government surplus or deficit in the same period. It is, however, government annual surpluses or deficits which have come to dominate government announcements in recent years. A trenchant criticism of relying on a single number to give an adequate measure of the government's impact on the economy will be found in Ashworth *et al.* (1984); see also Buiter (1985). The issue is taken up in the next section, The Relevance of the Debt. Governments have tended to produce annual targets for public spending, expressed as their share in GDP, for several years ahead, in Britain called the Medium Term Financial Strategy (MTFS). Targets may be expressed in terms of reducing government spending in real terms, or of holding expenditure constant. This will produce figures for the Public Sector Borrowing Requirement (PSBR) or more rarely the Public Sector Debt Repayment (PSDR). Governments have not been very successful in meeting their expenditure targets in spite of frequent target changes. Often this has been due to gross underestimating of the size of government expenditure due in part to the increase in transfer payments when there is a downturn in the economy, coupled with a decrease in tax revenue as workers are laid off. Predictions can also err in the opposite direction when the economy grows faster than is forecast. As detailed at the start of Chapter 2 the PSBR can be so manipulated by the inclusion and exclusion of various items that the figure by itself is pretty meaningless unless care is taken to make it compatible with previous years.

Most of the discussion that follows will centre on the National Debt rather than the annual change in the debt. The cumulative debt being larger than the current surplus or deficit can be considered the more fundamental problem, although the impact of the current balance may impose considerable strain on an economy; similar considerations apply to both aggregates.

Considerable portions of the debt are usually held by government funds and agencies and the total of debt including these holdings is referred to as Gross National Debt, the term Net National Debt being used when these holdings are excluded. The Gross concept is relevant when considering interest payments but the Net concept when considering the liquidity of the economy.

Figure 4.1 gives a picture of the Gross Public Debt as a percentage of GDP of the OECD countries from 1970 to 1989.

Until the mid-1970s debt was diminishing as a percentage of GDP – a continuation of a trend from 1950. From that period the ratio of debt rose in the OECD countries from a low of 36 per cent to a high of 56 per cent in 1987. There has since been a slight fall. In assessing the economic importance of these figures it needs to be borne in mind that debt levels have been very much higher in the past. Britain's, as a result of war financing, was 183 per cent of GNP in 1955 as opposed to some 50 per cent today. The amount of interest that has to be paid on the debt is also of economic relevance. The move to higher interest rates in the 1980s has increased the debt service costs but again these have been at higher levels in previous periods. In real terms, in several years in the 1960s and 1970s real interest rates were negative.

Faced with a deficit at worst the government issues banknotes to cover its expenditures. Since this requires no surrender of purchasing power by the private sector this will add a boost to the economy that, in an economy working to capacity, will be purely inflationary. Since the level of the note issue is normally circumscribed by law we concentrate on the issue of other types of government security which are sold on the market.

Just as it is necessary when looking at government spending and revenue carefully to define government in order to make meaningful comparisons, so also it is necessary when talking about the National Debt. The extent to which local government and state industry is included can be important. The subject of National Debt seems to arouse more irrational debate than most other economic topics. The size of the

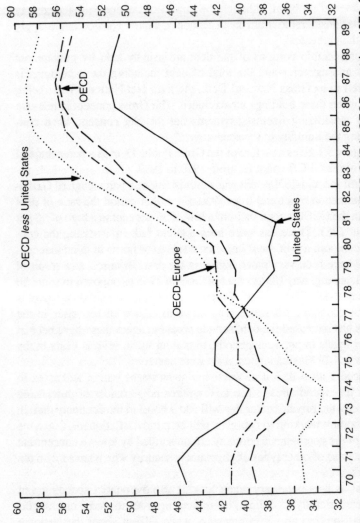

Figure 4.1 Gross public debt of OECD countries as a percentage of GDP/GNP in OECD countries, 1970–89
Source: OECD Secretariat estimates[1] General government

debt and its so called 'burden' come in for most comment. A frequent source of confusion is the carrying over of ideas about private debt to the public sector. Governments are expected to continue public debt; it is unlike most private debt in that it does not have to be repaid. A maturing issue is usually replaced with a new issue.

THE RELEVANCE OF THE DEBT

Can any valid comparisons be drawn between the debt of a nation and the debt of a company? Briefly the answer is 'yes'; but there are also pitfalls to be avoided.

A company balance sheet over time will normally show an increase in the liabilities of the company, which will be matched by corresponding increases on the asset side. Before a judgement is made that the increase in liabilities is good or bad, it is necessary to know a great deal more about the changes. For example, it makes a difference if it is the issued capital, reserves or bank overdraft which has increased; and it also makes a difference how the assets have changed. Has more been invested in plant, or is it that unwanted stocks are piling up?

It is also necessary to take account of both sides of a national balance sheet but this is almost never done. The National Debt has been primarily incurred as a result of war expenditures, and there are no physical assets corresponding to this expenditure. Nevertheless the public sector has many tangible assets. An increase in the PSBR because the government sector has invested in, say, the infrastructure of the economy, or because it is increasing investment in commercial undertakings under its control, may be viewed differently to an increase in PSBR caused by failure of governments to put up taxes to cover expenditures on current items. In a like fashion a reduction in debt by the sale of assets is one thing; a reduction because there is a revenue surplus is another. These vital distinctions are seldom made in public pronouncements which simply, and misleadingly, concentrate on the size of the PSBR.

Applying company balance sheet ideas to the national balance sheet has been labelled the 'cement and steel' concept. The purpose of business finance is to increase the company's profits and net worth, but this is not the case for government finance (with the possible exception of commercial activities which the government has undertaken). Assets held by the firm are the collateral against the firm's debt, but no such reasoning applies to government assets. Applying commercial ideas to the whole of government debt 'reinforces the ancient prejudice in favour of expenditure on hardware as distinct from services', the type of thinking that enjoins the building of schools and hospitals but jibs at paying those that run them adequate salaries. A symptom of this kind of thinking is the fondness of most governments for prestige development rather than undertaking less glamorous but more productive investment.

It is true that the economy will be worse off if a government increases the PSBR and uses the proceeds wastefully. But this argument has nothing to do with increasing the debt; it would be equally valid if the wasteful spending was made out of tax revenue.

THE TECHNICAL PROBLEMS OF DEBT MANAGEMENT

Debt presents problems of management. The PSBR, that is the net debt requirements of the government sector, have to be accommodated and the existing debt has to be managed by issuing new securities as old ones mature. The debt will have a certain time structure and is likely to be composed of some securities that can be cashed in on demand like National Savings, and a range of other securities with various redemption dates. Some will be due for early redemption (Treasury bills), some may be undated securities which simply pay interest (Consols), the bulk is likely to be medium- and long-dated. The pattern of indebtedness inherited from the past and the associated level of interest rates may well not fit in with current requirements and the structure may be manipulated at the short end to influence the money market or the long end by management of the gilt-edged market.

The cost of servicing the debt could be a problem either because it pre-empts too large a proportion of tax revenue or, if held abroad, because the outflow of interest payments could depress the price of the home currency. Many countries in the developing world have debt problems because they have borrowed on world markets, but for most developed countries this is not a serious problem. Debt levels are usually substantially below the levels shown at the end of the two world wars and, even with the general rise in interest rates in recent years, interest payments as a proportion of tax revenue are generally below levels that obtained in the past.

THE MANAGEMENT OF THE DEBT

On a day-to-day basis the debt has to be managed. Any fresh financial requirements plus any securities sold on the market have to be taken up by new holders in the private sector or by the government sector itself which means the release of cash into the economy. If the government fears the growth of liquidity in the economy it can attempt to:

1 fund, that is make long term securities more attractive;
2 increase taxes;
3 cut the use of real resources by the public sector by reducing government expenditure or investment.

All of these methods have been used and involve obvious drawbacks. The attempt to fund may mean increasing interest rates which may have other undesirable repercussions on the economy. Its success cannot be guaranteed and in setting interest rates political and external constraints have to be taken into consideration. Increasing taxes or cutting government expenditure can be politically unpopular and involve difficult choices. Changes in taxes can be aimed primarily at changing spending in the company sector, or at changing the level of personal spending. The latter is likely to reflect on the company sector if the change continues for any length of time. Changes in government expenditure to reduce debt requirements has been tried by many governments in the 1980s with very little success as shown in Chapter 3.

BURDEN OF THE DEBT

The phrase 'burden of the debt' is unfortunately one that seems to be embedded in any discussion about the National Debt. The implication of the word 'burden' is that life would be better if only the burden could be got rid of. Discussion about the debt is thus biased in advance. Confusion is made worse by differences about the meaning of burden.

What is meant by 'burden'?

Burden is sometimes construed to mean the current amount of goods and services which the private sector forgoes in order to enable the public sector to consume, termed *crowding out*. Crowding out may simply be a case of government expenditure substituting for private expenditure e.g. Government spending on health may be a substitute for private health spending. Crowding out may also occur because of the effect of increased government spending, and/or the way the increase is financed, on interest rates, exchange rates, imports and exports, wages or prices.

Crowding out may be nil in the case of an underemployed economy where the use of resources by the public sector need not be at the expense of private consumption but can come from increased production out of previously unused resources. Indeed government spending may *crowd in* private spending if the expectation is that increased government spending will bring about a recovery in a depressed economy. With full employment of resources, by definition, increased consumption by one sector is at the expense of another if imported goods remain unchanged. To make sense of the burden argument in conditions of full employment it is necessary, somehow, to evaluate the government's use of resources and its worth to individuals as opposed to leaving resources to be consumed as they were. It is clear that while this line of argument poses important issues, these have nothing specifically to do with debt financing; tax financing raises similar problems. The conclusion of Buiter was that:

> Probably more uninformed statements have been made on the issue of public sector debt and deficits than over any other topic in macroeconomics. Proof by repeated assertion has frequently appeared to be an acceptable substitute for the more conventional methods of proof by deduction or by induction.'

> (Buiter 1985)

Another concept of burden relates to the amount of goods and services forgone by people during the period of their lifetimes. Given full employment, capital projects which take a long time to fructify will lessen the amount of currently available consumer goods but increase the amount available, say, in ten or twenty years. Again it is clear that important issues are involved which have nothing specifically to do with the National Debt.

The concepts of debt so far approach the question from the side of the use of resources. They can be argued in terms of the real or money burden on the existing and future generations. Real economic issues also underlie the discussion in money terms, to be taken up shortly. Again these issues are misleading when confined to a discussion of debt financing, with the implied assumption that financing by other means do not also have similar implications.

Yet another concept of burden relates to the estimated effects that the debt has upon incentives to work, to save, to take risks, etc. Chapter 10 examines the incentive issues. What emerges from this discussion of the meaning of the debt burden is that government spending raises very important issues about the current use of real resources, the stock of capital we should aim to bequeath to the future, and the effect on incentives. The important point emerges that, however the government sector obtains the use of these resources, whether it is by commandeering them, by taxation, or by incurring debt, these important issues remain. To look at the so-called burden of the debt in isolation is a misleading exercise; it is necessary to consider the advantages and disadvantages of alternative methods of obtaining these resources.

INTERNAL AND EXTERNAL BORROWING

An important distinction to be made is between internally and externally held debt – that is, between internal and external borrowing. Internal borrowing is a rearrangement of assets. Citizens surrender current purchasing power in return for government securities, and no increase of real resources is directly created as a result. External borrowing, on the other hand, permits an import of real resources, either of consumption or capital goods. Likewise, interest and repayment of internal debt is the transfer of current purchasing power back to holders of the debt. However, interest and repayment of external borrowing means a corresponding outflow of goods and services, unless the external holders choose for a time to reinvest in securities of the country making the repayment. From the point of view of interest and repayment of external debt, it can be said that this constitutes a 'burden' on future output of goods and services. However, it must not be lost sight of that the initial borrowing increases resources. If these resources are used to increase the productive capacity of the economy, this may create a return over and above the ability to service the debt. The application of this to developing countries is obvious. It may at times be necessary to use foreign loans for increasing imports of consumer goods particularly in times of drought and other emergencies, but the use to increase productive capacity is to be preferred if at all possible, as this will help to create the output to repay and service the loan and improve the economy generally.

EQUITY ASPECTS OF THE DEBT

Probably the most frequently mentioned aspect of the internally held debt is the concern which is expressed over its effects on the distribution of income and wealth as securities form a larger part of the income and wealth of well off persons. The debt represents a transfer of income from those who pay taxes to those who own the securities. Since institutions such as pension and insurance companies own most of the securities and all citizens pay taxes of one sort or another, it is not easy to work out how much transference in fact takes place, who pays for it and who benefits from it. The presumption is that richer and older workers benefit somewhat more than younger and poorer persons as the former are likely to have larger interests in pension and insurance funds.

If the internally held debt were abolished overnight by decree, the government would be relieved of the obligation to pay interest on the undated stock and the obligation to pay interest and make repayment of other securities. Repayment of stock in practice means the refunding of debt by making a fresh security issue. The cost to the government of interest payments is not normally large enough to cause concern particularly when account is taken of the fact that governments often relend a portion of the capital at market rates to other sectors, and interest payments to the private sector will be taxed. There have been cases of countries in exceptional circumstances such as wartime issuing so much debt, usually in the shape of currency, as to cause a breakdown of the economy but these circumstances stand out because they are exceptional. Even in the United States, where the budget deficit has been in the news so much in recent years, the federal interest bill in 1987 was only about 3 per cent of GNP, or 13 per cent of the budget total.

The real objection that seems to be at the back of this type of argument is an objection to the very unequal distribution of wealth and income in most economies. This is a question which is worth discussing in its own right, but interest payments on the National Debt are of only subsidiary importance to the topic.

FUTURE GENERATIONS

A long-debated question is whether, and in what senses, raising money by debt can be said to burden future generations. Does public debt put a 'chain around the necks' of our children or is it a case of imposing no burden since future generations, as well as having the obligation to pay, also inherit the securities on which payment is made? The debt existing at the present time has the effect of redistributing income from existing taxpayers to existing holders of the securities. In 100 years from now both the holders of the debt (assuming debt repayment is financed by the issue of new securities) and the taxpayers will be different people. If we take a shorter time span, say 30 years, the argument can be looked at in terms of inter-generation equity – that sons and daughters will be paying for the debts of their parents. This point has some validity, but does not boil down to anything more than the truism that our actions today will affect the future in a number of ways, some of them calculable and some of them not. *In particular, the argument that raising funds by taxation today, instead of by debt, imposes no burden on the future is clearly false.* If a person's wealth or income is taxed today, while it is true that no 'tax burden' is left to future generations, it is also true that the assets of the individual to spend on, or bequeath to, his or her dependants will be less. In order to make sense of the argument that raising money by debt finance is a burden on the future, the stream of consequences stemming from raising finance in this way has to be compared with the stream of consequences stemming from raising finance in alternative ways. The number of alternative ways are innumerable, as they can take the form of various combinations of different taxes. In a trivial sense, however we raise the money imposes a burden on the future. In the sense that this question is usually phrased: i.e. that raising money by debt imposes more of a burden on the future than raising it by taxation, the question is not capable of a precise answer, as different assumptions about present and future behaviour will yield different answers.

In this question we come back again to a more fundamental issue that appears to underlie much argument on this subject; that is the question of the perpetuation of the existing structure of wealth by inheritance, and once more it seems that discussion of this question directly is more fruitful than a roundabout discussion of imprecise 'burdens' caused by this or that method of financing.[1]

Some other meanings of burden are now considered.

TAX FRICTION

It is possible that the proportion of taxes needed to be raised to service the National Debt could cause serious disincentives. The argument is valid but not normally of significance to most developed economies. In the context of considering a block of government expenditure financed by taxes or debt, the disincentives of both must be taken into account and are likely to be higher for direct tax finance.

REDUCED CAPITAL FORMATION

It is possible that debt and tax finance have different effects on investment and hence the growth of the economy. A general presumption would be that taxes on individuals are likely to have their major impact initially on consumption expenditure (impacting later on investment of firms as consumer demand drops) while debt would fall more on investment. To the extent that this is true it is implied that the future tax burden lies in having a smaller endowment of capital. This argument appears theoretically sound. Its practical importance lies directly in the extent to which the two methods of finance have a different impact on private investment. Few would be prepared to argue that this difference is likely to be large and in any case differences could be compensated for by other government polices.

MONETARY AND FISCAL IMPLICATIONS OF THE DEBT

Composition of the debt

In particular, the government (or central bank if this has delegated powers) are concerned with the liquidity of the debt: with the ratio of short- to long-term debt. Although holders can obtain cash by selling both types of security on the market, only short-term debt has a fairly certain value. Government concerns are twofold: one is that the private sector will be tempted to convert its assets into spending power; and the second that banks and other financial institutions may use the assets as a base on which to expand credit. In both cases what is important is the relationship between the government and private sector. A sale of assets from a private individual to another individual, or a sale from a bank to a private individual, is merely a rearrangement of assets within the private sector. This is not of monetary significance unless this implies a change in interest rates. This would come about if the new holders of securities were only induced to take up the securities at lower bond prices, an action which necessarily implies increased yields on the securities. These increased yields in turn could force a rise in interest rates on newly issued securities. If, however, the government buys the securities then this is directly increasing the purchasing power of the private sector. It may have to buy the securities because they are re-payable on demand or it may buy marketable securities because it wishes to maintain the current level of interest rates.

Total of the debt

Fears are often expressed about the absolute size of the national debt, or the size of interest payments. If interest payments are a large proportion of the budget it is possible that this will form a constraint on other government spending because it fears to put up taxes, but this does not as a rule happen. While the nominal size of the debt in most developed countries is large, when price changes are taken into account by –

expressing the debt for example as a percentage of National Income – the proportions are much lower than they were in the early post-war years after 1945.

Interest rates

Changes in interest rates affect the economy in various ways but these effects are not felt in any simple and direct manner. The government must bear in mind the effect on the demand for money by borrowers, on the supply of money, and more directly on the flow of money into or out of the country from overseas. One of the paradoxes of the 1980s was that, as governments came to rely more on interest rates to control their economies, they were at the same time relaxing many controls on banks and financial institutions which made it much easier for customers to obtain credit. High interest rates by themselves often failed to deter borrowers.

SUMMARY

The aggregation of government securities over time, less redemptions, is called the National Debt. The PSBR, or PSDR, is the net annual borrowing, or repayment, of the public sector to be added to or subtracted from the total of National Debt. Care needs to be taken in interpreting the PSBR. The nominal size of the debt in most developed countries is large. When price changes are allowed for by expressing the debt, for example, as a percentage of National Income, the proportions are much lower than they were in the early post-war years after 1945. Similar remarks apply to the interest that has to be paid on the debt, in general although payments have risen in the 1980s, as interest rates were increased, these payments are a lower proportion of National Income than in the immediate post-war period.

The relevance of the debt was discussed and technical problems of debt management outlined. In discussing the debt, a distinction should be drawn between debt held internally and debt held by foreigners. The former involves a monetary, not a real, transfer between citizens of one country; the latter enables an import of real resources and repayment involves a transfer of current purchasing power back to the foreign holders.

The discussion of 'burden' unearthed some important problems: the use of resources by the public sector; the amount of capital investment being undertaken; the effect on incentives; the distribution of wealth and income; the perpetuation of the existing structure of wealth by inheritance; and the effect on future generations. In all cases it was found that discussion of these problems solely in terms of debt financing obscured rather than illuminated the issues.

The monetary and fiscal implications of National Debt were examined. These are concerned particularly with the liquidity of the debt, and its effect on interest rates.

Part II

Aims and principles of public finance

Chapter 5

Aims and principles of public finance

A fiscal system serves a number of purposes beside the obvious one of providing revenue. Following Musgrave (1959), these will be collected under three headings: allocation of resources, distribution of resources and stabilization of the economy.

On the revenue side a tax system can be judged on how well it achieves economic efficiency. By economic efficiency is meant the collection of taxes in a way that distorts the economy as little as possible, or that moves the economy only in the direction deliberately intended. Ideally it should have low compliance and enforcement costs.

ALLOCATION OF RESOURCES

This aspect of the budget is concerned with the allocation of resources in the economy. As Chapter 1 has shown not all goods can be provided, or provided in the right quantities, through the market system and governments are concerned to correct for these deficiencies. Also of concern to governments will be the split between investment and consumption goods. Governments try to correct deficiencies in the pricing mechanism due, for example, to monopoly elements, the existence of external economies or diseconomies, and cases where social costs diverge sharply from private costs.

DISTRIBUTION OF RESOURCES

As indicated in Chapter 1 the distribution of income and wealth depends on a number of factors including work, educational opportunities, inheritance, gifts and government tax and spending policies. The distribution of income and wealth is also distinctly skewed in most countries. Under this heading of Distribution of Resources can be collected the adjustments that society decides to make in order to correct for deficiencies in the distribution of income and wealth. This part of the budget arouses considerable passion. No neat calculus is widely accepted which would help the debate. Some of the issues are taken up later in this chapter.

STABILIZATION OF THE ECONOMY

Stabilization objectives are concerned with achieving current government objectives. Current objectives may include: obtaining and maintaining a satisfactory level of growth, maintaining high employment, ensuring stability in the value of money, maintaining a satisfactory exchange rate and balance of payments. The mix of objectives changes with time with some being left, more or less, to free markets. Where government intervention takes place the hope is that this will achieve better results than non-intervention.

The listing of the aims of budgetary policy does not, unfortunately, necessarily mean that they can all be achieved. Often there will be direct conflict and the legislature has the tough job of weighing up the alternatives.

Within the aims selected by society as being relevant, persons have been looking for centuries for a general principle that could be used as a guide to apportion taxes. Two principles, the benefit principle and ability to pay have long been canvassed and are discussed later.

FISCAL NEUTRALITY

In recent years fiscal neutrality has come into increasing prominence as a government objective. Fiscal neutrality seeks the laudable aim of raising tax revenue in a non-distortionary manner, unless the distortion effect is deliberately sought, e.g. to correct for some harmful externality. The term tax neutrality can be used in a number of ways. At one extreme, if elevated to prime place, it would override stabilization objectives. More moderate views see the object of neutrality as eliminating, or at least reducing, some of the gross anomalies that have grown up in the tax system particularly in the area of savings and investment. To this end most developed economies have, we have seen, reduced income tax rates particularly at the top end, and reduced the number of marginal rates. Both the consumption tax base and company tax base has also been broadened. The changes in income tax and company tax has been partly achieved by broadening their bases by eliminating a number of exemptions and allowances, and partly by increasing taxes in other areas.

A tax that achieves neutrality would leave individuals and organizations making the same decision whether they look at pre-tax or post-tax returns. Neutrality applies both to the choice of assets and the use of assets by companies – the tax of a company should be the same whether profits are retained or distributed to owners. Neutrality also implies that the timing and amount of decisions remain the same: economic units should not, for example, be able to reduce tax by merely postponing action. An important source of neutrality would be to tax income from all sources equally, to prevent resources being devoted to activities subject to lower taxes or not taxed at all. Likewise tax liability should not depend on how income is spent. Uniform treatment of all sources and uses of income implies a comprehensive definition of income. An examination of proposed tax legislation to try to ensure that new anomalies are not introduced is also desirable. All taxes have some distortionary implications and fiscal neutrality has to be traded against other objectives. It is certainly right that they ought to be considered and that present tax systems have too many gross distortions in them. It was estimated that in the UK the proportion of net worth held in the most tax-privileged forms, including pensions, life insurance and owner-occupied housing, grew from 45 per cent to 75 per cent between 1957 and 1981. In 1987 these tax-priviledged assets attracted about three-quarters of the total flow of savings, see Leape (1990).

OPTIMAL TAXES

The main approach adopted in Chapter 7 is to regard as important the overall impact of the tax and benefit system. Some taxes may be extremely regressive, or have other undesirable features, but the effects may be swamped by other measures in looking at overall tax burdens. However, it remains true that public perception that a tax is unfair can have a significant impact, as the history of the Community Charge outlined in the Appendix to Chapter 12 illustrates.

A complementary approach is to ask what is the optimal structure of a tax, and what is the optimal mix of taxes? What, for example, is the optimal marginal rate of income taxation and is it the same for all income levels? Would a uniform rate of value added tax be optimal or should it vary by commodity? The debate raises issues about the efficiency of the system – that is, its effects on aggregate output, and also questions about the equity of a system.

Considerable work has been done in this area in recent years, it is highly abstract and mathematical. Although, unfortunately, as yet, it yields few results that are of practical application the work even so has considerable value. As Atkinson and Stiglitz (1980) say, 'The aim is not to provide a definite numerical answer to the question, "how progressive should the income tax be?" . . . the purpose is rather to explore the implications of different beliefs about how the world works and how governments behave.' For example, the literature has failed to find simple tax rules with wide applicability and thus shows that some popular preconceptions about taxes are not necessarily correct. Thus a popular view is that uniform rates of indirect tax are to be preferred on both grounds of horizontal equity and efficiency: the literature casts doubt on this finding as a universal rule by showing cases where the rule does not hold.

Even if an optimal tax system could be devised there are considerable difficulties in achieving this state because existing tax concessions will have become capitalized in asset values and withdrawing these concessions could have arbitrary and inequitable consequences.

The optimal tax debate of necessity involves setting out the criteria on which optimality is to be judged. In considering distribution the principal of least sacrifice has a long history and equally long criticism. A Pareto improvement is made when a change makes somebody better off without making anybody worse off. This makes the assumption that the welfare preference of the better off does not include the welfare of others. Another criterion would be if the welfare loss of the loser is less than the welfare gain of the person made better off. In order to judge these criteria, gain and loss need to be measurable and interpersonal comparisons of utility are necessary – the means to do either are lacking. The minimum sacrifice theory also neglects possible disincentive effects which could be important in determining the size of GDP.

Other criteria have been put forward, such as Rawls (1971). While accepting comparability he rejects the idea of maximizing the sum of individual utilities in favour of maximization of that of the least fortunate person. Social welfare functions impose a majority political view over that of individual utilities. Equalitarian social welfare functions might for example judge results on the effect the measures have on the gap between the rich and the poor. The literature explores the results of adapting alternative welfare criteria. Further reading will be found in Stern (1976) and Mirrlees (1977).

Even if an optimal tax can be agreed this is not the same as having it from the beginning. People and companies make decisions based on existing tax laws and changing the system can impose costly and arbitrary adjustment on society.

HORIZONTAL AND VERTICAL EQUITY

Underlying much of the discussion of public finance is the treatment of persons relative to each other. One of the few generalizations in public finance that commands wide acceptance is the idea that persons in equal positions shall be treated equally, termed 'horizontal equity': a proposition that requires a comprehensive definition of income. It follows logically from this that persons in unequal positions shall be treated differently, termed 'vertical equity'.

Equal treatment of equals is usually regarded in terms of equal sacrifice, or equal welfare loss. The rationalization behind the rule is the assumption that welfare between individuals can be compared, that welfare is a function of income and/or wealth, and that the marginal utility of income is the same for all taxpayers. Given these assumptions, it follows that people in equal positions should be called upon to pay equal taxes (and receive equal benefits) and that people in unequal positions should pay different taxes (and receive unequal benefits).

It will be seen how fragile is the underpining for tax and benefit discussion on these grounds. The difficulties of making interpersonal comparisons have already been noted. The assumption that economic welfare is a function of income may be regarded by many as a sufficiently close approximation to the truth, but the assumption that the marginal utility of income is the same for all taxpayers will leave many unsatisfied. As well as disagreements over these assumptions, the criteria on which equal positions are to be judged needs to be reached. Should it be some abstract definition of income, or wealth, or both; or consumption? More contentious is how people in unequal positions shall be treated. Regressive, proportional and progressive taxes have all been advocated at different times. There is probably widespread agreement now that taxes that fall on the 'better off' rather than the 'worse off', and are progressive rather than proportional, are to be preferred. These questions will be examined further.

In the previous discussion on the redistribution of income and wealth a social-welfare function was implied, it was inferred that society does make decisions of an interpersonal nature and that these decisions imply a set of preferences for social welfare at a particular time. These preferences may change over time, and may indeed be inconsistent. Part of the task of a study of public finance is to try and understand the reason for the changes and point out the consequences of the inconsistencies of the particular social-welfare function that is being applied. In particular, there may be a trade-off between horizontal equity and vertical redistribution;[1] for example, society may be willing to accept some horizontal inequality as the price of redistributing income from the rich to the poor. Thus a higher rate of value added tax on goods such as luxury yachts which are purchased by the rich, but only some of the rich, violates horizontal equity but may be accepted by society in general as a means of obtaining revenue to achieve some vertical redistribution of income. On the other hand, many violations of equity occur because of tax loopholes which enable persons in the same economic position as others legally to avoid paying as much tax. This is particularly true in respect of capital gains tax and the taxation of wealth at death.

The discussion of equity so far has been in terms of the individual but the taxpaying unit is equally important. Should the taxpaying unit be the individual or the household and how should the household be defined? Consideration of this matter will be deferred until the next chapter.

THE BENEFIT PRINCIPLE AND ABILITY TO PAY PRINCIPLE

Discussions of tax principles have been mainly in relation to the allocation of resources since distribution and stabilization aims have been accepted as government objectives only in this century. When the aims of public finance are drawn more widely than just considering the allocation of resources, neither principle will be found without fault, but both can contribute to our understanding of the problems involved.

Benefit principle

The benefit approach dictates that taxes are apportioned to individuals according to the benefits they derive from government activity and spending. Directly charging for a service where this is feasible, or imposing some other fee, is most likely to be the way in which 'taxes' are apportioned according to use. The weakness of benefit taxation as a universal principle is evident. Much government expenditure such as on defence could only be allocated in an arbitrary manner. Taxes can be used as a substitute for pricing where the latter is not feasible or difficult, but such taxes may have little correspondence with benefit received. For example, a tax on fuel for transport may be looked on as part payment for road expenditure and taxes on alcohol and tobacco as part payment for the health costs caused by these products.

Benefit taxation, where it can be applied means that the provision of government goods and services, like the provision of private goods and services, will be dictated by market demand when full costs are imposed on users. In a society where the aims of government are conceived in minimum terms of defence against external aggression and in the administration of justice, as during eighteenth-century Britain, this approach is understandable. The existing structure of wealth and income was taken as given, and the economy was conceived as self-regulating. On the grounds that the wealthy had more to lose from external or internal threat, the benefit principle could be used to justify higher taxes on them.

These ideas have given ground on many fronts. It is generally conceded that private provision in the absence of government intervention will be seriously deficient where there are strong positive externalities and will be over-supplied where there are strong negative externalities. Some redistribution of income and usually of wealth is granted as necessary in all developed countries and stabilization of the economy has been generally accepted since the 1930s.

With these wider aims the benefit rule is clearly inadmissible as a sole principle of general application. The more the government did to help the needy, the more the needy would have to pay. The whole transfer process which has been taking place, particularly in this century, would be frustrated. Again the allocation of some benefits, for example defence, would be an arbitrary process; and the aims of stabilization would not necessarily be carried out by following the benefit principle of taxation.

Nevertheless, the benefit principle has application in areas where a close relationship between outlay and benefit can be established, externalities are weak and where consumption is rival. Thus where the government undertakes the provision of a service which could equally well be undertaken privately, and there are no strong externalities, the danger of not charging according to the benefit principle is that demand for that service is likely to be stimulated. A serious misallocation of resources may result. A case in point is provided by the UK at the end of the 1960s when electricity prices were held down on the grounds that poor pensioners were dying of hypothermia because they couldn't afford to heat their houses properly. As a result electricity became the cheapest fuel and demand for it shot up as people and firms switched to it away from other fuels. The electricity board came up with the need for an investment programme of many billions of pounds which had it been undertaken would have been the largest investment project ever undertaken in the UK. When electricity prices were allowed to rise demand dropped back. Helping the poor directly to meet their bills by an increase in their pensions or other income, or by subsidizing their electricity bills, seems much the better way of helping them rather than distorting the whole infrastructure of the economy by holding down electricity prices for all.

For some services, for example health and education, the extension of demand which 'free' or subsidized prices give is deliberately aimed to capture the positive externalities.

No general solution emerges to the question of when it is desirable to apply the benefit principle. It is necessary in each particular case to weigh up the social costs and benefits involved in charging users for the costs of the service and in meeting all or some of those costs out of general taxation, or of some compromise whereby some users are charged market prices and others are subsidized.

Ability-to-pay

The ability-to-pay approach is concerned with the equitable distribution of taxes according to the stated taxable capacity, or ability to pay, of an individual or group. This rule, in terms of the objectives stated at the beginning of this section, enables the distribution and stabilization objectives to be carried out in an equitable manner. The allocation objective – how much to produce – has to be decided through the political process since prices are either absent or do not reflect market conditions.

With the ability-to-pay principle the criterion on which ability is to be judged has to be set out – i.e. whether it is to be income, wealth, income and wealth, or consumption. This will form the main concern of Chapter 6. In their usual formulations these criteria do not take into account benefits from government expenditure that accrue to the individual. However it is possible to do so and this approach is examined in Chapter 7.

SUMMARY

A fiscal system serves a number of purposes besides the obvious one of providing revenue. These were examined under three headings. The first was the allocation of resources between various uses such as investment and consumption. The second was the distribution of resources: how society decides to make adjustment in order to correct for deficiencies in the distribution of income and wealth. The final heading concerns the stabilization of the economy in terms of current government objectives. The idea of fiscal neutrality as a government objective was then examined.

The fiscal treatment of persons relative to each other was discussed using the concepts of horizontal and vertical equity. The 'benefit' and 'ability to pay' principles of taxation were examined. Neither is without fault as a general taxation rule, but an understanding of them is useful in trying to formulate a satisfactory tax system.

Chapter 6

The criterion of 'ability to pay'

From the discussion in Chapter 5 of the benefit and ability to pay approaches it is clear that, given the current objectives of society, the benefit principle by itself cannot serve as an adequate guide to taxation. Some form of criterion based on ability to pay is needed and this is now examined.

ABILITY TO PAY

In the search for a criterion to judge ability to pay, in order to achieve horizontal equity, claims are put forward for income, wealth and expenditure.

By wealth is meant the accumulated assets of a person or institution; by income is meant receipts that accrue per period of time. Wealth taxation is sometimes taken to mean the taxation of any income that wealth earns in a period, but it should refer to a tax on the underlying assets and will be so used here. Earnings from wealth are properly regarded as part of income. In practice few countries raise much revenue from wealth taxation as a result this base is unlikely to provide sufficient revenue by itself. This raises a number of problems which will be deferred until Chapter 8.

An expenditure base

Expenditure as a base for taxation has a long history. The idea was taken up by Kaldor (1955), and more recently by the Meade Committee (Meade 1977). An expenditure tax base makes the distinction between income and wealth irrelevant: this is a big advantage and simplification. Another is that, since consumption occurs out of current purchasing power many of the inflationary distortions present in existing systems are overcome. The source of spending power whether income or wealth can be ignored. In a general way, using consumption (i.e. expenditure) as a base is taxing according to what a person takes out of the common pool, and income with what he puts into the common pool. Transfer payments are an exception to the latter point. Whether transfer payments should form part of the tax base is a separate issue. An expenditure tax relieves saving of tax, the tax is postponed until it is spent.

The issue between an income and expenditure base is not, it should be stressed, one of progressiveness. It is possible to build into a tax system on either base whatever degree of progressiveness is required by a system of allowances and rates of tax. A progressive expenditure tax by exempting savings and investment from tax provides a stimulus to economic growth, at the same time it could levy substantial charges on those who consume most. Proponents of the tax suggest that it could lead to considerable tax simplification and have fewer economic disincentives.

Also a comprehensive expenditure-based tax does not entail the detailed recording of expenditures. Expenditures can be computed as the difference between money incomings and new savings. In practice certain assets would be designated as savings and new purchases of these 'registered' assets would be deducted from income to arrive at a figure for expenditure. Forms to calculate expenditures in this way would be somewhat more complicated than the current income-tax form, but not unduly so. They would be of the form:

1 *Personal incomes*: wages, salaries, dividends, etc.;
2 *Capital receipts*: sale of capital assets, borrowing, etc.;
3 *Windfalls*: inheritances, gifts, gambling winnings.
From the total of items 1 to 3 deduct:
4 *Savings*: These would comprise the purchase of registered assets, i.e. savings, lending etc.

The balance i.e. consumption expenditure would be taxed at whatever rates were considered appropriate.

Items 1 to 3 already appear in some way in the tax system and the problems of identifying income, dealing with fringe benefits, separating personal and business expenses and the like have to be solved just as with an income base.

Like most possible changes in taxation there is also a negative side. Existing wealth would be subject to taxation when it is spent. A particular problem for wealth which has been saved out of taxed income, as opposed to being inherited. At the time of transition those on retirement incomes or those who had saved to make a large purchase such as a house would be aggrieved. Spending out of pensions would not fall into this category since the bulk of pension contributions have tax relief and are subject to tax when the pension is received. Suggestions for transitional relief to overcome this double tax problem inevitably lead to a more complicated tax system. It may be largely a transitional problem during the period of change from the old to the new tax base, but the transition itself could be a lengthy one and complicated enough to raise doubts about the wisdom of making the move.

Difficulties also arise with goods which involve both a consumption and investment aspect such as education and housing. The taxable unit would be important because of the possibilities for high consumption individuals transferring income to low consumption individuals to buy goods for them. Further difficulties with an expenditure tax is the compatibility with a company tax based on income-related measures of profit and the probable need to change to a cash-flow basis but this is a move that has merits on its own. Moving to an expenditure base for any one country alone would be difficult as there would be a tendency for people to save in the expenditure-taxed country where saving is not taxed and move to an income-based country on retirement.

An income base

The concept of income that has gained wide acceptance is termed *total accretion*. Income is defined to equal consumption during a given period, plus the increase in net worth valued at market prices for the beginning and the end of the period. Income is thus defined as consumption, savings and changes in wealth. The principle is uncompromising: all accretions to wealth are included, in whatever form they are received or from whatever source they accrue. In practice, the principle may have to be modified, but if it is accepted as a principle it gives a basis from which to judge our present tax system and any proposed changes. The principle accepts that a change in net worth may be negative; in other words gains and losses should be allowed for.

The Memorandum of Dissent to the Royal Commission on the Taxation of Profits and Income (1955) Final Report sets out very clearly the rationale behind this definition:

> In our view the taxable capacity of an individual consists in his power to satisfy his own material needs, i.e., to obtain a particular living standard. We know of no alternative definition that is capable of

satisfying society's prevailing sense of fairness and equity. Thus the ruling test to be applied in deciding whether any particular receipt should or should not be reckoned as taxable is whether it contributes or not, or how far it contributes, to an individual's 'spending power' during a period. When set beside this standard, most of the principles that have been applied at one time or another, to determine whether particular types of receipt constitute income (whether the receipts are regular recurrent or causal, or whether they proceed from a separate and identifiable source, or whether they are payments for services rendered, or whether they constitute profit 'on sound accountancy principles', or whether, in the words of the Majority they fall 'within the limited class of receipts that are identified as income by their own nature') appear to us to be irrelevant. In fact no concept of income can be really equitable that stops short of the comprehensive definition which embraces all receipts which increase an individual's command over the use of society's scarce resources – in other words his 'net accretion of economic power between two points of time'.

(para. 5)

It cannot be emphasized too strongly that the consequences of adopting this definition of income would be that current rates of income tax, or some other tax could be reduced without a loss in revenue. In other words, at present, income, in the narrow sense, bears a disproportionate share of tax precisely because spending power that falls outside the tax definition of income is taxed less or not at all. Some countries, as second best, have taken, or have proposed, measures that would ensure high income groups pay at least a minimum amount of tax as a way of improving vertical equity. In 1983 in the United States this was taken as 20 per cent of income subject to tax minus $30,000 for single people and $40,000 for married persons. Some countries, particularly those with graduated net wealth tax (Denmark, Finland, the Netherlands, Norway, Spain and Sweden), also have provisions to ensure that no more than a maximum specified percentage of income is paid in income tax plus net wealth tax.

The imperfections of current income concepts can be illustrated by the UK where the first £5,500 in the fiscal year 1991 of real capital gains (that is after allowing for inflation) are not taxed, a concession that with separate taxation of husband and wife means that in 1991 £11,000 p.a. of household gains can go untaxed. Also capital gains are not collected on bequests at death. Betting and gambling are, on the whole, taxed at flat rates. Gifts and inherited wealth are not taxed according to the position of the recipient but according to the wealth of the donor.

DRAWBACKS TO THE PRESENT SYSTEM

The trend in many countries over the past decade is for a widening of the income tax base through reducing tax allowances so reducing the need for high tax rates when the base is narrowly drawn. There is though a tendency for new tax concessions to creep back. For example the UK has introduced very substantial tax concessions in savings and pensions and concessions to persons over 60 for private health care.

The process of widening the tax base could be taken much further particularly for example in the UK and United States where housing receives exceptional tax privileges. Widening the tax base helps remove the so-called 'blight' of modern times, the amount of time, money and resources which goes into tax avoidance. Avoidance means using legal means to reduce tax by, for example, exploiting every tax loophole. Tax avoidance has always, and probably always will be, a profitable occupation, but the greater the loopholes the more the industry is likely to thrive. Most countries have made some attempts to limit or tax fringe benefits which can form a substantial part of the remuneration of some employees, generous non-contributory pensions, share options, housing benefits, lavish entertainment expenses being examples.

DIFFICULTIES WITH A PURE BASE

Most income bases do not include unrealized capital gains largely because of administrative difficulties. The taxation of fringe benefits differs widely, and few tax the imputed income from owner occupied housing. The treatment of private pensions under an income base, for example, whereby contributions are made from pre-tax income but subject to tax when the pension is received conforms to an expenditure base. Judged from an income base, pension payments and other saving should not be tax deductible when made and only the interest component taxed when benefits are received. Failure to do this leaves savers with a dual benefit. They can receive interest on the postponed tax and they may well be in a lower tax bracket when benefits are received.

Many allowances have no place in either an income or a expenditure base. They have the effect of greatly narrowing the tax base and therefore result in higher tax rates in order to achieve a given revenue.

One reason put forward for a pure base is that this would simplify the tax system and reduce the reams of legislation designed to limit tax avoidance. While this could be true in the long run it is probably a chimera to expect any legislature not to enact exceptions to the tax base which would leave loopholes for tax avoidance and hence the need for further legislation. The battle between those who want to avoid tax and the tax authorities is likely to be a continuing one under any tax system.

An income base holds that all income should be taxed; an expenditure base holds that savings should be exempt and only consumption should be taxed. Both hold in common that taxes apply to total resources and both are capable of graduation. In practice no country has adopted a pure expenditure or a pure income tax based system. They have a hybrid system with elements of both and indeed elements of taxation that are consistent with neither, a situation that is likely to continue.

Whatever the tax base and the only major difference between an income and an expenditure base lies in the treatment of saving, both start from a wide definition of income. There are a number of common problems presented by valuation, inflation and deflation, fluctuating income and the taxpaying unit. These are now discussed in turn.

COMMON TAXATION PROBLEMS WITH ANY TAX BASE

Valuation

As anybody who has anything to do with valuation for purposes of probate will know, valuation can cause a great deal of work and involve a great deal of arbitrariness. There is little problem with items which are standardized and traded regularly, such as quoted company shares. Unquoted shares, unique items such as original paintings, antiques, plots of land, and to a lesser extent housing, are much more difficult to value, short of actual sale in the market place. On the grounds of practicality it seems that annual valuation is ruled out. An alternative is to bring the item into the tax net on sale, or on the death of the owner, when valuation has to take place in any case. It is argued against this that such a process discriminates in favour of people who enjoy unrealized gains. This is true but it seems to have little weight against the far bigger distortion of not taxing these items at all. Similar considerations apply to the argument that taxing at this point will interfere with the market process of buying and selling. Once again it is necessary to weigh the small loss likely to be caused in this way with the much bigger losses at present generated by different tax treatment of different assets. A valid argument is that taxing an asset in this way, rather than on an annual basis, can cause the tax payment to be higher under progressive rates. This is a valid point dealt with under 'fluctuating incomes' below.

Inflation and deflation

Pro and con

The reasons put forward for adjustment for inflation centre on equity and control of government expenditure; deflation has seldom been a problem in recent years. Adjustment may be by means of indexation or a series of ad hoc measures. Inflation adjustment for some, but not all, items is one of the most important ways that fiscal neutrality has been breached in recent years. It has caused serious distortions in savings and investment decisions and in the motivation to obtain capital gains rather than earned income.

In the absence of offsetting action, the tax burden is arbitrarily redistributed by inflation as taxpayers get sucked into the tax system, or into higher tax brackets by nominal increases in income. Real income may be considered a more appropriate measure of ability to pay than nominal income. It is also asserted that the extra revenue procured by inflation may induce extra government spending. Those who favour greater accountability of governments to their electorate feel that extra spending should have to be justified with an opportunity for Parliament to vote on increased taxes. They also see it as strengthening the will of governments to control inflation and possibly as helping to keep wage increases under control.

The disadvantages of indexation are that partial indexation may worsen rather than improve the equity of the tax system by leaving large loopholes through which the astute can avoid tax, it reduces the flexibility of the government to respond to economic changes and that it may, depending on the method adopted, be complex and costly to administer.

At a practical level it has to be decided what index to use. Usual cost of living indexes include indirect taxes and subsidies and it may be thought appropriate to exclude both from an inflationary adjustment. Practices vary in different countries. Similar considerations arise within the inflation index. Should it, or should it not, include adjustments for changes in the values of imported goods, of which oil is clearly important for many countries. Denmark used an index based on hourly earnings of industrial workers between 1975 and 1979 but this too gives rise to anomalies during structural changes in the labour market. More importantly there would be overcompensation for inflation if earnings rise faster than inflation. Inflation adjustment and its interaction with the tax system can result, especially for companies, in a large carry over of tax losses which can lead to considerable distortion in the allocation of resources. This was one of the main reasons for the UK change in corporation tax in 1986.

At low levels of inflation distortions are generally felt to be mild compared to the costs of indexing, but during periods of high inflation pressure builds up for protection. Practices in various countries are divergent Australia, Denmark, and Sweden abandoned inflationary adjustment in the early 1980s, Switzerland and the United States introduced it in 1985. The issues are examined in relation first to persons and then companies.

Persons

In principle, changes due to alteration in the value of money should be allowed *for all receipts* whether income, capital gains or anything else, that is a tax should be applied to a tax base in real terms. However, in practical terms money values with no inflationary adjustment are most often used except for a few privileged assets. The difficulties of finding a correct index, with which to obtain real values are a serious deterrent to working with deflated values, and allowing for inflation would be administratively complex and costly. Because of these difficulties, it is by no means clear that a system which attempts to take account of inflation and deflation would be more equitable than one that does not.

To argue that it would be equitable to compensate for changes in the value of money for all receipts is not a good argument for compensation for some of these receipts – a point that is frequently overlooked. It is argued that a gain of, say, £1,000 on selling shares may be a gain in money terms only, that what should be relevant is the gain in real terms, i.e. the gain in command over goods and services. In inflationary conditions this gain will clearly be less than £1,000 and in deflation conditions it will be more.

A capital gain can be contrasted with a wage increase. A money wage increase which restores the real purchasing power of wages to the level of the previous year nevertheless results in more tax being paid if tax rates are unaltered. A number of countries have indexation provisions for income taxes but in some, like the UK, the indexation is not mandatory. If capital gains are indexed, this will be a further incentive to secure income in the form of gains rather than wages. The claim that capital gains should be indexed, unless it is accompanied by general indexation, looks like special pleading by interested parties. Similar reasoning applies to other special interest groups pleading that their particular slice of income should be protected from changes in the value of money. If the principle of indexing is good for one, it is good for all, but of course adjustment for all loses much of its point. Governments start out with clear ideas of the amount of revenue they want from the economy; if adjustments are made on the income side for price changes, adjustments would have to be made on the revenue side to tax rates to ensure that the tax revenue target was reached. The only change, from the present, where adjustment may not be made, is that the government obtains more nominal revenue from inflation at the moment if tax rates are unaltered. If adjustments were made automatically to rates then the present hidden increase in nominal tax revenue would not occur.

The argument about inflation adjustment is frequently confused with the fact that receipts may occur at irregular intervals. For example, the argument is used that, as capital gains can accrue over a long period of time, it is therefore unjust to tax that part of the gain due to inflation. The valid point in this argument is the realization that large receipts of any kind under a progressive tax structure, raise the tax liability in the year in which the receipts are received. The tax paid in this case is likely to exceed the liability which would have resulted if the gain had been realized evenly over time. The remedy for this is some form of averaging for tax purposes, a measure which is desirable under any form of progressive tax. If averaging was achieved the assertion that capital gains are different from other income cannot be sustained. During a year both capital gains and income are subject to the same rate of inflation. Equity would dictate that both are adjusted for inflation or neither. Comprehensive adjustment for inflation is one thing, adjustment for one particular asset is special pleading.

It is also argued that a capital gain is illusory if the proceeds are to be reinvested in a similar asset. Thus in the case of an owner-occupied house purchased for £100,000 and sold for £150,000, it is probable that the whole of the proceeds will be needed to buy a similar type of property. This is easily seen as a case of special pleading, that house-owners should be protected against inflation and price changes as opposed to non-house-owners. The person who invests £100,000 in a house in the above example gains over the person who invests the same amount of money in securities and makes the same gain. The latter person in the UK and many other countries will pay tax on some of their gains and be at a disadvantage in entering the housing market in competition with the householder. The fact that owner-occupied houses are exempt from capital gains in many countries should not be allowed to obscure the fact that once an owner obtains a house (assuming, what is generally the case, that the property moves in line with the general market trend in house prices), then the owner is largely indifferent to the subsequent trend in house prices. A wedge is driven between those who have houses, and are largely protected from subsequent inflation in house prices, and those who subsequently enter the market for the first time.

Although housing was selected as an example, the principles involved apply to any asset: exemption from tax confers benefit on the existing owners of the asset vis-à-vis the rest of the population. It is difficult to establish any presumptive economic argument that particular assets merit exemption.

In the mass of words on the subject of inflation adjustment, particularly in respect of capital gains and the treatment of company assets, the assumptions of the protagonists are seldom made explicit.

Those who argue that inflation should be taken into account for particular assets presumably have in mind some concept akin to 'keeping capital intact'. If this is the correct premise, it is clear that taxing a paper gain is unjust.

Those who argue against this view take as their starting-point that what is relevant for taxation and equity purposes is the relative income positions of taxpayers. If this is the correct premise, a person who has a capital gain is, in money terms, better off than a person who has no such gain or a loss and should be taxed, after averaging the gains over time if the asset has been held for more than a year. On this assumption not to tax a paper gain is unjust, *or* alternatively everything should be adjusted for price changes.

This argument seems particularly protracted because the principle of 'keeping capital intact', while it may be an excellent accounting principle, is an unsound principle of public finance. The viewpoint adopted here is that however desirable it may be for the individual or company to maintain its asset position intact, it is not part of the fiscal system to do this for them. The aim of the fiscal system should not be to maintain the status of those who happen to have wealth or make capital gains. On the contrary, at any one time society aims for a certain degree of progression and a certain redistribution of income and wealth. The argument adopted here for the rejection of compensation for inflation, unless it is done for all, is clear: inflationary and deflationary conditions affect all sectors of the community, and compensation for one sector only results in less equity, not more, and moreover results in serious distortionary economic effects.

Companies

The principles that have just been discussed in relation to indexation for inflation for individuals apply equally well to companies. However, it is commonly asserted that companies should have provision for inflation adjustment. One argument put forward is that bargaining over earned incomes takes inflation into account and company profits will be adversely affected if this is not allowed for in the amount of tax companies are called on to pay.

At times when there is high inflation interest in indexation increases. The subject has been more or less under debate since the early 1970s in most developed countries. Different countries have introduced a variety of inflationary adjustments but there have been no solutions that are generally acceptable.

The problem for firms is particularly acute in respect of depreciation allowances and the tax treatment of stocks. The treatment of capital gains and losses and interest income raising the same considerations as personal tax.

Depreciation

In an inflationary period investment in a fixed asset that lasts for many years means that the replacement cost of the asset, at least in nominal terms, will have increased and depreciation provisions based on historic costs will not be sufficient to replace the asset. (A parallel argument can be used for personal durable consumer goods.) Using a price index, or basing depreciation on replacement cost, would be a way of allowing for inflation but the complexities involved have deterred most countries from doing this comprehensively and partial adjustment has led to some severe distortions and misallocation of resources. It was for this reason that the UK in 1984 introduced major company tax changes phasing out stock relief provision and changed depreciation provisions.

There may be a case for basing company financial information on replacement values, although these values may be very subjective, but to base taxation on replacement values risks confusing relative and general price movements. Inflation is a movement in the general price level not in this or that specific price. This point is taken up below.

The profit or loss of a business depends on the value placed upon the cost of goods sold. Consider the case where stocks are held for an average of six months, and inflation has increased by 5 per cent in this period. Then stocks valued at their original cost, will overstate the real profit of the business as it will cost them more to replenish their stock. An accounting method that values inventories according to their original cost indexed for inflation, would be a way of correcting for this. At one stage in the UK the Sandilands Committee (Inflation Accounting Committee 1975) suggested that the government statistical service should make available a series of price indices for stocks purchased by specific industries.

The provision that separate price indexes be used for specific industries is a particularly dangerous one if such adjustment is brought into a company's tax position. It amounts to insulating a company from *relative* price changes rather than insulating them from movements in *average* prices. Movements in relative prices occur independently of the levels of inflation or deflation and it is economically desirable that firms should take account of relative price movements. Thus when the price of an input, say oil, is increased the increase in price can be expected to lead to desirable adjustments that economise in oil use. Partially to isolate a firm via a tax adjustment for this change would be highly damaging to the economy.

Conclusion

Many countries, because of the complexities involved, do not take inflation into account in their tax structures or do so only in a limited way. The position adopted here, is not the one generally accepted. Inflation adjustment for all can be justified but inflation adjustment for just some assets or some groups is special pleading. Comprehensive adjustment runs the risk of building in inflation in an economy. Adjustment, whether total or partial, is in any case complicated and in the case of partial adjustment likely to lead to misallocation of resources to the more tax favoured assets.

Fluctuating income or expenditure

The difficulty posed by any progressive tax is the inequity between those whose income fluctuates from year to year and those who receive their income in regular amounts. Similar arguments apply on the expenditure side.

The income side

Looking at the income side, authors, artists, sportspeople, farmers, fishermen and a number in professional occupations who rely on fees are likely to have fluctuating incomes. They are likely to pay sub-stantially more in tax than a person who receives the same income in equal annual amounts. This has long been recognized as a problem with existing systems and most countries have adopted some limited forms of averaging for certain categories of person. Under a fully fledged total accretion principle of income the problem would be more acute as more income will be volatile. Legacies and gifts are examples of receipts which would count as income, could be large, and cannot be expected regularly.

The seemingly straightforward solution of aggregating income over, say, a five-year period or a lifetime, is usually considered unacceptable because if a person has a drop in income in any year, his tax bill in that year will be based on his average income over the relevant period – which may be higher than his current income. The fact that a rising income gives a lower tax bill does not compensate for the hardship which is likely to be involved in meeting high tax payments during periods of reduced income.

The usual assumption of averaging is that the total sum of taxes paid over the averaging period should be the same as if the income had been received in equal amounts in each year of the averaging period. With a five-year plan, tax could be computed by finding the average income over this period (i.e. total income for the five years divided by five) and reworking the tax liability for each of the past years on the basis of this average. Even in the computer age this reworking of tax liability is not considered administratively desirable nor is it necessary. The Report of the Canadian Royal Commission on Taxation (1966) suggested the use of special averaging tax schedules which would mean that only one computation of tax would be necessary, instead of a new computation for each year averaged. An alternative, using the current year's cumulative average income and subtracting from this the amount of taxes already paid for earlier years of the averaging period, is outlined by Vickrey (1974: 172–95, 417–27).

The expenditure side

Under an expenditure tax irregular receipts of income do not matter. It is the expenditure pattern which is relevant for the tax. Unfortunately an expenditure based tax faces an even more serious bunching problem than an income based system. Expenditures do not proceed smoothly over a person's lifetime. Purchases of consumer durables, cars, houses, etc. may all be bunched and therefore cause a high tax bill in a particular year in which the expenditure takes place and averaging would be necessary.

In principle an expenditure tax should tax consumption as it occurs and exempt amounts of future consumption until such time as it occurs. Such an approach for a durable good would be treating the purchaser as if renting the good. This would involve imputing values of the services provided, say that of a house, on an annual basis and few legislatures appear willing to contemplate this step.

One solution would be to treat outlays on durables, including housing, as expenditures when they occur and therefore subject to tax. Imputed yields would be ignored, and any profit on sale would be counted in income. Amounts borrowed would not be included in receipts and repayments of principal and interest would be subject to tax. This doesn't avoid the lumpiness problem when tax will be concentrated in the year of purchase and this solution does not seem feasible.

THE TAXPAYING UNIT

If the structure of society is such that the composition of all taxpaying units is the same, say each lives in a household composed of working husband, wife who stays at home and two children there is little difficulty in setting up a taxpaying unit. But taxpayers differ greatly: from those who are single with no dependants to look after, to persons with large families and many dependants. It seems impossible to devise a system which does not appear to be 'unfair' to some sector or another.

The UK Royal Commission on the Taxation of Profits and Income reported in 1954:

> We have come to the conclusion that the taxation of the combined incomes of husband and wife as one unit is to be preferred to their separate taxation as separate units because the aggregate income provides a unit of taxation that is fairer to those concerned. That is why we do not recommend a departure from the present system. The combined incomes of married persons are sometimes described as a joint purse. We do not think that so wide a generalisation can safely be made on such a question of social habit: but it does appear to us, on the one hand, that marriage creates a social unit which is not only truly analogous with other associations involving some measure of joint living expenses and that to tax the incomes of two married people living together as if each were equivalent to the income of a single individual would give a less satisfactory distribution than that

which results from the present rule. Such a method of taxation would mean that one married couple bore a greater or less burden of tax than another according to what must surely be an irrelevant distinction for this purpose, namely, the proportion in which the combined income was divided between the partners.

(1954: para.119)

Aggregation of income brings the couple into the higher tax bracket(s) sooner than a single person, although it was possible in the UK for a couple to opt for separate taxation by forgoing the married person's allowance. It also means that if couples did not opt for separate tax, wives had to make their incomes known to their husbands for tax purposes so that he could complete a tax return.

The Commission was sensitive to the tax advantage that some married couples can enjoy when there is separate assessment for husband and wife. The transfer of unearned income from the spouse with the higher income (and therefore under a progressive tax system the higher tax) to the partner with the lower income, or without an income, can result in substantial tax savings.

By 1990 in the UK the arguments put forward by the Commission no longer carried weight with the government and separate taxation of husband and wife was brought in. While many taxpayers will be unaffected a substantial number will benefit. The balance of advantage in taxation has switched to married persons especially where the partners have substantial unearned income as this, in the UK system, will no longer be aggregated when calculating tax. The practice in some countries is to treat earned income on a single taxation basis but to aggregate unearned income. There are also advantages for the couple where one partner's income is below the tax threshold and the other spouse is able and willing to devolve income earning assets to the other to make use of their tax allowance. The retention of a married couple's allowance in a system where the unit of taxation is the individual seems anachronistic. Wives will also have the (dubious?) advantage of being responsible for their own tax returns.

Should the tax paying unit aggregate the income of children with that of the parents? Failure to aggregate unearned income leaves a big loophole for parents to give their children sufficient income earning assets to use up their personal tax allowances and so escape tax. In the UK children's earned income is not aggregated with that of the parents' income. They are taxed in their own right, but unearned income which is received from capital given by the parent is included in the parents' tax liability.

Difficult questions are raised by present social mores, where many couples cohabit outside marriage and may or may not have children, and also by the treatment of single parent families, whether through death of one partner, divorce, or choice. In the UK single-parent families are able to claim an 'additional personal allowance' for a child. In general, cohabiting couples are treated as single persons for tax purposes. If the couple have a child they too can claim the additional personal allowance.

THE TAXATION MIX

Setting up either the total accretion or the expenditure tax principle is an attempt to judge horizontal equity. In both the assumption is made that the source of income is a matter of indifference: whatever the source, it represents potential purchasing power. The receipt is counted as income under total accretion and under an expenditure tax is taxed when spent instead of when received.

It is clear that no tax system has a 'pure' form of taxation but is a mixture. It should also be clear that other types of tax involve more or less violence to the principle of horizontal equity. Excise and value added taxes will fall unequally on persons in equal positions if they have different consumption patterns. Most noticeably, if tobacco and alcohol are to retain their present high rates of tax for social reasons, then two individuals in equal positions, except that one smokes and drinks and the other does not, will pay very different amounts of tax. In Chapter 3 the benefit principle of tax and social-cost arguments were examined. It is clear that the application of either is likely to violate equity. However this does not negate a discussion of principles, rather it forces a consideration of why such departures are justified. There may well be social and other reasons for deliberately departing from a principle in particular cases. It should make it much harder for particular groups to indulge in special pleading.

SUMMARY

In order to implement the 'ability to pay' principle it is necessary to judge ability. The claims of income, wealth and expenditure as measures of ability to pay were examined. On its own wealth taxation cannot provide all the revenue modern governments require so the choice for a comprehensive tax base come down to a choice between income or expenditure as a tax base. Under an expenditure tax wealth is taxed as it is spent, under an income tax a separate wealth tax is needed if it is desired to tax wealth.

The only other major difference between an income and expenditure based tax system lies in the treatment of saving, since both start from a wide definition of income. They both present a number of common problems which were examined under the headings of: valuation, inflation and deflation, fluctuating income or expenditure and the tax-paying unit.

Chapter 7

Incidence

INTRODUCTION

The classical concept of 'incidence' deals with the problem of trying to sort out who really pays a particular tax and what are the effects of a tax change. For example, should taxes on companies be considered as being paid by the shareholders, the employees, the customers of the company, or in some proportion by all of them? Are capital gains paid by the seller on whom the tax is imposed, or the buyer, or in some measure between them?

Incidence has two aspects: one is concerned with the financial consequences – who actually pays out the money; the other is concerned with a possible transfer of real resources in the economy. If the tax proceeds are spent on real resources, as opposed to making transfer payments, there may well be a loss of resources available for the private sector. This is certain in a fully employed economy '*crowding out*', less certain in a less than full-employment situation where government expenditure may be activating what were previously idle resources and may further stimulate the private sector '*crowding in*'. If a transfer of real resources is involved, then notions of burden will involve the evaluation of the gains and losses resulting from the changes in private and public activity.

Financial incidence refers to the location of the '*ultimate*', as opposed to the '*direct*', burden of the tax. The direct location of a tax is the person on whom the legal liability is imposed, the ultimate location is the person who finally pays it. '*Shifting*' refers to the process by which the direct burden is pushed along through price or wage adjustments from the point of impact (i.e. where statutory liability is imposed) to the final resting place. '*Effects*' refers to all other changes that the tax may bring about, for example inflation, changes in output or incomes, and transfer effects.

It should be noted that it is not possible to make practical measurements of the 'ultimate' burden of a tax. Take, for example, a tax on cigarettes. The consumption of cigarettes can be measured and some assumption about incidence made, for instance, that the consumer pays the whole of the tax. It is then possible to say that this individual pays so much tobacco tax compared with that one. But this does not measure the 'burden' on the person who never takes up smoking because of the cost, or has had to reduce, or stop, smoking because of the tax.

Although a great deal of work has been done on incidence definitive answers to questions should not be expected. Take, for example, Atkinson and Stiglitz (1980). This advanced work consists in part of the development of a general theoretical framework used to evaluate specific tax changes in a general equilibrium setting. The importance of particular assumptions, for example, the degree of monopoly power being exercised, the elasticities of supply and demand, factor mobility, etc., can then be investigated.

A basic distinction is incidence on the *sources-of-income* side and incidence of the *uses-of-income* side. The former refers to taxes that alter the returns from wages, interest, profits or rents, the latter to taxes that alter the prices of goods and services. It is known, for example, that the proportion of income that comes from dividends and interest payments increases as one goes up the income scale, so that a tax that falls on wages will have a very different incidence to an equal yield tax that falls on interest recipients. Taxes that fall on goods and services are generally held to be regressive but for any particular tax such a generalization might fail to hold. If, for example, the amount spent on alcohol increases with income, then a tax on alcohol may be progressive, at least over some income range.

Incidence can be looked at in different contexts. Following the widely accepted work of Musgrave, we can look at absolute, differential and budget incidence. Attempts have also been made to look at dynamic incidence.

ABSOLUTE INCIDENCE

Absolute incidence is the examination of the distributional effects of a particular tax, or a change in a particular tax, with no change in government spending or other taxes. Absolute-incidence studies could be used to analyse the effects of a change in taxation on inflation or unemployment. As such, the task is daunting in its complexity and will not be taken up here.

DIFFERENTIAL TAX INCIDENCE

Differential tax incidence examines the distributional effects brought about by substituting one tax for another of equal yield while keeping government expenditure constant. This approach therefore avoids the problems associated with a switch of resources to the public sector. Since political factors frequently involve the decision whether to raise or lower this or that particular tax, efforts on these lines have practical relevance. The concept of incidence that emerges from studies on these lines is a relative one, describing how the incidence of one tax differs from that of some other tax.

Strictly speaking, a differential tax study does not overcome the complexity of the interrelationships in the economy that were referred to in the discussion of the concept of absolute incidence: different taxes are likely to have different impacts on private consumption, and so on. These changes are likely to be smaller than in the absolute-incidence case, but it is an empirical matter in each case whether these effects are small enough to be ignored.

OTHER CONCEPTS OF INCIDENCE

Dynamic incidence was used by Dosser (1961) to refer to the effects of fiscal measures on the rates of change of individual and group real incomes, with emphasis on the pattern of change over time. Groups can be defined in various ways such as rich and poor, or the division between labour and profits. For example, it is possible that a tax measure that succeeds initially in redistributing income to the poor may over time, due to adjustments made because of the tax, have opposite effects. Others have looked at the tax effects on the amount and timing of an individual's lifetime earnings (Polinsky 1973). Polinsky points to the possibility that a tax system could be progressive in respect of annual income but regressive looked at from the point of view of lifetime earnings.

From this brief introduction to incidence it is apparent that definitive answers will not emerge from theoretical work alone. The theorist can, for example, try to distinguish between the conditions that must be met for a tax on corporations to be passed on to the shareholder and those that must be met if it is to be passed on to the consumer or worker. The presumption is that if all markets are profit maximizing the shareholder will bear the burden. If markets are monopolistic, or firms adopt sales or other than profit maximizing rules, the consumer or worker is more

likely to bear the cost. Models can be constructed with various behavioural assumptions to see how fiscal burdens are distributed. If this
is the approach adopted, the model must then be selected which most
closely mirrors the economy. Empirical studies of incidence so far
unfortunately produce conflicting evidence. This is not surprising as
many non-tax variables influence behaviour. In addition the rate of tax
will also depend on many factors such as the structure of tax and
allowances and the degree of inflation or deflation in an economy.

BUDGET INCIDENCE

The concepts of incidence used so far are attempts to look at the effects
that flow from government taxation. Even if we assume that such studies
yield meaningful results, many would hold that such an approach is
seriously misleading. Citizens may benefit from government spending
as well as having burdens from the taxes they pay. The concept of
budget incidence is thus an attempt to look at the net impact on the
individual of government activity: is the taxpayer a gainer or loser on
balance from the incidence of government expenditure and revenue
collection? Budget studies which incorporate the benefits that flow from
government expenditure must also incorporate ideas about the incidence
of these benefits. The problems here may be less acute, but some
benefits – those that flow to companies, for example – may be just as
difficult to allocate as it is to find the incidence of company taxation.
The budget studies below do not attempt to allocate corporate taxes and
benefits. Budget incidence, the attempt to take the effects that flow from
the tax and the expenditure side, is so important that these issues will
now be examined.

THE INCIDENCE OF TAXES AND BENEFITS: GENERAL CONSIDERATIONS

The study of incidence is thus turned away from an investigation of a
particular tax change into a study of the costs (i.e. who pays) and the
benefits of the whole fiscal system which can be allocated to individuals. Criticism of this approach has been made on a number of
grounds (see Prest 1968; Peacock and Shannon 1968; and Peacock
1974). The criticisms concern the general methodology used, assumptions about the incidence of taxes and benefits, and the need to improve
the data. This method is here put forward as the one that approaches
most nearly the concept of the standard of living of a person or family.

It does so by taking the income of the unit, adding to it a money value of services received where it is sensible to allocate these on an individual basis, and subtracting taxes paid. The value of nearly half of government expenditure, on items such as defence and roads, is not allocated and is therefore ignored as a benefit, about 35 per cent of taxation is also unallocated, this will be mainly taxes where the formal incidence is on companies. This is, it is suggested, a useful approach in the context of measuring poverty. Alternative assumptions can be made for other purposes. For example, Gillespie (1965), in a study of Canadian conditions, has tried allocating defence and other general expenditures on the basis of equal benefit, according to gross income, capital income and disposable income. A similar study for Britain was carried out by Nicholson and Britton (1976); see also Boreham and Semple (1976).

There is still the problem of deciding who ultimately pays the tax and receives the benefit. Studies must obviously make assumptions about this and also about what these benefits are worth to the recipient. However, these problems can be seen in perspective. The importance or otherwise of a particular tax or benefit in relation to the whole can be judged. In particular, it would be feasible to set up alternative assumptions about the incidence of various taxes and benefits to see what overall difference this makes to the 'burden'.

It should be clear that studies of this kind cannot show a comparison with a 'state of nature' where there is no government taxing or spending, because government activity alters incomes, prices, the supply and demand for various factors, and so on. They are likely to be of most use in showing the effect of marginal changes in the level of taxes and benefits, where the secondary effects on factor prices and adjustments are small. Large changes in taxes and benefits need behavioural assumptions to be made about reactions to shifts in the circumstances affecting factors. Budget studies could be broadened out in this way but have not yet done so.

THE INCIDENCE OF TAXES AND BENEFITS IN THE UK IN 1987

Since the early 1960s the Central Statistical Office in its Economic Trends, has published on an annual basis detailed tax and benefit figures for particular income groups. Information was divided into the effects on single persons, married persons without children, and families with varying numbers of children. Economic Trends (May 1990) gives information for 1987 and has changed the basis of presenting the information. This unfortunately makes 1987 figures completely incompatible with previous years. We are promised sometime in the future that some of the past data will be recalculated on the new basis to make such comparisons possible.

The new series presents information on what is called an equivalization basis. This means that household income is adjusted to allow for household size and composition (to recognize different needs). A household of five adults needs a higher income than a single person living alone to achieve the same 'standard of living'. A distribution of

Table 7.1   Equivalence values used for 1987 data

Type of household member	Equivalence value	
Married head of household (i.e. a married couple of 2 adults)	1.00	
1st additional adult	0.42	
2nd (or more) additional adult	0.36	(per adult)
Single head of household (i.e. 1 adult)	0.61	
1st additional adult	0.46	
2nd additional adult	0.42	
3rd (or more) additional adult	0.36	(per adult)
Child aged:		
16–18	0.36	
13–15	0.27	
11–12	0.25	
8–10	0.23	
5–7	0.21	
2–4	0.18	
under 2	0.09	

Source: Economic Trends May 1990.

Note: The values for each household member are added together to give the total equivalence number for that household. This number is then divided into the disposable income for that household to give equivalized disposable income. For example, if a household has a married couple with 2 children (aged 6 and 9) plus one adult lodger. The household's equivalence number is 1.0+0.21+0.23+0.42=1.86. If the household's disposable income is £20,000, its equivalied disposable income is £10,753 (=£20,000/1.86).

equivalized income, where all households are put on an equal footing regardless of size and composition, provides the CSO suggests, a more meaningful way of comparing the income of households. Table 7.1 sets out the equivalence values used.

In any exercise of this nature the inclusion or exclusion of particular taxes and benefits can make a difference to the results. In 1987 some 66 per cent of total government receipts and 51 per cent of total government expenditure were allocated. Included on the receipts side are income tax; employees', employers' and self-employed contributions to National Insurance; domestic rates; VAT and customs and excise duties. The major items not allocated are corporation tax, commercial rates, and the relative small amount received from capital taxes, i.e. capital gains and capital transfer tax.

On the expenditure side benefits are subdivided into cash benefits and benefits in kind. Cash benefits include family benefits, pensions, National Insurance payments and social security benefits. Benefits in kind include the National Health Service, state education, housing and travel subsidies. The method of allocating the benefits from state education is to impute to each child the average cost per child of education in the particular category of school he or she is attending. Benefits of the National Health Service are allocated in a similar manner, it being assumed that the total value of all the services (except maternity services, which are allocated separately) is the same for all persons in each household type.

The benefits derived from government expenditure on administration, defence, police, museums, libraries, parks, roads and capital items are not allocated. By their nature, allocation of benefits of these services to individuals would be a haphazard affair. The value of the analysis is somewhat lessened because of under-representation of the top income range.

A recapitulation is in order before commenting on these figures. The estimates gather up the diverse strand present in the British system of taxation and government spending. The Central Statistical Office (CSO) estimate that value added tax and oil duty are both somewhat progressive taxes, since the demand for the products to which they relate tend to rise more than proportionally with income. Excise duty on tobacco is slightly regressive but that on drink is broadly neutral. However, it is important to remember that these findings would be modified if the range of incomes investigated was extended. Employees' insurance contributions reach a ceiling, while income tax is progressive. On the expenditure side, benefits will normally be progressive – that is,

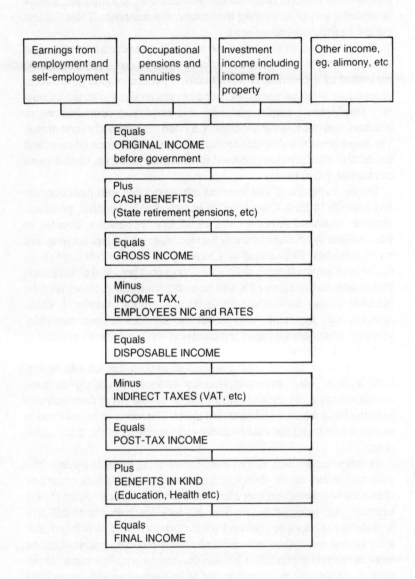

Earnings from employment and self-employment

Occupational pensions and annuities

Investment income including income from property

Other income, eg, alimony, etc

Equals
ORIGINAL INCOME
before government

Plus
CASH BENEFITS
(State retirement pensions, etc)

Equals
GROSS INCOME

Minus
INCOME TAX,
EMPLOYEES NIC and RATES

Equals
DISPOSABLE INCOME

Minus
INDIRECT TAXES (VAT, etc)

Equals
POST-TAX INCOME

Plus
BENEFITS IN KIND
(Education, Health etc)

Equals
FINAL INCOME

Figure 7.1 Stages of redistribution
Source: *Economic Trends*, May 1991

forming a larger percentage of lower incomes than of higher incomes –
with the important exception of benefits received via tax allowances.

Figure 7.1 shows the stages of redistribution considered. The top line
gives four boxes which together add up to produce Original Income.
When cash benefits are added in we reach Gross Income. Direct taxes
are subtracted to arrive at Disposable Income.

Indirect taxes subtracted to arrive at Post-tax Income and finally
adding in benefits in kind produces Final Income.

The information is given for quintile groups. This means that households are ranked by equivalized disposable income and then divided into
five equal segments. So that the bottom quintile gives the average
income of the 20 per cent of households at the bottom of the equivalized
income range and pro rata.

Figure 7.2 shows for all households the effect of these changes.
Equivalized original income varies from an average of £1,220 per
annum in the bottom quintile range to £25,470 in the highest range.
After all the changes have been made the range of final average incomes
is reduced to the range £4,820 to £17,660.

Table 7.2 gives an alternative illustration of income redistribution.
The lowest 20 per cent of income households receive 2.1 per cent of
equivalized original income as opposed to the top 20 per cent which
received half. In the post-tax income situation this percentage had
changed to 7.6 and 43 per cent respectively.

Table 7.3 shows the effect of these changes in more detail. On the top
of the table are non-retired households and at the bottom are retired
households. Taking the non-retired households the range of original
income varies from an average of £2,760 in the bottom quintile to
£27,700 at the top. Partly this will reflect the increase in economically
active people shown in the upper quintile groups. Final incomes average
from £6,250 to £18,980. The retired households had an original income
range from £380 to £10,600 with final incomes from £3,270 to £9,640.

From Table 7.3 can be abstracted the amount of direct taxes and
indirect taxes paid by each quintile group. Table 7.4 presents the results
as a percentage of income.

Taking indirect taxes in the top section of Table 7.4 we find that
indirect taxes are very regressive when expressed as a percentage of
original income. For non-retired households they are 51 per cent for the
lowest quintile and 12 per cent for the highest income group. For retired
households the extremes vary from 192 per cent to 19 per cent. Adding
in cash benefits to original income to arrive at gross income this

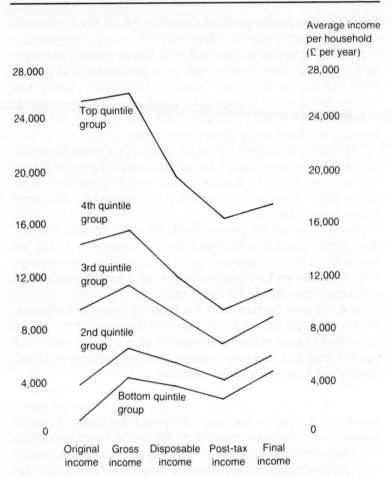

Average income
per household
(£ per year)

Figure 7.2 The effects of taxes and benefits on quintile groups[1] of
households, 1987

Source: *Economic Trends*, May 1990
1 Households are ranked throughout by their equivalized disposable incomes.

regression is still present but on a much reduced scale, as it is for all
other income definitions.

Direct taxes except when expressed as a percentage of original income are progressive except for retired households where the lowest
quintile group pays more than the next three quintile groups.

The final section of the table totals direct and indirect taxes. Expressed as a percentage of original income we have marked regression

Table 7.2 Percentage shares of total equivalized income for households ranked by equivalized disposable income

Quintile group	Original income	Gross income	Disposable income	Post-tax income
Bottom	2.1	7.5	8.2	7.6
2nd	7.0	11.0	12.0	12.0
3rd	16.0	16.0	16.0	16.0
4th	25.0	23.0	23.0	22.0
Top	50.0	43.0	41.0	43.0
All households	100.0	100.0	100.0	100.0

Source: *Economic Trends* May 1990.

and for final income a somewhat progressive picture. However for gross income, disposable income and post-tax income the impression is one of near proportionality for non-retired households except at the top income range who pay less in taxes than the next lower quintile. Retired households show a U-shape with higher taxes at the lower and upper ends.

Should we be complacent about these results? That is to say, do they accord with current ideas about equity? It may be questioned, for example, whether it is the general wish for the near proportional level of tax (49–54 per cent), taking direct and indirect taxes together, which is imposed on all but the bottom of the income range of non-retired households. Also for retired households on the bottom range having so much of their income taken out in taxation. These tables show fairly conclusively that the tax and benefit systems in the UK, in spite of a considerable amount of effort, are neither equitable nor succeeding very well in achieving their declared object of relieving poverty. Chapter 9 examines poverty in detail.

Table 7.3 Summary of the effects of taxes and benefits on non-retired households, 1987

Average per non-retired household (£ per year)	Quintile groups of households ranked by equivalized disposable income					All households
	Bottom	2nd	3rd	4th	Top	
Original income	2,760	8,400	12,670	17,070	27,700	13,720
plus cash benefits	3,050	1,840	1,180	720	480	1,450
Gross income	5,810	10,240	13,850	17,790	28,180	15,170
less direct taxes [1] and employees' NIC	840	1,970	2,920	4,040	6,890	3,330
Disposable income	4,970	8,270	10,930	13,740	21,290	11,840
less indirect taxes	1,400	2,060	2,430	2,810	3,350	2,410
Post-tax income	3,560	6,210	8,500	10,930	17,940	9,430
plus benefits in kind	2,680	2,040	1,850	1,450	1,040	1,810
Final income	6,250	8,250	10,350	12,380	18,980	11,240
Retired households						
Original income	380	560	920	2,390	10,600	2,970
plus cash benefits	2,790	3,360	3,340	3,570	2,960	3,200
Gross income	3,170	3,920	4,260	5,960	13,560	6,170
less direct tax and employees' NIC	460	470	530	810	3,130	1,080
Disposable income	2,710	3,460	3,730	5,160	10,420	5,090
less indirect taxes	730	690	670	1,060	1,990	1,030
Post tax income	1,980	2,770	3,060	4,100	8,440	4,070
plus benefits in kind	1,290	1,350	1,270	1,330	1,200	1,290
Final income	3,270	4,120	4,330	5,430	9,640	5,360

Source: Economic Trends, May 1990

Note: 1 After tax relief at source on morgage interest and life assurance premiums

Table 7.4 Direct and indirect taxes as a percentage of income paid by quintile groups

Quintile	Non-retired households					Retired households				
	(1)	(2)	(3)	(4)	(5)	(1)	(2)	(3)	(4)	(5)
Indirect taxes as a percentage of income										
Bottom	51	24	28	39	22	192	23	26	37	22
2nd	24	20	24	33	25	123	17	20	25	17
3rd	19	17	22	28	23	72	16	18	22	15
4th	16	15	20	26	23	44	18	20	26	19
Top	12	12	15	19	18	19	15	19	24	20
Direct taxes as a percentage of income										
Bottom	30	14	17	23	13	121	15	17	23	14
2nd	23	19	24	32	24	83	12	14	17	11
3rd	23	21	27	34	28	57	12	14	17	12
4th	23	22	29	37	33	34	14	16	20	15
Top	24	24	32	38	36	29	23	30	37	32
Direct and indirect taxes as a percentage of income										
Bottom	81	38	45	62	35	313	38	43	60	36
2nd	47	39	48	65	49	206	29	34	42	28
3rd	42	38	49	62	51	129	28	32	39	37
4th	39	37	49	63	56	78	32	36	46	34
Top	36	36	47	57	54	48	38	49	61	52

Source: *Economic Trends*, May 1990

Notes: (1) Original income   (4) Post-tax income
       (2) Gross income   (5) Final income
       (3) Disposable income

SUMMARY

Incidence is the problem of trying to sort out who really pays a particular tax, or receives a particular benefit and the other effects of a tax or benefit. More recently attempts have been made to analyse the impact of the whole budgetary system. The ideas of 'crowding out', 'crowding in', shifting and various concepts of incidence were examined. The UK pioneered the use of budgetary studies and most of this chapter was taken up with detailing this method and giving some of the results.

Chapter 8

Wealth

INTRODUCTION

In all countries the distribution of wealth is more unequal than the distribution of income, sometimes markedly so. This is the case even when the figures are adjusted for different earning patterns and the life cycle pattern of wealth. Typically wealth holdings will be near a peak just before retirement. Inheritance plays the largest part in the perpetuation of wealth inequality (Harbury and Hitchens 1979). Since wealth is heavily concentrated among those with high incomes there is therefore an argument for a wealth tax on the grounds of ability to pay. Under a pure income based system only changes in wealth would automatically form part of the tax base, leaving open the question of a tax on the underlying wealth. Under a pure expenditure base both the stock of wealth, and increments in this wealth, would be taxed as it is spent. Redistribution arguments to reduce the heavy concentration of wealth and the benefits that this brings are also put forward for a wealth tax. On benefit principles, costs of protection of wealth would be charged to wealth holdings but a more powerful argument on benefit lines is that the value of land and property, which form a significant part of wealth, can be greatly influenced by decisions of the community.

WHAT IS WEALTH?

In principle wealth can be distinguished from income by the time element. Income as a concept only makes sense if a period of time is specified, say income per week or per annum. Wealth, on the other hand, has to be dated. Individuals can add up all their assets and subtract their liabilities at a particularly time on a particular day. The result will be their wealth or net worth at that time, positive if they have wealth, negative if their liabilities outweigh their assets. If the assets are valued the following day a different figure for wealth is likely, particularly if the assets consist of items such as shares and property, which have volatile prices.

Wealth then consists of assets less liabilities, so the concept of wealth is essentially arbitrary, depending on what assets and liabilities are considered wealth. Personal possessions such as houses, land, property, stocks and shares, cars and other consumer durables and objects of art may present valuation problems, but not problems of principle: they are wealth. Rights accruing to the individual such as occupational pension rights or, more widely, state pension and welfare rights can also be considered as wealth. Actuarial values can be put on these and these values attributed to the individual. There is no right definition of wealth. Figures can be presented on a wide or narrow definition.

A further difficulty with defining wealth is the possibility of overlap with income. A simple example will make this clear. Competitions frequently offer prizes such as £10,000 a year for life or a lump sum of £100,000. If interest rates on bonds are 10 per cent then £100,000 invested in a bond will yield £10,000, so the company will be largely indifferent to which prize is chosen. Should the prize be considered as income of £10,000 per annum, or wealth of £100,000?

A one-dimensional picture of differences could be presented in which information on wealth included information on capitalized income streams. Alternatively income statistics could impute a return to the net assets of a person and include these in income statistics. Separate information on income and wealth is probably to be preferred provided double counting is avoided by using figures of income and wealth that are drawn up on a mutually exclusive basis.

Land and housing are clearly wealth and present some special features that will be discussed before examining the taxation of wealth.

LAND

The meanings attached to 'ownership'

The land and real property laws of a country usually exhibit a long standing struggle of rival interests. Mankind, even at a primitive stage of development, showed an acute interest in land and territorial rights. Ownership itself is not a simple issue, it presents a highly complex tangle of privileges, rights and duties. By way of illustration, does ownership confer: the right of alienation, i.e. to sell or give land away;

the right of bequest; the right of franchise; the right to mineral wealth below ground; the right to hunt and fish; the right to erect buildings on land; the right to neglect land to the detriment of neighbours and future generations; rights above ground; or right to sunlight?[1]

In addition: What happens on intestacy? Are services or taxes required of the owner? Does it accord social status? Are improvements made by a tenant the property of the owner, or must the tenant be compensated? Does the community reserve any public rights, e.g. of access? Has the community the right to acquire the land for the public good?

Very important in a fiscal context is the treatment of changes to the value of land brought about by the community with no part being played by the owner. Should increases in value by acts of the community be taxed and should decreases in value be compensated? Large changes in value can occur due to acts such as sea defences, drainage, town expansion, siting of airports and roads and the granting or withholding of planning permission.

'Ownership' is the rag-bag into which all aspects are bundled. The history of land and the privileges, rights and duties that attach thereto exhibit a rich variety of solutions to be found at different times and in different places. Much of history is a record of this changing nexus of privilege and responsibility. A brief account of the UK situation is found in the Appendix at the end of the chapter.

The economics of land

David Ricardo, an economist of the early nineteenth century, developed the idea that land is in a separate category from other factors of production since its supply could neither be diminished nor increased – an idea encapsulated in Mark Twain's advice to a friend: 'Buy land, they've stopped making it.' Ricardo argued that a tax on land could not reduce the available supply and hence could have no adverse effect on production: therefore, 'rent' should be treated differently from other factor payments. Fundamentally, the quantity of land is limited in supply. A community with a growing population is likely to experience an increasing demand for the limited amount of land available for food-growing, dwellings, transport and amenities – which will raise its real value. This 'unearned income' may not accrue to every landowner but it will accrue to landowners en masse. We have here the germ of later ideas developed by 'single taxers', such as George (1879), that land need be the only item to bear tax, an idea which today, even if acceptable, would not yield the amount of revenue required.

Ricardo's ideas have been modified on two fronts. The effective supply of land can be greatly modified by the action of persons, so the absolute fixity of the quantity of land needs to be modified. Services from land can be increased by, for example, better agricultural methods or increasing the height of buildings; it can also be reduced by, for example, soil erosion. Secondly, other factors may be akin to land, in that the supply cannot immediately be changed in response to an increase in demand, and these factors will also enjoy an enhanced price, or 'quasi-rent', for a period.

The degree to which the price of land is affected by population pressures and socially created values is the chief attribute that marks land off from most other assets. In the UK a government Commission reported:

> There is no novelty in proposals to secure for the community at least a share in the values it has itself created. An act of 1427 sought to recover increases in the value of property attributable to public expenditure on works for sea defence, and in the reign of Charles II, there was statutory appropriation of a part of landowners' unearned enhancement or 'melioration' assessed upon the benefits of street widening in London.
>
> (Land Commission 1965: para. 2)

With increased government activity today, the scope for great changes in land values which accrue without effort on the landowners' part is very much increased. Proposals to build new towns, the reconstruction of existing towns, new road links, the closing of railway lines, siting of power stations, nuclear plant, airports and seaports, the planning regulations which permit or prohibit certain types of development, are but a few of the more obvious examples of community decisions which can greatly increase, or decrease, the value of land.

Should land be treated differently from other assets?

From the fiscal viewpoint it is necessary to decide whether the relative uniqueness of land, that is its relative 'fixed quantity' and change in value which can occur through public action, is sufficiently marked to call for special tax treatment. In a country which is sparsely populated the question may seem an academic one; in a well-populated country it becomes more acute. The problem, as has been indicated, is made more complex since a wide variety of planning regulations has grown up. The redesignation of land from the 'green belt', that is land that shall not be built upon, to a housing area can increase the price of land many hundredfold overnight. In a similar way, the price may be adversely affected by planning permission which goes the other way.

Summary

Land, it is clear, is a scarce resource: it is part of wealth and as such should form part of a wealth tax base. Land is different from most forms of wealth in that community action can very significantly alter its value, up or down, without any action by the owner. Unfortunately, no economic or political consensus seems to have emerged in the UK on the form that such taxation or compensation should take.

There now seems a general consensus that some form of planning is required, and that compensation should be paid for those adversely affected by community decisions. It therefore seems equitable for those who receive benefits in this way to contribute to the community. Details of the changes since 1947 in the UK are given in the Appendix of this chapter. Unfortunately, the two major political parties in Britain seem to have devoted more time to undoing the work of the other party when they achieve power than they do in trying to find a permanent solution that would be acceptable to both.

OTHER ASSETS GENERATING ECONOMIC RENT

It was noted above that other scarce factors can generate economic rent and the discussion above on land applies with little modification to these assets. Where the right to exploit the scarcity is regulated, licensed or controlled by the government, a case for taxation of the economic rent applies. Raw materials, such as oil and gas, form an important case. With these type of assets it is important to arrange a tax regime which encourages rather than discourages firms to extract the maximum economic resources from each site. A tax which is simply in proportion to the quantity of material extracted would not do this as the cost of extracting marginal supplies is likely to rise. Another aspect is a tax regime which leaves firms with sufficient incentive to explore for new sources. The complexity of the taxation of North Sea oil and gas in the UK (Royalties, Petroleum Revenue Tax, Mainstream Corporation Tax, Advanced Petroleum Revenue Tax) and the large number of changes thereto that have been made paints a sad picture of administrative incompetence and muddle but it also points out the difficulties of reconciling the various aims listed above.

HOUSING

The theoretically correct treatment of housing

The theoretically correct treatment of housing with an income-based tax is to include the rental value of the house, net of interest, depreciation and maintenance, in taxable income. Few countries do so effectively. The chief difficulty is in assessing the rental value of owner-occupied houses. There is also the problem with owner-occupied houses that tax would be payable on income not received in cash.

Under an expenditure base there are two alternatives. Since housing is a form of consumption, the net rental value of owner-occupied housing should be included in the tax base, but this leaves it open to the objections just outlined. Alternatively, the purchase of the house would be treated in the tax base and on sale only the gain would be a taxable receipt. This alternative is not a serious contender as at the same time as most purchases were committing themselves to large contractual outlays they would find themselves liable for large amounts of tax.

Like a virus, housing has come to infect or distort whole economies in various degrees. The UK, where housing has long been treated favourably, is used as an example. The proportion of mortgage debt as a proportion of GDP increased from 32.1 per cent in 1982 to 58.3 per cent in 1989, compared to approximately constant ratios of 20 per cent in Germany, Japan and France. (See Bank on England Quarterly Bulletin, February 1991.) A number of countries allow tax deductability on consumer loans; this could offset the bias towards housing but at the same time it is likely to depress savings ratios. Denmark, Luxembourg, the Netherlands, New Zealand, Norway, Portugal, Switzerland and the United States allow full deductability on consumer loans, with partial deductability in Belgium, Finland and Ireland.

In the UK most tenants of council houses receive subsidies but these are small in relation to direct housing subsidies for owner occupation which are estimated to have reached £7.8 billion in the tax year 1990–1. Taxes on owner occupiers have been reduced or abolished. The value of the services from a house to the owner occupier goes untaxed, since imputed rent is no longer included in the tax base, so they have an advantage over people who rent these services and have to pay for this out of taxed income. Sale of the main residence incurs no liability to income or capital gains tax either during the houseowner's life or at death. Only at death will the value of the house be aggregated with the other assets of the deceased and if large enough will be subject to tax.

The shift from rates to a Community Charge was another signal that investment in a bigger property will not be penalized since the Community Charge is not differentiated according to value or size of the property, although this will be reversed somewhat in 1993 if the proposed Council Tax is implemented.

The distortions these tax concessions and subsidies introduce to the economy are very high. The effect of this largeness is to redistribute income from the 35 per cent of the population who are non-home owners to home owners. The former are likely to be on average poorer than home owners. Within the house-owning group, on average, those on income of £40,000 or more received twice the benefit of £560 per annum received by those with an income between £10,000 and £15,000. It is not surprising that the UK authorities bemoan the lack of industrial investment when investment in housing for one's own use has so many advantages. Britain is the only country in which institutions are prepared to lend up to 100 per cent of the value of the property. In the United States loans up to 95 per cent age of the value are allowed but most European countries and Japan only allow a smaller proportion. In Germany and Japan the figure is 60 per cent. The first £30,000 of borrowing for an owner occupier receives tax relief at the standard rate of tax – currently 25 per cent. Until 1991 higher rate taxpayers received relief at their marginal rate of tax or 40 per cent. This was scrapped but high-income earners were compensated by an increase in the rate at which the higher rate was payable: a benefit to all high-income earners not just those with mortgages. Non-taxpayers benefit by having a lower rate of interest equivalent to income tax relief at the standard rate. This relief is without time limit and applies to all not just first-time buyers. Even when the tax relief on the first segment of borrowing is ignored, interest rates for housing loans are for most the cheapest source of finance, usually several percentage points below other bank loans and less than half the cost of credit card finance. Not surprisingly a proportion of this borrowing gets channelled into non-housing consumption, a process described by the Bank of England as 'equity extraction'. It defines this as 'the difference between the net increase in the stock of house purchase loans and the private sector's net expenditure on housing', and comments that it has become more widespread.

On the other hand, private rented accommodation has suffered from rent restrictions since the time of the First World War – although these have been relaxed somewhat recently – and tenancy laws that make it extremely difficult for a landlord to obtain possession of his property.

The taxpayer has responded to these incentives and the UK has over 65 per cent owner occupation while the private rented sector has fallen to less than 5 per cent of the total housing stock. Britain's personal saving ratio has fallen from 11.6 per cent to 5.0 per cent, the lowest seen in any leading country.

The result of this surge in home ownership is that house prices between 1969 and 1989 rose at over twice the rate of retail prices. There have been three periods of real falls – 1973–7, 1980–2 and 1990 (continuing) – but these were largely the result of previous speculative splurges in prices (Flemming and Nellis 1990).

Macro-effects

The macro-effects of this largesse are now serious in a number of countries. Chapter 1 has already referred to the serious problems in the United States on the lending side where the S & Ls need on some estimates a $500 billion bailout.

In the UK differential price movements in different parts of the country restrict the mobility of labour, and the cyclical nature of the price movements causes considerable disruption to the building sector with a multiplier impact on the rest of the economy. The government is finding it extremely difficult to damp down consumer spending as householders have found ways to unlock some of the substantial real increase in capital values to provide finance for other spending. The freeing of financial markets has seen financial institutions more than willing to lend on the security of property. A considerable proportion of housing changes hands each year and this gives the opportunity for borrowers to borrow more and in excess of their housing need – a process referred to above as equity extraction. Those who stay put can often renegotiate a bigger mortgage on the increased capital value of their property or at worst (because it tends to be somewhat more expensive) take out a second mortgage. Because of the lower rates of interest on housing finance, sensible buyers borrow as much as they need, and are able to, and use the surplus money for general purchases. Fear of the political repercussions may inhibit governments from putting up interest rates as much as they would like, so making it more difficult to achieve monetary control. Political consideration can result in governments inducing instability into the economy if they reduce interest rates to engineer a pre-election boom. This can push up inflation and consequently produce the need to damp down the economy after the election.

Housing summary

Housing now represents a major tax expenditure in many economies and reversing this expenditure could add substantially to government revenue or allow big tax reductions. Gradual rather than abrupt change is to be preferred as large numbers of people have made their decisions on the basis of existing legislation and undue hardship could be caused if these tax concessions were abruptly changed. In the UK in 1991 tax relief was confined to the standard rate of tax and the figure for relief has not been increased in line with inflation for several years. A further step would be to announce a gradual tapering reduction in the level of relief over a period of years. Confining relief to first-time buyers and limiting the number of years the relief can be claimed is an alternative that could be phased in. Subjecting the capital gain in housing to tax at the death of the owner would cause least disruption.

TAXING WEALTH

An annual wealth tax?

Wealth, being much more unequally spread than income, appears to offer a good base for an annual tax. A number of European countries do tax wealth or have done so: Austria, France, Ireland, the Netherlands, Norway, Spain, Sweden and Germany.

The experience with an annual wealth tax is that yields are low, costs of collection and compliance costs are high and market distortions result as wealth is redistributed into tax favoured forms. The reasons for high collection costs are not hard to see. Unless assets are uniform and regularly traded, valuation can be difficult and costly. The result is that many assets are excluded from the tax base or included at arbitrary values. Dwellings and small businesses are usually treated favourably. Differential tax treatment of assets results in distortions in asset holdings. Seepage of assets abroad in a way that escapes tax is likely. The ability of rich individuals to avoid tax should never be under-estimated. A further difficulty with a wealth tax is that, as many assets such as owner-occupied houses, jewellery, works of art, etc. do not yield income, even modest rates of tax can lead to the necessity to sell off some of the assets to meet the tax. Administrative rules to meet the cash flow problems of payers add further complications to the tax.

The relative ineffectiveness of most attempts to have an annual wealth tax have led many to believe that taxing wealth when it is transferred is the better route.

The case against taxing wealth

Barry Bracewell-Milnes (hereafter BBM), in a series of booklets (1982, 1989a, 1989b), has taken support for Midas to the limits and beyond. He takes the intangible benefit the owner gets from giving and calls this wealth. Lumping this intangible benefit together with tangible wealth enables BBM to assert his case, which is that all taxes on gifts and bequests should be abolished. We should not tax the wealthy so that we can increase their psychic satisfaction from giving.

BBM starts with the totally unprovable assumption that: 'The value or "utility" obtained by the donor from his giving is strictly comparable with the value or "utility" obtained by the consumer from his consumption.'

BBM uses the example of the transfer of a financial asset with a market value of 100 which is gained by the recipient. The donor loses this sum but gains by altruistic satisfaction. He asserts the two satisfactions are commensurate, and the latter must exceed the former or the gift will not be made. So '*the process of giving at least doubles the value of the gift*'. It follows logically if this is accepted that a tax on giving can destroy wealth by damping down altruism and tax relief can increase it.

There follow a couple of biblical quotations about the blessings of giving which point to another weakness of the analysis. Those with a Midas touch get satisfaction from keeping not giving. The assumption that taxes do not yield satisfaction to the taxpayer is also subject to challenge. Empirical studies show that faced with a choice between tax cuts and improvements in government services people often vote for a considerable increase in services. (Hockley and Harbour 1982 and 1983). Public goods are provided from general taxation precisely because relying on charity is likely to result in serious under-provision of these services. One reason people agree to taxation is that they are willing to provide their share of revenue provided they know others will also contribute. Private altruism is likely to be most generous to close relatives, the perpetuation of wealth in fewer hands with greater inequality in society is the likely result of BBM's suggestions.

BBM does correctly point to the administrative and compliance costs of compulsory redistribution through the tax system and the distortions that can be introduced as wealthy people seek to escape taxation. These are separate arguments. The costs need to be evaluated and to be weighed against the benefits. They do not provide a presumptive argument for or against wealth taxation.

Taxing wealth transfers

Taxing wealth when it is transferred by gift or inheritance has advantages over an annual wealth tax. (See, for example, Meade 1978.) The latter will tax those who build up fortunes as well as those who inherit and may have disincentive effects as a result. Valuation has to take place at death and these values can form the basis for a tax on wealth transfers. Inheritance tax has long formed part of the tax base of many countries. Bringing gifts into the tax net as well is an obvious closure of what otherwise would be a loophole for the wealthy to escape tax by giving away this wealth before they die.

Inheritance taxes may be based on the wealth of the donor or on the wealth and/or the cumulative amount of gifts and inheritance already received by the recipient. Under a donor-based system the donor has no incentive to spread his wealth to a number of recipients; the tax bill is the same whether one or a hundred people benefit. If one of the aims of wealth taxation is to ensure a more equal distribution of wealth then a cumulative recipient-based tax is the better method of achieving this.

SUMMARY

In all countries the distribution of wealth is more unequal than the distribution of income, sometimes markedly so. Inheritance plays a major role in the perpetuation of wealth inequality.

The distinguishing characteristics of wealth were examined, which points up the impossibility of having a single definition of wealth. Land and housing are clearly wealth and present some special features that were examined.

Land is a scarce resource and its supply cannot readily be increased, an argument put forward by Ricardo for taxing rent differently from other assets. An idea which is examined together with that of 'quasi-rents'. Of more importance today is the extent to which is price can be affected, up or down, by many actions of the community.

APPENDIX: A BRIEF HISTORY OF LAND IN BRITAIN

The subject of land abounds in legal subtleties. A short summary, or outline, certainly cannot do justice to the niceties that have developed. In Great Britain the Norman Conquest of 1066 brought great changes. After the Conquest the normal position was for the Crown to own land, and others to hold an estate under various forms of tenure, either directly from the Crown or from an intermediate holder who himself had tenure directly or indirectly from the Crown.[2] Feudal tenure involved the granting of an estate for services. These were in the form of military, spiritual or agricultural obligations. Wills of land were not permitted; descent in the male line predominated.

This situation was gradually changed in a number of ways. Feudal services tended to be commuted into annual payments or 'rents'. The trust device came to be used to get around the ban on bequeathing land; this right was not legally established until 1540. The freehold, as a freely marketable commodity unencumbered by onerous feudal rights, was achieved by statute in 1660. The system thus established was, speaking very broadly, the one existing until 1947, although there were numerous alterations in the laws affecting land during this time, some of considerable importance. Since 1947 land has become something of a political football. The Labour government enacted in 1947 the main recommendations of the Expert Committee on Compensation and Betterment (1942), known as the Uthwatt Committee, and vested in the state all development rights in land. Anyone wishing to develop land had to recover the right by payment of a charge. The act was bureaucratic and attempted to tax land betterment at 100 per cent. The Conservative government changed the system in 1953, 1954 and 1959. By the last date a free market for land was the practice, which resulted in high prices for land with development value. Gains made from land were then generally untaxed until 1962, except when undertaken 'by way of trade', when they were taxed under normal company taxation rules. In 1962 capital gains in land and building were taxed if realized within three years of purchase. The 1965 Act charged all gains. A Labour government introduced a Land Commission Act of 1967, which attempted to charge a betterment levy on land when its use was changed. The charge was originally at 40 per cent of the increase in value from existing use to a new use. The Act envisaged the Land Commission's being an active body acquiring land to hold, manage and sell to developers. A Conservative government abolished the Land Commission in 1971 and gains on land were treated in the same way as other gains and subject to capital gains tax and estate duty.

Chapter 9

Social security, taxation and poverty

THE MEANING OF SOCIAL SECURITY

The term social security may be used in a broad or narrow sense in developed countries. Table 9.1 provides a list of what are usually considered major social services. The emphasis in each developed country may vary, the United States for example has no comprehensive public health service and practice over state pension provisions differs considerably.

All 12 member-states of the EC in 1988 had the services listed in Table 9.1; there were, however, considerable differences.

The narrower meaning of social security in developed countries is normally confined to state programmes, usually but not exclusively, of cash transfers to meet contingencies such as old age, accident, sickness, unemployment and family responsibilities. One of the aims of a social security system is to prevent persons falling into poverty through adverse circumstances like those listed, and to aid those that are in poverty.

Whether the term '*National Insurance*' or '*Social Insurance*' is a good one to use has been long debated. There are two basic principles of private insurance, the less important one being that the premium to be paid should be based on an assessment of the risks involved. Thus a thatched house pays a higher premium against fire risk than a similar house with a tiled roof, motor insurance premiums may vary with the age of the insured, their accident record, occupation, type of car, etc. A person in chronic poor health, or over a certain age, is unlikely to be accepted at all in a private medical-care scheme. In contrast state insurance was instituted on the principle of collective risk and either flat-rate contributions or contributions graded in some way to ability to pay, but not graded by risk.

Table 9.1   List of main social security benefits

Cash benefits
Retirement pensions
Unemployment benefit
Sickness, maternity and invalidity benefit
Industrial injuries
Family allowances
Poverty and low-income assistance

Public health
Hospital and general practitioner services
Environmental health services
   sewerage, refuse collection, water supply, etc.

Education

Housing

Other services
Employment exchanges, retraining, parks, and a variety of Personal Social Services.

The more important principle of private insurance is the actuarial aim that premiums should more than cover the claims paid out. With national insurance most countries supplement funds out of general taxation and do not build up funds to meet future payment obligations. The payees, with their social security contributions, build up a series of rights to benefit which they hope future payers will honour.

EUROPEAN CONSENSUS

A survey 'The Perception of Poverty in Europe in 1989' (1990) of 11,819 people in the EC found a consensus on what is necessary to lead a proper life in a European country in 1989. Eight out of every ten persons sampled thought indispensable: basic home facilities (tap water, electricity, etc.), welfare, housing and education. The survey showed a dramatic change in the explanation of poverty. Considerably less support was given to the idea that poverty was a consequence of laziness and unwillingness. For instance the proportion of people in Britain who held this idea fell from 43 per cent in 1976 to 18 per cent in 1989. One

European in three thought poverty was the result of social injustice, another third considered it to be due to fate, misfortune or to the inherent structure of the modern world.

INCREASING OR DECREASING INEQUALITY?

A study 'Comparative Tables of the Social Security Schemes' (1989) covered France, UK, Germany, Italy and Spain. It looked at changes in incomes between 1973, 1979 and 1984 and found that the UK was the only country where a significant increase in inequality occurred between these dates. The inequality applied not only to original income but also to gross and disposable incomes. The study found that after 1979 a marked rise in the inequality of original income was not balanced by taxes and social transfers. These trends have been accentuated since 1984 by greater salary increases to the well off, tax reductions that benefit them more than the poor and failure to upgrade many social benefits in line with the cost of living. The final straw for many persons appeared to be the introduction of the Community Charge in 1989 in Scotland and 1990 in the rest of the UK details are given in the Appendix of Chapter 12. This provoked street disturbances and an estimated 20 per cent of persons, in mid-1990, who had withheld payments.

A recent study Johnson and Stark (1989a, 1989b) for the politically independent Institute for Fiscal Studies studied the effect in the UK of changes to the tax and benefit system on households made by the Conservative government in the 10 years from 1979 to 1989.

Table 9.2 shows the average gains in pounds per week for UK households in various income ranges. Income is gross household income before taxes and benefits. While all sectors gained, the poorest by £1.65 per week, those at the top gained a massive £286.53 a week. Another way of looking at these gains shows that half of all the money spent on changes to the tax and benefit system accrued to those on incomes of £500 per week or more.

These findings were confirmed by a report by Professor Townsend reported in *The Times* (28 March 1991), which looked at real disposable income. 'Contrary to the claims made by Mrs Thatcher when prime minister, and by other ministers, the poorest sections of the population experienced a fall in real disposable income during the decade 1979 to 1989.' The groups worst hit were families with children and single adults under pension age, particularly under-25. During this period the real annual income changed as shown on Table 9.3.

Table 9.2 Average gains in gross household income 1979–89 due to tax and benefit changes

Income range (£/week)	Average gain (£/week)
Below 10.00	1.65
10.00 to 49.99	0.33
50.00 to 99.99	1.42
100.00 to 149.99	3.57
150.00 to 199.99	4.27
200.00 to 249.99	4.20
250.00 to 299.99	4.79
300.00 to 399.99	5.85
400.00 to 499.99	9.17
500.00 to 599.99	14.12
600.00 to 999.99	34.98
1000.0 and above	286.53
All	7.18

Source: Paul Johnson and Graham Stark *Taxation and Social Security 1979–89: The Impact on Household Incomes* (Institute of Fiscal Studies 1989).

The same copy of *The Times* also had a report on another page that Mrs Thatcher, prime minister during the time these changes favouring the well off were put in effect, was to have an additional annual allowance of £29,000 after leaving office and ceasing to enjoy the formidable back-up provided by the civil service. Other former prime ministers would also benefit. Mrs Thatcher is already entitled to an index-linked former prime minister's pension of £25,362 a year, an MP's salary of £21,000 and secretarial and office allowance of £27,000 provided to all MPs plus a £10,500 cost-of-living allowance for having a constituency

Table 9.3 Change in real income of average household 1979–89 at 1989 prices

	1979 (£)	1989 (£)	% Change
Poorest 20%	3,442	3,282	– 4.6
Average	10,561	13,084	+ 23.9
Richest 20%	20,138	28,124	+ 39.6

outside inner London. 'Although nothing as vulgar as public lobbying took place, Mr Major acted after friends of Mrs Thatcher let the considerable difficulties she faced on leaving office be known at Westminster.' Unfortunately, letting the considerable difficulties of the least well off in society be known at Westminster doesn't get the same generous treatment for them.

A study by Jenkins (1991) is in broad agreement with the above finding. He found that while real incomes in the UK increased during the 1970s and 1980s these gains have been most marked among the rich, with the poorest gaining little. Whatever measure of inequality he used, 'the income distribution was more unequal in the mid-to-late 1980s than in the early 1980s'.

An official study by the House of Commons Social Security Committee (1991) again confirms the above findings. Those with incomes below half the average income grew from 5.4 million to 9.1 million between 1979 and 1988 with many in this group being slightly worse off at the end of the period than they were at the beginning.

STATE OR PRIVATE PROVISION?

A few persons, such as Nozick (1974), believe that the role of the state should be minimal; limited to the narrow functions of protection against force, theft, fraud, enforcement of contracts and so on. They see any more extensive role for the state as violating persons' rights not to be forced to do certain things, and as unjustified. Such views leave no room for social insurance, which is seen as a violation of individual liberty.

The case for the state rather than the private sector managing social security schemes rests in part on the arguments listed in Chapter 1 that the private sector would fail to provide these services at all, or do so in a sub-optimum and inefficient way. These ideas came under increasing criticism in the 1980s from those who saw an increasing role for private insurance and wanted a switch to income-tested rather than universal benefits. Private insurance was seen as a way of achieving greater choice and claims were made about administrative savings. Both claims were largely unsubstantiated. Most state schemes allow individuals to supplement state provision by private insurance if they wish, so it is hard to see how a purely private system can add much to this. It seems highly unlikely that private provisions by a variety of companies would have lower administrative costs than a centrally administered scheme of compulsory insurance. State provision (financial or by the provision of services) would still be necessary to sweep up those who were ineligible at the start or who fell out of the private system because their rights had been exhausted. Advocates of state provision tend to see private provision as creating harmful divisions in society and emphasize the unifying role played by universal compulsory state provision.

Most state schemes also differ from private schemes in that premiums are not based on individual risk. In the absence of regulation, and probably state subsidy, private schemes would, for example, either refuse to insure, or charge higher premiums for health insurance, to those who were chronically sick. They would also be much more likely to have ceilings on both the length of time over which they would make payment and the total amount of payment they would make on any claim. Another departure of state-run schemes is that they may well incorporate an element of redistribution so that, for example, the lower paid may receive a pension that pays out a greater proportion of their contributions than that of the higher paid.

With state schemes the terms of payment may be altered in a way that contractual private schemes may not be able to, although private companies can go bankrupt. The alteration in the terms of state schemes may be to the benefit of potential and actual recipients, such as an upgrading of pensions. Alternatively the terms may be worsened as when the terms for making payments are tightened. In the UK, in the period 1979–88 there were 17 significant changes in National Insurance unemployment benefit, some favourable but most unfavourable to the unemployed, for details see Atkinson (1989). The UK had a major change in the system of income-related benefits, as well as changes to the structure and level of both state and private pensions in 1988. These changes, including the abolition of earnings-related supplement, make Britain unique in the European Community in this respect and in the taxation of benefits. For an overview see Dilnot and Webb (1988).

RELATIVE POVERTY

It is clear from this discussion that fortunately, in most of the developed world, we are not discussing what is termed absolute poverty but relative poverty. Absolute poverty refers to those who are unable to maintain the basic essentials for life, are destitute, and face death due to starvation, lack of shelter or other causes.

Relative poverty has been concisely defined by Townsend (1974):

Poverty can be defined objectively and applied only in terms of the concept of relative deprivation . . . Individuals, families and groups

in the population can be said to be in poverty when . . . their resources
are so seriously below those commanded by the average individual or
family that they are, in effect, excluded from ordinary living patterns,
customs and activities.

Relative poverty raises many questions about how it should be measured
which will not be taken up here, a recent discussion of these can be
found in Atkinson (1989).

TAX AND BENEFIT OVERLAP

It is difficult to see how the overlap of the systems of taxes and benefit
could be avoided, without excessive costs. The difficulties have been
highlighted under the term *poverty trap*, embracing both the earnings and
unemployment traps. It is important, however, to put this in perspective.
The numbers caught in either trap are estimated in the UK to be small –
about 500,000 persons. The economic consequences are probably not
serious but the importance to the individual concerned can be significant. It is important for this reason to keep the numbers involved as low
as possible, but complete elimination is very difficult.

The *earnings trap* refers to the fact that as income increases so
entitlement to means-tested benefits falls. The loss of benefits added to
the tax and social insurance contributions on income can result in very
high implicit marginal rates of tax. Rates over 100 per cent have been
noted; that is, an increase in income can actually make a person worse
off.

The poverty trap can affect both those in work and those not employed. A low-income employed person may not be much better off
even if he succeeds in doubling or trebling his income. For those not in
employment, say the retired, unless there is a adjustment in benefit
levels an increase in pension can be eroded by loss of other benefit
entitlement.

The unemployment trap operates in the same way as the earnings trap
but in this case refers to the effect on the willingness of the unemployed
to seek work. The unemployed who are able to find only low-paid jobs
may then find themselves worse off or no better off. Tax and National
Insurance payments, combined with loss of benefits and costs of going
to work such as travel, can erode their income to below their previous
assisted level.

DIVERSITY OF SOCIAL PROVISION

Developed countries accept the need for social services but ideas and practice of how best to achieve a desirable social outcome differ widely on both the provision and financing of activities.

On the one hand are those countries, such as the United States, which believe strongly in fostering the individual ethic so that persons are encouraged to make their own provision for health care; state provision tends to be meagre or confined to selected groups such as war veterans. A recent study of seven countries (the United States, Canada, Israel, Norway, West Germany, UK and Sweden), where considerable efforts had been made to use comparable data, found that state transfers in the United States, Canada and Israel formed less than 10 per cent of gross income of the inhabitants and that levels of poverty in these countries were relatively high (Smeeding *et al.* 1990). At the other extreme, transfers in Sweden were 30 per cent, with low poverty. West Germany and the UK transfers were some 15–20 per cent and had medium poverty levels. Norway was also a medium transfer country but achieved a low poverty level. The inverse relationship between the level of state transfers and poverty is subject to many reservations but it seems safe to conclude that the state has an important role to play and the way the state intervenes affects the categories of those in poverty. Thus in the UK, of those in poverty a large number are elderly, reflecting the low basic state level of pension. Poverty in single-parent, largely female-headed, families were found to be a major problem in all countries except Israel where there are not many families in this category.

As well as the differences just noted, in the extent of services provided by the state, there are differences both between and within countries about the nature of the provisions. Should they be universal, available to all, or selective, subject to a means test? Universal benefits avoid administrative complexity and remove the stigma attached to means testing. On the other hand, paying benefits to all regardless of their income means that tax rates have to be higher. Means testing enables benefits to be targeted at lower cost, but targets are often missed because of serious problems of low take up. This may be due to the stigma felt to be involved and perhaps deliberately fostered by governments to deter claims, ignorance of the benefits available or the costs in time and effort in making claims.

METHODS OF FINANCIAL HELP

Basic income guarantee

The nature of benefits needed is not independent of the manner in which they are paid. Most countries have a mixed system of tax allowances and benefit payments, which causes a number of problems.

A number of advocates would like to see a basic income guarantee provided for all citizens, whether employed or not. In the UK, Williams (1943) put forward the idea of a 'social dividend' and many variations of this basic idea have been suggested since, including Meade (1972) and Parker (1989). This would enable all or some tax allowances and benefit payments to be cashed out. All income above the basic guaranteed level would be subject to tax. This would extend the scheme in the UK whereby child tax allowances were replaced by cash payments. Tax allowances have the disadvantage of not helping the poorest since they benefit only those with sufficient income above the basic tax allowance level and are of most benefit to high-rate taxpayers.

The basic income payment might be a flat rate for all or differentiated by a small number of criteria such as age, family circumstances and disability. With everyone guaranteed a minimum income the need for other provisions would be reduced.

Tax credits and negative income tax

Under a refundable tax credit scheme a person receives a tax credit instead of a tax allowance. This is used to offset tax, or if their tax is less than the credit, the difference is received as a cash payment. A significant difference of a tax credit over a tax allowance is that the credit has the same value for all whereas a tax allowance reduces a person's marginal rate of tax and so is of most benefit to higher-rate taxpayers.

A negative income tax (NIT) may be confined to tax allowances or encompass also a range of other benefits paid by the state. Persons would pay tax if their incomes were sufficient, or receive payments related to the level their income was below the tax allowances and any other benefits that were included in the scheme. This latter broader-based NIT raises the possibility of being able to iron out at least some of the incompatibilities and difficulties that occur because of the overlap of social security benefits and tax payments.

Tax credit and negative income tax proposals extend the benefits of tax allowances, or some portion of the benefits, (usually at the level obtained by the standard rate taxpayer), by means of a cash payment to those who incomes are too low to benefit from the tax allowances. In contrast minimum income schemes buy out all or some tax allowances.

Drawbacks to support schemes

The major drawback of minimum income schemes is that high levels of tax are needed to finance payments to all. Unless the minimum income is set sufficiently high, poverty will not be eliminated and high-income levels imply tax rates, probably of 50 per cent or more.

The tax credit and narrow NIT proposals would not be sufficient to take many people out of the poverty level. Broader-based NIT proposals that encompass social security payments as well as tax allowances do not necessarily have this drawback. Also, it should be noted that the more benefits that remain outside the NIT system the greater is the problem of high effective marginal tax rates, (tax paid plus loss of benefits) as small-income increases can result in the loss of several benefits. NIT allowances used to offset tax have the advantage of reducing two-way flows of funds between the government and individual and of overcoming the difficulty of low take up of some benefits.

The extent to which any of these schemes secure administrative savings, if at all, depends on the level of the payments made and the relation of this to the poverty level. Hopes that the present complex systems of payment for adverse and emergency contingencies can be dismantled are probably illusory. Countries without a withholding system for payment of income tax would find it more difficult to implement an NIT than those with a withholding system and all countries would find it more difficult to use the tax system for demand-management purposes. The presence of a large number of self-employed persons makes their inclusion in an NIT scheme difficult as their incomes may well fluctuate sharply from one period to another.

These schemes also need to be evaluated on their incentive effects. The implicit marginal rate of tax may be quite high as income rises benefits are lost and tax is payable.

A number of other problems have to be settled with an NIT. There is general agreement that the family should be the basic unit, of any plan. Otherwise a non-working spouse of a millionaire could qualify for benefit. Agreement has to be reached on what consists a family unit, e.g. the position of adult children living at home, or children living with adults who are not their parents, single parent families and couples living together outside marriage.

For couples, particularly those with children, who receives the benefit can be important. From the incentive and administrative point of view payment to the main wage earner, usually the male, is preferred. On social grounds payment to the mother may be preferred as she is more likely to be directly responsible for the family welfare. The definition of income for tax purposes and for social benefit purposes usually differs in several important respects and this can create problems.

In trying to integrate tax and social payments should the wealth of the potential recipient be included? Failure to do so gives the opportunity for wealth holders to seek unrealized capital gains rather than income. On the other hand, the main wealth holding of many people is the house they are living in and it seems inequitable, and inefficient, to require them to sell this before they are eligible for assistance. The problem mainly affects those who have modest levels of wealth. Wealthy individuals for the most part will have incomes that put them beyond the level of assistance and they are able to live on their income without reducing their capital. Those with modest amounts of capital will in adverse circumstances, such as having to live for a long period in a nursing or retirement home, find their capital eroded. Countries normally take some assets into account before assistance is provided. Perhaps a better alternative would be a tax on those assets so that people would not have to consume all of their wealth above the assistance level before they become eligible for some help.

METHODS OF FINANCING SCHEMES

European countries, with the exception of Denmark, which meets cost out of national taxation, finance services by a mixture of taxes. These include contributions from employers, employees and user charges. The contributions arise from social security payments, payments out of general taxation and from local authority sources, together with part payment from users of some of the services. Social security taxes are usually at graduated rates with ceilings on contributions common but not universal. With the exception of Portugal, which has the most rudimentary social security system, all countries make contributions towards the cost out of general taxation. Long-term benefits are financed on a 'pay-as-you-go' system with the exception of Luxembourg, where the schemes are funded. A few countries have mixed systems for employment injuries and occupational diseases. The pay-as-you-go systems may be supplemented out of general taxation.

The most common practice for retirement is to pay pensions at 65 for men and 60 for women. However, there is a common pension age of 60 in France, of 65 in the Netherlands, Spain and Luxembourg, and of 67 in Denmark. Germany allows a choice between the ages of 63 and 67 and Portugal has a retirement age of 65 for men and 62 for women. The amount of pension depends on a number of factors such as length of contributions and number of dependants. In general, the richer countries of the Community have more generous basic pensions. The UK rates are relatively low and unlike most Community countries do not take account of average earnings in the annual updates. Instead, the UK uses a price index, which has the effect of holding down pension increases.

THE DUAL INCOME TAX SYSTEM

Most countries now have a curious dual system of income tax. The tax called 'income tax' is a tax on income drawn on a fairly narrow base, with considerable efforts made by means of tax allowances and graduated rates to achieve a degree of equity. The other tax, National or Social Insurance, is on income, as a rule even more narrowly drawn than the income tax base. It is on wages and salaries over the lower earnings limit but often excludes fringe benefits and unearned income. Rates start at low earned-income levels with no further exemptions and usually have maximum payment ceilings. Therefore at high-income levels the progressive nature of income tax tends to be offset by the regressive nature of social insurance contributions.

It would be relatively easy to transform NI contributions into a progressive tax by abolishing the upper earnings limit. In the UK the earnings limit for the employers' contribution was abolished some time ago so that companies pay NI on all wages above the limit.

Amalgamation of income tax and social insurance contributions is, fairly obviously, a strong candidate for consideration on several grounds not least administrative simplicity and equity. If, as seems reasonable, it is desired to exempt retirement incomes from social insurance contributions this could be achieved by a change in allowances or tax coding for the retired. The position of the unemployed and sick who are exempt from such contributions could again be met in a similar manner.

The arguments against amalgamation tend to cluster round the idea of benefit taxation: that certain services should be paid for by the user. For example, an increase in pensions should be met by an increase in the pension component of the social security system. It has already been shown that the connection between charges and benefits is very tenuous, varying amounts being contributed out of general taxation to all these services. In particular there are very few funded schemes. Amalgamation would not stop governments announcing that so much of a change in income tax was due to the change in social benefits. It need not stop separate parliamentary accountability of the social accounts.

The argument sometimes used is that people would not be willing to pay in increased income tax what they are currently paying by way of social contributions. The argument that people regard social contributions as being less onerous than the same amount deducted by way of income tax, with a portion of income tax earmarked for insurance, is not very convincing, particularly now that for most people both are deducted by way of PAYE.

Another argument is of the kind put forward to the UK House of Commons in 1975 by the Secretary of State for Social Services:

> there has been an enduring feeling in this country particularly among the trade unions, that there is a kind of guarantee about a contributory system – a guarantee that would not obtain in the same way if the scheme were financed entirely out of taxation. It gives some assurance that Governments will not use the lack of a contributory principle as an excuse to economise in the important matter of pensions.

The argument seems to be that the system cannot be changed because people are under the illusion that guarantees exist within the present system. The counter argument is that people should be educated to the true facts. The sentiment of the last sentence of the quotation is clearly contradicted in the UK. From the start pensions have been subject to economies. They have never been implemented on much more than subsistence level and indexation is in line not with earnings but with prices so that pensions have failed to keep up with higher living standards.

In 1990 the Netherlands proposed an integration of income tax and social security contributions as part of a major reform of the tax system. Certain social security contributions, currently payable by the employer, will be paid by the employee with a proposal for grossing up of salaries to compensate for the change.

SUMMARY

The term social security may be used to describe a wide range of services usually provided by the state or more narrowly to cash or other transfers to meet contingencies like old age, sickness and unemployment.

Whether the term 'national' or 'social' insurance is a good one to use, or whether contributions are better considered part of the normal tax system was discussed.

Studies show that Britain is the only European country to show a significant increase in inequality in the 1980s. On average the real income of the poorest 20 per cent has fallen 4.6 per cent, those on average incomes have gained by 23.9 per cent while the richest 20 per cent of the population have gained 39.6 per cent.

The merits of state versus private provision were examined. The concept of relative poverty was introduced and the problems caused by the overlap of the tax and benefit systems notable the poverty trap embracing both the earnings and unemployment traps. The diversity of social provision between countries was noted, together with methods of giving help and alternatives ways of financing that help. The oddities produced by having two taxes on income, an income tax and social insurance contributions was noted.

Part III

Policy

Chapter 10

Introduction to policy considerations

INTRODUCTION

The consensus in the post-war period until the end of the 1970s was to treat tax policy as part of demand management as a means to achieve a more equal distribution of income, to correct for market failures such as unemployment, to help the balance of payments and to encourage growth in the economy. Since then more emphasis has been placed on the distortionary and disincentive effects of high (income) tax rates. Many countries, as shown in Chapter 3, have attempted reforms aimed at correcting for these perceived defects.

AVERAGE AND MARGINAL RATES OF TAX

Incentives may be affected by both average and marginal rates of tax, but the latter is usually more important in the context of incentives. The average income tax rate is simply tax paid divided by total income, it gives the proportion of income taken in tax. The marginal rate of tax is the amount paid on additional earnings. Largely because income tax has a system of allowances which are deducted from gross income to arrive at taxable income, marginal rates are higher than average rates.

RATIONAL EXPECTATIONS

The 'rational expectations' model has come to prominence in recent years. The highjacking of the term 'rational' with its implication that other theories of how expectations are formed must be irrational, is unfortunate. The hypothesis of rational expectations, instead of assuming for example that people extrapolate from past data, assumes that on average people guess the future correctly. Any tendency for systematic error will, it is assumed, be quickly spotted and corrected. Expectations will most of the time be incorrect, but this will be due to factors that could not have been foreseen at the time the expectations were formed.

When the rational expectations hypothesis is coupled with the assumption of instantaneously flexible prices the conclusion is reached that demand-management measures are ineffective and that apparent differences between policies that used to be thought important do not exist. The model takes one back to the pre-Keynesian model of nearly 60 years ago where whatever the level of unemployment observed, that must be the natural rate of unemployment, consisting only of people who are between jobs. The natural rate will change with time as micro-economic incentives alter the natural rate itself. A good introduction to rational expectations theory is found in Shaw (1984).

In such a model there is no place for stabilization policy. Government action, to change say unemployment or prices, will be correctly antici-pated and people will take counter action so that real variables in the economy will not change. Only random policies of the government, which cannot be predicted, will have real effects and random policies are hardly suitable for stabilization purposes.

The theory of rational expectations has a number of interesting applications in economics but it has not yielded much help in the stabilization area. It has to be coupled with the strong assumption of instantaneous price adjustment to yield the result that stabilization policy is ineffective and this condition is clearly violated in practice even if it is accepted that expectations are formed rationally.

STABILIZATION POLICIES

Much has been written about the effects that are likely to flow from different monetary and fiscal changes. The analysis is frequently con-ducted at great length with an impressive array of geometric and mathe-matical expertise. Within the assumptions adopted by the authors the conclusions can seldom be faulted. As an exercise in logic this work probably has value, but as a guide to the best policy to adopt at any one time unfortunately it yields few results. It is seldom that the conclusions can be shown to hold once the restrictive assumptions have been removed.

An added difficulty is the lack of general agreement on a theory explaining the variables usually selected as important for study. The usual variables on which it is desired to see the effects of monetary or fiscal changes are: consumption and saving; investment; prices and output; and work effort. Since the theories explaining these variables are in dispute, it is not surprising that an explanation of the effect of this or that budgetary change is, at best, imprecise and subject to doubt.

This chapter looks briefly at each of these variables. It does not attempt to provide precise answers to the question as to what would happen to each of these if, say, a particular tax was changed. In our present state of knowledge such a precise answer is impossible. Neither does it attempt a detailed assessment of the use of monetary and fiscal methods in the post-1945 period. Rather, it looks at some of the problems involved in getting even approximate estimates. The concern is with resource use – the allocation side of the fiscal process. In a fully employed economy, resource use by the public sector involves the opportunity cost of fewer resources being available for the private sector. In addition, there may be extra costs because of distortion introduced by taxes which alter the choices of economic units. There may also be benefits to consider; for example, when a tax reduces consumption of some product that society considers harmful, although the analysis usually concentrates on the 'excess burden' of a tax, i.e. the excess cost or loss of welfare that results from that tax compared with what would have been the burden if a non-distorting tax had been used to raise the revenue. A lump-sum tax is the only one held to be neutral since the liability to such a tax is in no way related to economic behaviour. All other taxes interfere in some way with choice among consumer goods, or between present and future consumption, or between goods (income) and leisure. On the production side they may cause less than efficient, i.e. least factor cost, production.

Other costs associated with taxes are administration and compliance costs: the former are costs of the revenue-collecting agency, the latter of those who have to pay the taxes and these were discussed in Chapter 3. VAT, company taxation and the Community Charge come in for particular criticism under this head, and an annual wealth tax would be likely to have high costs on both levels.

In considering tax changes nobody doubts that favourable tax treatment of particular assets can be a powerful tool in redirecting assets to those that are tax-favoured. Thus housing enjoys considerable tax advantages in most countries and investment in housing is larger as a result. Deposits in institutions which enjoy tax privileges are likewise enhanced over what they would otherwise be. What is much less clear, and what is of importance for overall demand management, is the extent to which tax privileges raise the total assets in a particular category as opposed to merely redirecting existing funds, e.g. do tax-exempt savings instruments increase the aggregate level of savings or merely redirect savings away from other securities? Studies find it easy to establish the latter but much harder to find the former effect.

PERSONAL CONSUMPTION AND SAVING

Most economies have seen a wide variety of measures used in the post-1945 period to try to influence economic conduct, e.g. from direct measures, such as rationing to price and wage control, to a variety of monetary and fiscal policies. Fiscal policy impinges on monetary policy and vice versa. For example, a change in income tax, by altering the return from investment income, will have some of the effects of changing interest rates. Economic theory does not predict the direction of a change in savings of a tax change because there are both income and substitution effects, which work in opposite directions. For a recent study see Starrett (1988). A tax increase on savings may induce more saving from those who are seeking a set level of income for retirement or other purposes. The substitution effect of a tax increase reduces the rate of return on savings and lowers the rate at which the saver can substitute future for present consumption, which is adverse to savings.

To get somewhere it is necessary to have a theory to work with, even if it is no stronger than the feeling that 'consumption and saving can be changed by altering income'. Keynes stated:

> The fundamental psychological law upon which we are entitled to rely with great confidence both *a priori* from our knowledge of human nature and from detailed facts of experience, is that men are disposed as a rule and on the average to increase their consumption as their income increases, but not by as much as the increase in income.
>
> (Keynes 1936: 96)

Since this was written over 50 years ago, this 'law' has been the subject of much debate and investigation. In particular, many of these studies attempt to reconcile studies which use cross-section data on household income, which support the Keynesian viewpoint of a declining marginal propensity to consume as income rises, and time-series data which suggest a constant marginal propensity. Another puzzle is the empirical observation that consumption is less volatile than income. Attempts have been made to modify the law to take account of the structure of wealth as well as of income and the effect of changing interest rates. It has been suggested that past levels of income need to be taken into account as well as current levels, as these will determine habitual consumption standards. Friedman (1957) suggested that it is 'permanent' or normal income which is the relevant concept. This is defined as that annuity income which would finance a flow of consumption which is perceived to leave wealth intact. Others have stressed the importance of the flow of income over the life cycle of the individual. Many of these alternative statements are concerned with the long-run trend in consumption and the influences, economic and social, which bear on this. Rational expectations have caused a reworking of many of these ideas. Management of the economy, as we are concerned with it, is largely a matter of year-to-year control, and here we are on safe ground in asserting that a change in income will be of major importance and will change consumption and saving in the same direction as the change in income. The size of the change will depend on many factors. One of the most important is likely to be the way the income change is distributed over different income groups. Budget studies inform us that, as we move up the income scale, out of each addition to income more is likely to be saved – in economic terms, the marginal propensity to save increases with income. It follows that a pound paid in tax by a person with a high income will tend to reduce saving more than a pound paid by a taxpayer with a small income. Thus a progressive income tax is likely to reduce saving more than a flat-rate tax. Put the other way, taxes which fall mainly on the poor are likely to have more impact on consumption, pound for pound, than taxes which fall mainly on the rich. These generalizations are frequently invoked by advocates of tax changes, for example those who advocate reducing the rates of income tax in order to increase savings.

Unfortunately, there is no clear empirical evidence on the effect of the magnitude of the difference on savings or on consumption. If the difference is small, then arguments for tax changes on these grounds can be ignored.[1] If they are large, it is necessary to take them into account. American studies, for example Musgrave (1989), suggest that although taxes that affect high-income earners are likely to affect savings more than consumption, the effect is easily overstated because, although low- and high-income earners are likely to have very different average rates of saving, their marginal rates differ much less. An early study by Dow (1964: 270–5) lists British investigations which in general give more weight to the effect on savings. In view of the uncertain nature of the data and the assumptions that have to be made, authoritative statements on the relationships of changes in tax and effects of consumption and saving must await further investigation.

Let us consider a fully employed economy where the need is to increase saving (i.e. reduce consumption expenditure) in order that resources may be released from the consumption to the investment sector. Even if the argument is accepted that the effect of taxing high incomes is to affect savings to a significant extent, it does not necessarily follow that flat-rate or regressive taxes are to be preferred to progressive ones. There is an obvious clash between the objective of control over the economy and of redistribution of income and wealth. Political judgements here come to the fore. From the point of view of controlling the economy, it does not matter whether the savings are undertaken by individuals or the government. If a decision has already been made about the desired degree of progression of the tax system, and if it is then desired to reduce consumption, then tax rates can be increased but in such a way as to leave the degree of progression of the system unchanged. If this is expected to result in less private saving, or a slower increase in private saving, this effect can be allowed for in the new rates. This results in the desired level of saving being obtained through a government surplus, or reduced deficit.

It is possible, but not very likely, that this increase in savings of the government sector would result in a shortage of funds for private investment. Numerous ways are available whereby these funds can be channelled back to private investment. The decision is once more primarily a political judgement. The government could undertake direct investment in firms, or the resources of private lenders could be supplemented. Alternatively, taxes on companies could be reduced or investment incentives increased.

One further illustration will be given. At first sight a change in the taxing of wealth is a clear-cut case of a change in taxation that will affect saving more than consumption. However, one way of avoiding taxes at death may be, as in the UK, to give away one's wealth at least seven years before death. To the extent that wealth is given away to younger persons sooner than it would otherwise be given, the consumption patterns of these younger persons are likely to change. In particular tax reductions aimed to increase savings may backfire if the reductions result in wealth gains in stock markets and housing prices and this wealth enhancement leads to a spending increase. This seems to have been the case in the United States after their 1981 tax reforms and in the UK in the late 1980s. In both countries savings ratios fell to low levels after measures that would normally be expected to raise savings ratios.

A consideration therefore of the impact of monetary and fiscal changes on consumption and saving should take account of the impact on different income groups because they are likely to have different propensities to consume. Ideally the effects of different amounts of wealth should also be taken into account and allowance made for shifts of money and assets to different age groups who are likely to have different spending habits. Dow (1964: 275) has suggested that an important category to separate out is the self-employed, whose propensity to consume is lower than that of comparable income groups because of higher saving to provide investment for their own business.

The above brief discussion shows some of the more important difficulties that have to be faced if 'hunches' about the effects of tax or monetary changes are to be turned into objective facts. In Britain the matter is further bedevilled by a lack of adequate statistical data, in particular in relation to savings figures. Those that appear in the National Income and Expenditure tables are completely unreliable, because no attempt is made to arrive at independent estimates of saving. The figure is arrived at by taking estimates of income and deducting estimates of consumption. The resulting residual figure is called 'saving'. Since income and consumption are big magnitudes, even small errors in these estimates can make a large difference in the residual figure. Independent estimates of savings are beginning to be built up but these have yet to be incorporated in the National Income and Expenditure tables. The amount of savings in the community and who undertakes it is therefore uncertain. There is a need for statistics which better reflect what is actually taking place and for more consideration of the motives for saving, and how these motives change in response to different economic and social pressures. What is certain is that a considerable part of savings has now been institutionalized through pension funds and insurance companies.

Public expenditure can affect consumption and saving as well as changes in tax or monetary policy. The most important part in this respect is likely to be the extent of transfer payments. These have increased in recent years to a greater extent than other forms of government expenditure. The greater provision of social security payments by the government, in the form of pensions, children's allowances, and the like, reduce the need for private provision for these needs, although the extent to which the private sector would voluntarily save to provide for these contingencies is uncertain. Similar considerations apply to so-called free services, such as medical care, but the effect is weaker in that much would be spent directly on these services by individuals in the absence of schemes financed out of taxation. The overlap of social benefits and taxation, which we have already noted, makes the incentive effects of tax changes even harder to evaluate.

COMPANY SAVING AND INVESTMENT

The post-1945 period has seen a variety of methods used to influence investment, from direct controls such as licensing and planning permission, to various monetary and fiscal policies. Even if there were agreement about a theory of investment, which there is not, the presence of so many variables makes it very difficult to pin down the effect of any one of them.

The 'accelerator principle' makes investment a function of changes in demand. The truth in this principle, that a permanent change in demand calls for a different stock of investment goods, should not blind us to the obvious defects of the principle as a guide to short-term investment decisions. An increase in demand can often be met from previous resources that were idle or not working to capacity. The length of time required to adjust the capital stock, up or down, may run into years. Much investment needs to be planned for a number of years ahead. For example, once a decision has been made in principle to go ahead with a new factory, a suitable site has to be found, planning permission obtained, contractors engaged before work can commence and the construction itself may take years. Under these circumstances it might be thought that investment of this type would be insensitive to temporary changes in demand brought about by a government that was pledged to maintain employment, rather than intending permanently to alter demand patterns.

Present evidence is far from conclusive, but from surveys of British industry it seems that investment plans do fluctuate considerably according to the current condition of the economy, whether, that is, the period is one of expansion or contraction: 'stop' or 'go'. There are several possible explanations for this. The most unfavourable interpretation for British industry would be that not many firms plan very far ahead or calculate their intended investments in a very rational manner, since many appear not to take tax or investment incentives into account. However, other factors must also play a part. Some forms of investment have a short time before fruition and it is then more realistic to expect fluctuation in investment according to fluctuations in demand. Again, the cut-back during times of low demand may be due to difficulties in obtaining finance rather than deliberate intentions to cut investment.

There is also business confidence to take into account, which may be unduly pessimistic about investment prospects at a time of contraction of demand, and unduly optimistic at a time of buoyant demand.

Other explanations of investment lay more stress on the availability of particular types of saving, for example ploughed-back profits, or the buoyancy of the stock market. British policy, by its past discrimination against distributed profits, changes in tax allowances and experiments with initial allowances, investment allowances, investment grants, depreciation provisions and business expansion schemes, has tried hard to influence investment policy. Dividend discrimination appeared to have little success. Other incentives suffered from several drawbacks and now both company tax and incentives have been reduced.

Another theory of investment makes it a function of rate of return on investment compared with the rate of interest. If the return from real investment is above the cost of borrowing (or above the best return that can be obtained from putting surplus funds into financial assets), then the inducement to invest is strong and vice versa. One way that the rate of interest can be important is via the stock market and its influence on the willingness and ability of firms to raise fresh capital, and on the flow of new money into the market.

Input–output studies approach the problem of investment by trying to unravel the inter-connections between industries. For example, for every £100 of final output in the metal manufacturing trades required net inputs might be estimated as £1.80 from coal, £0.70 from other mining, £3 from chemicals, £44.50 from metal, £4.70 from engineering, and so on. If, therefore, a decision is made to expand steel production by so many million tons, the details can be fed into the model and the requirements on the economy can be calculated. The shortfall or over-expansion of investment in particular sectors feeding the steel industry can then be seen. If industrialists can be convinced of the soundness of the calculations, they have a firmer base on which to plan their own investment. The firm is well aware intuitively that the success or otherwise of its own plans depends to a large extent on what is happening in the rest of the economy – the more facts can replace guess-work the more steady is investment likely to become. Too much should not be expected from what are admittedly crude models of the interactions in the economy. The hope is that more data will be forthcoming, improvements in method made and the predictions rendered more reliable.

A number of econometric studies of UK investment behaviour have been made and are surveyed by Lund (1975). Eleven out of the twelve studies cited by Lund give a positive role to tax allowances and investment grants in influencing investment, but no consistency on the size of this effect is yet forthcoming.

Alternative assumptions about the incidence of corporation tax can also yield different answers about investment effects. If taxes are fully passed on in changes in prices of goods, then they amount to a sales tax differentiated according to the ratio of profits to sales. Tax should not in this case affect investment. The incidence of tax focuses attention on the degree of competitiveness of the various sectors of the economy and the long-run adjustment mechanisms to changes in demand for particular products. The investment theories outlined concentrate attention on differing variables. They are not independent variables but interact with each other, and their respective importance is likely to change over time. Bearing this in mind it is not surprising that evidence of the quantitative effect of government measures on investment is hard to pin down.

In recent years a concept of 'crowding out' has been reintroduced to try and explain poor investment performance in a number of countries. The old pre-Keynesian concept of crowding out assumed full employment and that a pound of government expenditure would crowd out a pound of private expenditure and the economy would be no better off. Modern proponents of crowding out allege that debt finance of the government that is not accompanied by an increase in money either crowds out business by driving up prices, reduces finance for the private sector or drives up interest rates and reduces private investment that way. While it must be admitted as a theoretical possibility, the evidence for crowding out in British conditions is weak. There is plenty of evidence that businesses see little prospect of profitable returns and little evidence that finance is not available for sound prospects. Indeed, one of the things that went seriously wrong with the economy in the early 1970s was that the boom conditions, engendered in the economy on the premise that it would stimulate real investment, resulted in stock market and property speculation rather than industrial investment. Rates of interest in many economies in the 1970s were below the level of inflation, particularly when the net-of-tax cost to a company of fixed-interest payments is taken into account and this too failed to induce a real investment boom. A fuller discussion of crowding out is given in Blinder, Solow et al. (1974).

Conclusions on savings and investment

Many factors including taxation enter into the saving and investment decisions of firms and individuals. Taxation is a powerful tool in redirecting funds to particular ends but the impact on overall levels of saving and investment does not appear to be strong. In spite of countries having many similarities in their tax structures in the 1980s, they had very different levels of saving and investment. Low rates were experienced by the United States and UK and high rates by Japan. Most other EC countries had intermediate levels.

MICRO CHANGES IN PRICES AND OUTPUT

The adjustments in prices and output that businesses make in response to government policy changes are at least as difficult to sort out as any that have so far been considered.

Take the case of an increase in cost. At the micro level it is clear that if a manufacturer passes on to his customers the whole of an increase (whether this is due to an increase in VAT, in company tax or higher interest charges), the demand for his product may be affected. He may be forced therefore to reconsider his price and so in effect bear part of the increase, at least in the short run. In the long run, adjustments can be made to the size of the plant and the industry itself can also expand or contract by the movement of firms into and out of the industry.

Nor are the changes that occur in one sector of the economy likely to be confined to that sector. An increase in the price of, for example, cars may well lead to some substitution of other goods for cars and increased costs felt by business may be shifted to others.

The time element has so far been ignored for expositional purposes. Its presence adds considerable practical difficulties in sorting out the effects of a change. For example, after increases in the tax on tobacco the consumption of tobacco normally falls for a few weeks or months, only to come back to higher levels. One of the difficulties in sorting out the effects of a change is that the market for tobacco, as for many products, has been changing. Most noticeably the spread of smoking among women has increased while smoking among men has declined. To say that the consumption of tobacco surpasses its old level is not to say that in the absence of the tax change consumption might not be higher than its present level. It is very difficult to separate out statistically the underlying trend in consumption and the change due to the tax measure.

AGGREGATE CHANGES IN PRICES AND OUTPUT

The above reasoning deals with the response of an individual or manufacturer to a change. In trying to account for aggregate movements in prices and output a number of other considerations need to be borne in mind.

The impact of a change will depend in part on the state of the economy. In conditions of full employment the manufacturer is more likely to pass on increases, reasoning that competitors will follow suit, so relative market shares between himself and competitors in the same industry, and also the market share of his industry *vis-à-vis* other industries, will be affected slightly, if at all – that is, an increase in price in one sector may lead to a broad movement over a wide range of prices.

Many countries have experienced a general rise in prices, or inflation, in the post-1945 period. A number of theories have been developed to explain this phenomenon (see Johnson 1967; Bronfenbrenner and Holzmann 1963: 593–661; Laidler and Parkin 1975). Two theories have contended for pride of place: demand inflation, which concentrates on the pull that demand can exercise on prices; and cost inflation, which lays emphasis on increases in costs forcing up prices. In the latter case an interaction between wages and prices is seen as a process leading to the continual rise in prices. Major emphasis with cost inflation has been put on increases occurring in wages and salaries coming from union pressure and from increased oil costs. Employers may, however, bid up wages in order to try and secure scarce grades of labour.

The role assigned to fiscal policy in controlling prices is given different emphasis by these two theories, but both have in common the fact that relatively little emphasis is placed on monetary policy. A reaction against this can be discerned in the 1980s, when greater emphasis was laid on monetary control. Unfortunately the words of Johnson (1967) are still true:

> Policy to deal with inflation is a subject on which a great deal has been written and argued by eminent authorities without adding substantially to knowledge, and in some cases subtracting from it.

Inflation may be a problem with many similarities to cancer. It seems that cancer is not a single disease, nor has a single cause. Many types of cancer have been recognized and treatment of some of them has been successful. Inflation too may be of different kinds with different causes calling for different treatment.

CHOICE BETWEEN WORK AND LEISURE FOR AN INDIVIDUAL

The theory of how an individual selects between work and leisure is indeterminate as shown in Figure 10.1. The case illustrates an increase in tax on income, but similar considerations apply to other taxes which can have incentive effects. An increase in VAT reduces a person's income just as an increase in income tax would. A tax has two effects. One is termed an 'income effect': the individual can retain less income if taxes are increased, which may encourage him or her to work more in order to maintain their previous standard of living. The tax also generates a substitution effect, which works in the opposite direction: the cost of leisure (the amount of post-tax income earned by working) is reduced and so he or she may decide to increase leisure. *Pari passu* for a lowering of tax.

The amount of work/leisure is plotted along the horizontal axis. The origin 'O' represents the maximum hours of work which would give a maximum income 'Ob'. Assuming a constant wage, movement to the

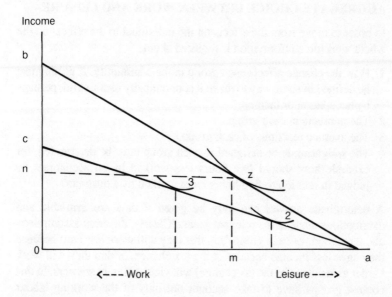

Figure 10.1   Individual choice between income and leisure

right along Oa increases an individual's leisure and reduces income. Point 'a' represents the amount of leisure when no work is done.

The straight line joining 'a' and 'b' indicates the various combinations of each that the individual can obtain by varying work time. Let us assume that the individual chooses point 'z', the point of tangency of their highest indifference curve (labelled 1), which gives a quantity of 'Om' work and 'ma' of of leisure and 'On' of income. Into this picture we now introduce an increase in tax which reduces maximum income to 'Oc' for the same hours spent at work. Hence we draw the new line 'ac' to indicate his new budget position after the tax change. Where on the new budget line 'ac' the individual will settle cannot be determined. If the indifference curve is represented by '2', leisure is increased and work diminished. The substitution effect exceeds the income effect. If the indifference curve is represented by '3', the individual will work more and have less leisure the income effect is stronger than the substitution effect. The position taken up by the individual on the budget line 'ac' depends on the combined results of the income and substitution effects: the individual may be motivated to work harder or less hard as a result of the tax change.

AGGREGATE CHOICE BETWEEN WORK AND LEISURE

In order to move from the effects on the individual to the effects on the whole workforce information is required about:

1 How the change affects each group in the community. A group must be defined in some way to make it economically meaningful, perhaps by occupation or income.
2 The numbers in each group.
3 The average reactions of each group.
4 The weighting to be assigned to each group must be determined, for example how should five hours less worked by an accountant be judged in relation to five hours more worked by a dustman?

A determinate answer can only be given if data are available and assumptions made at the relevant points. Clearly, different assumptions about reactions of each group (e.g. that they will work less hard because they have less income because of the tax change, or that they will work harder to make up for the tax change) will yield different answers. In this context groups have to take account not only of the working labour force, but also of the potential labour force.

The theoretical conclusion about tax changes is ambiguous; no prior assumption that they will increase or decrease work effort can be made. Nevertheless politicians frequently assert the work incentive effects they expect to follow from lower (usually income) taxes. It is to be expected that where the interests of the well off are concerned there will be no lack of justification for actions that clearly serve their interests. There will be no disappointment on this score when it comes to the adjustment in work effort to a fiscal change.

Long ago Keynes complained that:

> Practical men, who believe themselves to be quite exempt from any intellectual influences, are usually the slaves of some defunct economist. Madmen in authority, who hear voices in the air, are distilling their frenzy from some academic scribbler of a few years back.
>
> (Keynes 1936)

Things have now moved on and the latest idea, if it accords with current political wishes, seems to be adopted without further testing. These ideas may contain insights that seem obvious and so half truths get taken up without further justification. In the area of work effort one such famous, or infamous, idea is known as the Laffer-curve, drawn in Figure 10.2.

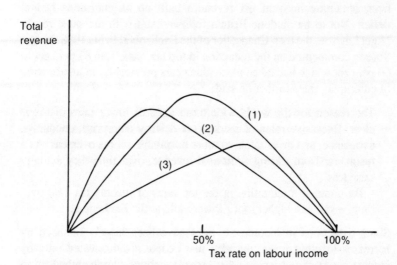

Figure 10.2 The Laffer-curve

In Figure 10.2 the vertical axis represents the total tax revenue while the horizontal axis represents tax rates as percentages of wage rates. The truth part of this curve is that a tax rate of zero yields no revenue and a tax rate at or near 100 per cent will also yield nothing or very little if the tax can be avoided. There may or may not be a single optimum rate of tax which yields a maximum revenue. Laffer drew his curve with a nice symmetry as curve 1, but whether the real world is better described by this curve or curve 2 or 3, or some other, is conjecture. It could well be the case that there is more than one peak or a relatively flat area over a wide spectrum of tax rates.

It follows, if the Laffer-curve holds, and tax rates are above the optimum point then a reduction in tax will actually increase revenue. Tax receipts may increase because the tax reductions increase the work effort by the existing labour force, and/or by greater numbers being drawn into work. Tax revenue may also increase when tax rates are reduced, if transactions that previously occurred in the black economy and therefore escaped tax, are induced to enter the official economy. This is termed the Gutman effect, after its author. Its importance depends on the extent of the black economy and the difference between the tax paid on legitimate business and the likelihood of being caught and punished in the black economy.

On the basis of such reasoning the United States cut taxes and far from obtaining buoyant tax revenues built up an enormous budget deficit. Not to be outdone Britain followed suit with the same result. Nigel Lawson, the then Chancellor of the Exchequer, in his 1988 Budget Speech commented on the reduction in top tax rates from 83 per cent to 60 per cent which had taken place nine years previously. In justification of cutting tax rates further he said:

> The reason for the world-wide trend towards lower rates of tax is clear. Excessive rates of income tax destroy enterprise, encourage avoidance, and drive talent to more hospitable shores overseas. As a result, far from raising additional revenue, over time they actually raise less.
>
> By contrast a reduction in the top rates of income tax can, over time, result in a higher, not a lower yield to the Exchequer.

Since reductions in income tax rates have been largely financed by increases in other taxes, the idea that people are motivated only by income tax rates and ignore other taxes is a popular myth embedded in this statement and this in spite of the fact that for years trade unions have used cost-of-living arguments for wage increases. Similarly doubtful is the implied suggestion that the bulk of highly paid people who work for employers actually have much control over the hours they work. Recent work in economics and psychology lends little support to taxes having much effect on work effort or on motivation of workers (Earl 1990).

Evidence about the effects of changes in tax can be obtained by interview, questionnaire, experimental methods and indirect methods. All have been used. Experimental methods are rare for obvious reasons but one was carried out in 1977 in New Jersey in the United States, by Professor Brown on a group of 1,300 taxpayers on the basis of a negative income tax. Indirect methods involve the formulation of a model from which changes stemming from tax alterations can be predicted. All methods have to be used with care.

EMPIRICAL STUDIES ON WORK EFFORT

Since the theory is indeterminate, it is necessary to look at empirical work. A large number of studies have been made. Recent summaries are found in Dilnot and Kell (1988), Brown (1988) and Brown and Sandford (1991). The results of these studies are fairly conclusive that the aggregate number of hours worked are little affected and, if anything, the results point to the income effects outweighing the substitution effects, so that higher taxes will be associated with a small increase in hours worked. An exception to this is the reaction of married women to joining the labour force and the number of hours they are prepared to work. Here it seems that there is a small impact. Since no study has been able to come up with strong disincentives on the number of hours worked, a number of investigators have postulated other undesirable effects of taxes. These take the form of suggesting that the quality of work will be adversely affected, or persons will be less willing to take on more responsible posts, or that tax is a significant cause of the 'brain drain' and that it increases tax evasion and avoidance. While these effects may be important, it has to be pointed out that the nature of these alleged effects are such as to make it extremely difficult to establish to what extent they have any validity. For example, most of us in answer to a questionnaire would probably be glad to blame the tax system, rather than ourselves, for our lack of a better job, or for our not having a higher position in our existing job. In the UK, while tax may be one factor influencing people's choice of a job abroad, more important than the tax rate are likely to be different levels of gross pay at home and abroad and the underfunded research and other facilities which professional groups such as doctors and academics complain about.

High rates of tax can certainly increase tax avoidance and evasion. There are few who would defend the 98 per cent rate that applied before 1979 to the investment income of top taxpayers in the UK. At current rates in the UK, as shown, the incentive has swung to the opposite extreme. It is now more advantageous to many persons to obtain investment income and capital gains rather than earnings. This reversal is the more surprising as the government in its economic policies have long stressed the ideas of Smith (1776). Adam Smith held that if there is to be discrimination it is better to discriminate against unearned rather than earned income.

SUMMARY

Before it is possible to analyse the effect of a change in government policy, it is necessary to have a theory about how the economy operates.[2]

In this chapter, consumption and saving, investment, prices and output, inflation, and work effort, have all been examined and treated in isolation from each other. In practice, they are closely interrelated. A change in government policy may cause significant changes in two or more of them. It is the overall effect that is important. Sometimes changes in different variables will operate in the same direction, for example causing a reduction in investment and in work effort, and sometimes changes will tend to cancel each other out.

In judging the implications for economic policy it has been shown that there is no generally agreed theory to work with. Thus, unfortunately, an analysis, even for an observer who is trying to be impartial, depends a great deal on which theory is selected and on the weight given to each of the variables. More unfortunately still it leaves the door wide open, for those with special interests, to select those theories that serve their causes best. This pessimistic conclusion is not intended as an apology for inaction. Given the size of the government sector, it is not possible for the government to be neutral. It is an indication of the need for care in accepting the claims put forward for this or that particular measure.

Chapter 11

Macro-economic policy

INTRODUCTION

Macro-economic policy is used to describe the actions of governments when they seek to alter the economy so as to try and achieve some aim of distribution, allocation or stabilization. Until the 1980s it was commonly accepted as a legitimate role for government. A number of challenges have gained prominence since then. Early intervention by governments tended to operate on the demand side of the economy mainly by means of fiscal policy. Since the 1980s measures have tended to operate on the supply side of the economy with more active intervention by means of monetary policy. The latter at first concentrated on monetary targets and when these largely failed turned to interest rates and exchange rate management. An up-to-date discussion of policy in the post-war period in the UK can be found in Gowland and James (1990).

CHALLENGES TO MACRO-ECONOMIC MANAGEMENT

It has always been accepted that because of poor timing government action may make things worse. That, for example, action to depress the economy in an attempt to bring inflation down may not work until the economy is in a downturn. The modern criticism is more substantial than this. Criticism by the rational expectation school has been looked at in Chapter 10. It was seen that the conclusion that policy measures would be ineffective relied on the assumption of instantaneous price adjustment and therefore government action to steer the economy may still be useful in a world that clearly does not fit this condition. Rational expectationalists and others argue that better results will be achieved by adherence to pre-announced rules rather than governments having discretion over policy measures. Milton Friedman has long advocated adherence to a monetary rule because of the lack of information about the economy and the time lags involved before policy changes work their effect.

A third line of attack on discretionary policy is elaborated by Kydland and Prescott (1977). They hold that optimal control theory is not an appropriate tool for dynamic economic planning. The former is the selection of that decision which is best, given the current situation and a correct evaluation of the end-period position. They believe this will result in sub-optimal positions in a dynamic economic planning situation because economic planning is a not a game against nature but against rational economic agents who will be trying to outguess government moves.

'Time reversal' is the term given to a policy which at the beginning seems optimal but subsequently turns out not to be. Governments, unless they are bound to follow a fixed rule, have the discretion to switch at a later time to what then seems a better policy. However if people know this they are likely to anticipate a policy change and frustrate the original intentions of the policy-makers. As an example governments may announce policies, such as limiting the money supply, which they hope will limit wage increases, in order to restrict inflation. Later high wage settlements can face the government with the choice between relaxation of the rule, or high unemployment. That the former is possible weakens the resolve of employers and employees to reach low wage settlements in the first place.

The obvious objection to rules is finding one that would give good results in today's complex and evolving economies. Proponents of rules have therefore suggested that rules should be elaborated to account for various exogenous contingencies. A monetary rule might, for example, vary the change in money supply according to the degree of inflation or deflation. This stretches the faith of many commentators to believe that adaptive rules of this type can be formulated in a way which would show a significant improvement on discretionary policy. The latter still leaves the government with the option of keeping, or changing, its previous policy: wage-makers and others can never be certain that governments will always validate their actions. There is also the problem of deciding if the contingency has in fact occurred in a manner that justifies using the rule. Policy-makers may cheat, for example by attributing an inflationary rise to some special and one-off factor. It is also the case that a free market system, especially in the financial sphere, is designed to lubricate the economic system: i.e. to circumvent restrictions. Thus the history of money control is one where successively targeted money variables proved less and less reliable as the financial system was able to expand other assets outside that partic- ular money definition.

Those that are opposed to rules argue it is easy to find a not too unrealistic set of circumstances that would produce very poor economic results. Discretion in their view enables 'learning by doing', so that future efforts to stabilize the economy should be able to avoid past mistakes.

Empirical evidence from 17 developed countries during the period 1973–86 by Alesina (1989) appears to support the contention that the more independence a central bank has, the more likely it is to be successful in combating inflation at a lower cost in unemployment. Thus at one extreme lie West Germany and Switzerland with low inflation; Italy and Spain lie at the other extreme. In such a complex matter as inflation it may be dangerous to make such a simple connection between inflation and central bank independence but the findings are certainly supportive of the time inconsistency arguments. The central bank may be operating discretionary policy but the more independent of govern- ment influence a central bank is the more its inflationary stance is likely to be believed. Britain's full entry into the European Exchange Rate Mechanism removes a lot of the government's power to manipulate monetary variables for political ends and will thus provide a market test of the arguments outlined. Joining the Exchange Rate Mechanism does not rule out political action but makes it more difficult for member governments to take unilateral action. Change has to be discussed at Community level and countries frequently have to modify their views to obtain a consensus.

POLICY INTERVENTION

The idea that governments can improve the economy by forgoing inde- pendent policy action in favour of rules is at best unproven – a look at the historical evidence shows examples of both harmful and beneficial intervention. It is also unrealistic, not only in expecting a government to forgo this power but also in its ability to do so. The size of the govern- ment sector, commonly about 40 per cent of GDP, means that govern- ments have to take a myriad of decisions that affect the economy. The rest of this chapter examines the difficulties of intervention.

DIFFICULTIES OF INTERVENTION

Ideally we set out to ask: if a given change is put into effect, what will be the resulting changes and adjustments in the economy? Or, alternatively, what must be changed in order to achieve some desired objective? The change can be in monetary policy, in government spending, revenue and debt, or in direct type of controls such as hire-purchase regulations. Our ideal has been called 'a state of bliss', and like most states of bliss it is difficult to obtain. The complexity nearly defeats us. There is so much to take into account – so little agreed theory and empirical knowledge to work with.

A recognition of this complexity is in itself an important point. The criticism that an economist will give at least two opinions is understandable. Given an objective, say to increase productive investment, there are usually countless ways of achieving this. There is first of all the decision, a political one, whether it is public or private investment, or both, which shall be increased. If some measure of encouragement of private investment is required, then consumer spending could be encouraged, which in turn would be expected to feed back a demand for investment, or alternatively investment could be encouraged directly. In either case there are numerous combinations of tax changes, monetary changes, or changes in regulations, which can bring this about. No two combinations are likely to have exactly the same repercussions on other parts of the economy. Under these circumstances it would be surprising if a unique 'best' method could be agreed on. A search for a unique solution is likely to be misleading in other ways; for example, it is unlikely that a solution which is satisfactory, given full employment of labour, will be satisfactory given a large measure of unemployment.

THE INFORMATION BASE

Managing the economy requires forecasts about the likely course of the relevant economic magnitudes and a first step in this is information about what has already happened. A look at Table 11.1, which shows Gross Domestic Expenditure for the UK in 1989, reveals the magnitudes on which the government can operate for stabilization purposes. Some 61 per cent of the total is made up by private consumers' expenditure on goods and services, 18 per cent by public current expenditure on goods and services of the central government and local authorities, and 20 per cent by gross investment. Of this gross investment, companies and financial institutions account for 12 per cent, persons for 5 per cent and the balance of 3 per cent is made by the public sector.

If we suppose that the government wishes to use fiscal or other measures to cut expenditure by £1 billion for stabilization purposes, this represents a cut in customers' expenditure of about 0.3 per cent. The same reduction on central government expenditure is a cut of 1.6 per cent. If imposed on local authorities it is a cut of 2.6 per cent. Likewise, if persons' and companies' investment is to bear the whole of the cut, this would amount to a reduction of 1.4 per cent. Correspondingly, if public-sector investment is to bear the whole of this cut, it would amount to a reduction of 7.2 per cent. This simple illustration goes a long way to explain why adjustments are frequently carried out on private expenditure: because it is by far the largest component of GNP, a cut of a given magnitude is a smaller proportion of the total, and hence is likely to have a less disturbing effect. There are other reasons for attempting to regulate private consumer expenditure rather than the other components of national income. One is the speed with which

Table 11.1 Gross domestic expenditure at market prices, 1989

Type of expenditure			£ (million)	%
Private consumers' current expenditure on goods and services			328,453	61
Central government final consumption			60,850	11
Local authority final consumption			38,576	7
Gross investment:				
Persons	(26,054)	(5)		
Companies	(45,966)	(9)		
Finance companies and institutions	(14,565)	(3)		
Public corporations	(4,833)	(1)		
Central government	(5,071)	(1)		
Local government	(3,983)	(1)	100,452	20
Increase of stocks at average prices for the year			3,102	1
Total GDE at market prices*			531,453	100

Source: United Kingdom National Accounts (1990) HMSO, London.

* Market prices are increased by taxes on expenditure of £80,136 million and decreased by subsidies of £5,668 million.

measures can be put into effect: investment must be planned for some time ahead and cutting back can prove a very costly process. Another is the argument we have met before that can be summed up by the phrase 'Public squalor, private affluence'. Public spending, whether on current or capital account, is often held to be of an essential nature. There is no need to take this statement at its face-value: government spending needs examining in the same way as other magnitudes and we have seen that in recent years it has come under close scrutiny. Finally, since investment is likely to increase GNP in the future, a cut in current consumption of the private or public sector is usually preferred to a cut in investment, though nevertheless in recent years there have been frequent adjustments to public-sector investment plans.

It will be found that in practice adjustments are much more complicated than the above would imply. For example, whatever measures are used to reduce consumers' expenditure, these are likely to have differential effects on different commodities. Thus, to talk of a cut of £1 billion on consumers' expenditure only amounting to a reduction of 0.3 per cent is misleading. The impact on particular products and services may be severe. Also, of course, there are likely to be repercussions on other components of GNP. Account must also be taken of the extent that persons and companies are able to compensate for the changes by obtaining higher wages or higher prices.

Other economic factors may operate against cutting consumption, such as its expected effect on wage restraint. Political factors must also realistically be taken into account, and at times this may weigh against cutting private consumption. A cut in private consumption is obvious and may be actively resented, whereas a cut in public expenditure may be less obvious. A cut in investment, private or public, is followed by consequences that are remote and not easily related to the original cut.

Management by trying to restrict the money supply or changing interest rates cannot so easily be apportioned to sectors of the economy. One of the advantages claimed for monetary policy is that its effects will be broadly spread over the economy. However, in practice it has been shown that monetary policy of this type can be very disruptive to some sectors of the economy. Small businesses are particularly vulnerable because of their reliance on bank finance. The housing and property markets are likewise sharply affected by monetary conditions and the fluctuations can spread into the construction and building trades.

PRACTICAL DEMAND MANAGEMENT

The above account has been cast in terms of past figures, but in practice many of the difficulties of demand management arise because estimates are required of the relevant magnitudes for some 18 months to two years ahead. Forecasts are required for the behaviour of the economy if no policy changes are made and also for the effects of alternative policies.

In most countries forecasts will be produced by both government and private organizations. In the UK the Treasury and Bank of England make three forecasts a year. The National Institute of Economic and Social Research makes a quarterly forecast and publishes it in the National Institute Economic Review. The London Business School makes regular forecasts and their main results are published in the *Sunday Times*. The Department of Applied Economics at Cambridge University and Professor Minford of Liverpool University also have forecasting models together with a number of industrial consultants and big stockbroking firms. For a critical comment on forecasts, see Ramsey (1977).

The Treasury and the Bank of England make forecasts before the annual Budget, in the spring, in the summer and in the autumn. They are of world economic prospects, of output and expenditure at constant and current prices, including the current account of the balance of payments, of external capital movements, and of domestic financial flows.

The main requirements for a good forecast are:

1 accurate and up-to-date knowledge of the state of the economy, and of its past history;
2 where intentions and plans which will take effect in the future are already formed, accurate knowledge of them; and
3 where the future will be determined by decisions yet to be taken, a good quantitative understanding of the factors which will determine these decisions.

The difficulties of forecasting arise partly from the fact that none of these three requirements is more than very imperfectly met. The statistical information about expenditure, prices and output varies considerably in comprehensiveness, accuracy and up-to-dateness from one sector of the economy to another; in many cases the quality is rather low. This shows itself in the fact that in some cases early estimates are very substantially revised later on, and also in the fact that where a particular magnitude – GNP itself is a good example – can be measured by more than one route, the different approaches commonly yield very different measures of the quarter-to-quarter or year-to-year movements. Knowledge of intentions and plans is confined to certain special cases, in particular (i) government expenditure programmes, and (ii) companies' plans for fixed capital expenditure; in neither case has it been found that subsequent events can be relied upon to conform closely to the reported plans. On the third item, our understanding of the factors which determine spending and other economic behaviour, the achievements of econometric research have been rather modest. A weaker argument for forecasting is the assertion that it enables consistency of view so that plans are coherent.

In the context of short-term forecasting the centre and focus of forecasting is the estimate of Gross Domestic Product, from which can be derived estimates of demand, of unemployment, and forecasts of the balance of payments. Many of the components of GDP, such as consumption and industrial investment, are of interest in their own right.

One approach to this problem is the construction of models of the economy which can be put in mathematical terms and programmed on to a computer. Alternatives, for example different tax changes, or a different government borrowing requirement, can then be fed into the model and results compared. Economic models have long been used, but too much should not be expected. A model must be based on assumptions about how the economy works, the incidence of taxation, etc. It has been shown that there is a great deal of uncertainty about both the data and the relevant economic theories and therefore the reliability and robustness of any particular model cannot be taken for granted.

Recent mathematical work in chaos theory casts doubt on the ability of models to forecast very far ahead even with perfect data. Chaos is used not in the sense of formlessness but of endless variation. Many simple non-linear equations can be shown to have this property. This means that very small changes in the starting conditions, changes much smaller than the variation to be found in the data, can be shown to lead to quite different results as time unfolds. The Appendix at the end of the chapter gives further details.

THE BALANCED BUDGET AND PSBR

There have always been advocates for a balanced budget, i.e. the idea that a government is virtuous if it matches expenditure with revenue. More recently the idea of constraint has been popularized by the idea of a limit on the Public Sector Borrowing Requirement.

Economically this view is rejected if for no other reason that where a government is undertaking long-lived capital investment, debt finance is entirely appropriate. If it is granted that the government has a role to play in regulating the economy and no government has shown a willingness not to do so, although the means have tended to change from fiscal to monetary policy, then such regulation may call for budgets surpluses or deficits at any one time. Political reasons appear to underlie many objections to departing from a balanced budget. It is argued that government expenditure is too large already and anything which induces caution in government spending is to be welcomed. Give the government power to spend more than it raises in taxes, so it is argued, and any discipline over its spending is forfeited.

Some time has been spent in Chapter 2 in looking at government expenditures. The inadequacy of talking of government spending either as a given total or as a figure of the government borrowing requirement, without considering the components of government expenditure, is apparent. Useful service may be performed by attacking this or that component of government spending as being too high or too low, judging the grounds of the attack on their merits. To argue that there is some fixed percentage of government spending above which inflation or some other evil or evils sets in, as well as being a dubious statistical exercise, is not necessarily an argument for cutting government expenditure, any more than it is an argument for cutting private consumption. What matters, for stabilization purposes, is the total demands on the economy in relation to the real resources of the economy: if the former is above the latter, it is an indication that the demands from all sectors should be looked at anew. The decision that it is best to cut expenditure in one section or the other does not emerge from the statistics.

It is argued that unbalanced budgets can lead to currency depreciation. The argument is undoubtedly true: there are examples of governments, unable or unwilling to tax adequately, resorting to the printing press. To argue that a certain consequence can happen is not to argue that it must happen. If it is feared that the increase in the level of demand causes the inflationary pressure, this only points to the fact that offsetting action is required. If it is feared that deficits over a number of years will so add to the money supply as to be inflationary, a similar reply can be made, i.e. this is a pointer to the need for offsetting action, for example to tighten control of the monetary sector, to fund, or to take action to reduce the deficit, which can be done either by increased taxation or by reducing government expenditure. The latter solution of cutting government expenditure does not automatically emerge as the best solution.

A further assertion is that deficits are less painful than current taxes, in the sense that people take account of current taxes and discount future taxes to service debt. It is argued that this leads to overexpansion of government services. A counter-assertion is also put forward, i.e. that traditional concepts of budgeting have hindered the provision of much-needed services and that failure to separate the debt of the nationalized industries and local authorities (which debt will normally result in the creation of real assets) accentuates this trend to under-provision. While either of these assertions may be true for a particular historical time period, they become increasingly hard to demonstrate in a modern budgetary setting.

The concept of the balanced budget, or PSBR, has an intuitive appeal to the individual because of the analogy with the economy of the private household. It has no validity in the accounts of a nation. It is dangerous because it conceals the real issues of 'the best use of the nation's resources'. The injection of dogma merely helps to cloud this real issue.

THE FULL-EMPLOYMENT BUDGET CONCEPT

A new concept came into vogue in the 1970s, balance at full-employment levels of income. (See, for example, Friedman 1959; Committee for Economic Development 1972; and Blinder, Solow *et al.* 1974). The concept played a part in some US presidential budget messages and was mentioned by the UK Chancellor of the Exchequer in his Budget Speech in 1991 as a reason why the government was expected to go into deficit in the coming period.

The concept can be seen as a way of measuring the effect of the budget on the economy which attempts to abstract from cyclical changes. Government determines what level of government expenditure and tax rates should produce a balance at full employment. Another variant has suggested that given full employment the overall budget could be in surplus or deficit but any additional government spending should be of a balanced-budget type.

Objections can be made to rules of this kind on technical grounds: that a budget balance is no guarantee that there will not be deflationary or inflationary pressures in the economy; different types of government expenditure and taxes will, as we have seen, have different effects on the economy.

Advocates of budgetary rules rely on the value-judgement that rules like the above, imperfect though they may be, will give better results than the use of discretion, a judgement that many will disagree with.

SUPPLY MANAGEMENT

Supply-side policies are a mixture of economics and politics. The latter include a belief in leaving as much as possible to free markets and so encompass privatization, deregulation and the removal of trade union legal privileges. Primacy is given to monetary over fiscal policy. Jobs may need to be preserved by wage cuts rather than government hand-outs. On the economic side is the belief that the economy may be subject to inflationary pressure when there is an increase in demand because of supply inflexibility hence the advocacy of the political policies just mentioned. Tax cuts, meant to operate at the micro level, are advocated to boost work, saving and investment and were examined in Chapter 10. It is very difficult to judge the overall success or otherwise of these policies partly because they are so recent. Deregulation, as shown, is often more a replacement of one form of control by another with mixed results. Tax cuts have had few macro effects although particular meas- ures such as tax incentives for savings have diverted savings from one form to another their effect on overall savings is more problematic.

Denationalization has largely replaced public by private monopolies or oligopolies, although the process has revigorated many of them. The power of trade unions has been reduced and labour markets are freer as a result. The unwillingness of workers to accept wage cuts is, not unsurprisingly, very high. It is a problem of market failure: workers might, the point is debatable, see benefits in terms of higher employ- ment from wage cuts if all wages fell but have no means of ensuring this. So to accept a wage cut is a real loss for an uncertain gain. It is also the case that the unemployed are not a party to wage bargaining so have no means of enforcing a wish for employment by accepting a lower wage.

MONETARY CONTROL

The 1980s saw the assent of monetarism, a term with a number of meanings. At its heart is the belief that control over the money supply will control inflation. In the UK the authorities attempted monetary control by operating mainly on supply-side factors. The government's intentions were set out in Medium-Term Financial Strategy (MTFS) documents setting out targets for the subsequent four years with in the beginning monetary targets as the centre piece. The PSBR and interest rates were the chief means used to try and control demand for money and credit. Changes in tax rates, privatization and sales of debt were seen as adjuncts to help keep the PSBR low. The prior questions about what assets constitute money, and more importantly can they be controlled, received less attention. In Britain today the number of official monetary aggregates is getting crowded. M0 is the narrowest definition of money: it comprises notes and coin in circulation outside the Bank of England and bankers' operational balances with the Bank of England. Assets are added through definitions of M1, M2, M3, M3c, M4, M4c and M5, as well as various PSBR magnitudes. It was a paradox that as governments were committing themselves to monetary targets they were at the same time ending many restrictions on the financial sector. It is of little use controlling a money magnitude if potential spenders can obtain funds from another source that is not being targeted. The result in the UK was government reliance on controlling a particular money magnitude was never satisfactory achieved. The target was initially Sterling M3 (£M3). When this proved unreliable new monetary measures were introduced and multiple money measures were targeted in a rather desperate attempt to find something that was creditable. Quantitative controls over banks and financial institutions to limit money and credit expansion were against the political ethic of free markets and were not attempted.

In 1979 exchange controls were abandoned in the UK and for a time the exchange rate was floating, with its exchange value left to market forces. This was a period of strong demand for the pound and the high exchange rate had a devastating effect on British firms, unable to compete in export markets and many went bankrupt. As the exchange rate setting changed the government's policy shifted gradually towards managed exchanged rates, with interest rates playing a prominent part. The Prime Minister, Mrs Thatcher, was, however, a tenacious opponent of full membership of the European Monetary System and this was not achieved until 1990 when Britain entered at what many believed to be too high an exchange rate. As a result interest rates in Britain remained high for a long period and industry in 1990–1 was again in a depressed state with many bankruptcies, high unemployment and as a consequence a forecast public sector deficit, the first for several years.

PROBLEMS OF CONTROL

In trying to manipulate the economy whether monetary, fiscal or the exchange rate is seen as the major weapon, a fundamental problem is, as shown, to diagnose the trends on which future predictions about the economy will be based. After the prognostication, if action is thought to be necessary, the type of action to be taken must be decided upon.

Enough has been said to indicate that in most cases a number of alternatives are open which will effect a remedy. The choice of which course of action offers the 'best' solution involves both political and economic judgement. In both cases differences of opinion can legitimately occur. Of particular importance in assessing alternative measures is the time scale needed to put the measures into effect, and once put into effect the time for them to affect the economy. The latter may be very short if people are anticipating the results or very slow if people heavily discount the future or expect the decision to be reversed at a later date.

Another important consideration is how flexible the proposed action is. If the prognostication is wrong because it has either underestimated or overestimated the effects, can the action be changed so as to allow for these revised estimates?

Stabilization or management of the economy, however, is only one aim of government. Policies need also to be judged in relation to their effects on the allocation and distribution of resources.

Different policies will almost certainly affect the allocation of re-sources between private and public goods, between investment and consumption goods, and between types of goods in each category. A tax on labour is, for example, likely to lead to the substitution of capital for labour. Tracing the effects of different policies is likely to be difficult because not only is the stock, that is the amount already in existence, likely to be affected, but also the flow, that is the additional amount demanded or supplied over time. Different policies will also almost certainly affect the distribution of resources and move the economy towards, or away from, whatever degree of equity is considered desirable.

When the aims of government are considered as a whole, this limits the extent to which any one measure can be used. Favourable effects in one direction tend to be counterbalanced by unfavourable effects in other directions. The steps outlined can be summed up in a flow diagram (Figure 11.1). Once it has been decided that action is required, this leads to a consideration of alternative policies indicated by 1, 2, 3, 4, . . . , N. For each policy it is necessary to weigh the time and flexibility elements and their effects on stabilization, allocation and distribution.

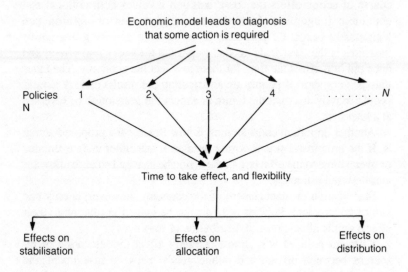

Figure 11.1 Flow diagram of the factors needing assessment in macro-economic management

SUMMARY

There is no unique way to achieve a particular economic objective, but a rich variety of means. Changes in monetary policy, government spending, revenue and debt, or in direct controls can all be used and will have different repercussions on the economy.

Economic models can be used for short-term forecasting but with so much uncertainty both about the data, and the theory of how the economy works, too much should not be expected. Chaos theory throws in doubt the validity of attempts at long term forecasting.

The main components of Gross Domestic Product were examined as these reveal the magnitudes on which government can operate for stabilization purposes. The practical problems of estimating these magnitudes for up two years ahead were examined.

Ideas about a balanced budget were taken up. These ideas have an intuitive appeal to the individual because of the false analogy often made between the economy of the state and that of the private household.

Practical difficulties in establishing just what is happening in the economy, and what measures should be taken if something needs correcting, were outlined and summarized.

APPENDIX: CHAOS THEORY

Recent work in mathematics throws doubt on the work of models that attempt to predict long-term behaviour of the economy. Most models involve linearizing non-linearities – simply put, this means assuming something that is not a straight line, can be approximated over a short section by a straight line – a powerful method that has enabled progress to be made in many sciences. However, chaos theory shows that even very simple non-linear equations can be unstable or chaotic, so that the small error involved in linearizing can lead to big errors in the final result. A straightforward and often-used population formula is useful as an example:

$$P_{n+1} = kP_n(1-P_n)$$ where P_{n+1} = next population
P_n = starting population a value between 0 and 1
k = any number

$(1-P_n)$ constrains the population between 0 and 1. Zero signifies the

Table 11.2 Iteration of the formula $P_{n+1} = kP_n(1-P_n)$

$k =$	0.5	1.2	2.0	3.1	3.5	4.0	4.0
$P_n =$	0.5	0.5	0.5	0.5	0.5	0.5	0.4
Iteration							
1	0.125	0.3	0.5	0.775	0.875	1	0.96
2	0.055	0.252	0.5	0.540	0.382	0	0.154
3	0.026	0.226	0.5	0.770	0.826	0	0.520
4	0.013	0.210	0.5	0.549	0.500	0	0.998
5	0.006	0.199	0.5	0.768	0.874	0	0.006
6	0.003	0.191	0.5	0.553	0.382	0	0.025
7	0.001	0.186	0.5	0.776	0.826	0	0.099
8	0.000	0.181	0.5	0.555	0.500	0	0.358
	.			.	.		
	.			.	.		
Eventual repeated value(s)	0.168	0.5		0.765	0.874	0	No pattern
				0.557	0.500		
					0.826		
					0.382		

population has died out, 1 that it has reached capacity.

Pencil and paper, a small hand calculator or computer, can be used to show that using values of k up to 3 and a starting population of 0.5 yields stable values of the populations after a few iterations. Table 11.2 sets out a few of the values.

When $k = 0.5$ and $Pn = 0.5$ the first iteration gives a value of 0.125 for population in the next period. This value gives a population of 0.55 for the following period. By the ninth iteration the population has crashed to zero or extinction. If $k = 2$ and $Pn = 0.5$ the population is always the same at 0.5. However, a value of k of 3.1 leads to alternating values of 0.765 and 0.557 and a value of k of 3.5 to four alternating values. Values of k between 3.5 and 4.0 lead to an increasing number of values to which the itereations tend and random numbers occur – the iterations never settle to a pattern – a chaotic picture. Other values can be experimented with, for example, a value of $k = 4.0$ and a starting population of 0.4 shown in the last column also yields a string of random values that never settles down however many thousands of times the calculation is performed.

The conclusion is that in non-linear systems even minute changes in the data can lead to completely different results. Lorenz, one of the pioneers in this area, named it the 'butterfly effect'. The flapping of a single butterfly's wing in Asia produces a minute change in the state of the atmosphere. Over time the state of the atmosphere diverges from what it would have been. So in a month's time a cyclone may, or may not, happen in the West as a result. Meteorologists for this reason seem to have accepted that, using present methods, weather prediction, even if they had perfect data, would be little better than guesswork for periods beyond about six or seven days.

Economists have been slower to accept the ramifications of chaos theory for their predictive models, although the theory has yielded insights in a number of economic areas. An exception must be made for a recent work by Goodwin (1990), which starts 'Why is economics like the weather?: because both are highly irregular if not chaotic, thus making prediction unreliable or even impossible.' An advanced paper is given by Barnett and Choi (1989).

Unless the economic world is linear it is hard to escape the conclusion that economic prediction has about as much power to predict the long-term future as that of a witch-doctor stirring the entrails and is rather less colourful. An account of the origin of chaos theory is provided by Gleick (1987). A mathematician, Stewart (1990), has provided a thought provoking introduction for the layman.

Part IV

Multi-level government

Chapter 12

The mix of centralized, local and regional government

INTRODUCTION

Most citizens are subject to at least several of the following jurisdictions:

- local government
- some form of regional authority
- central government
- broader grouping such as North America, EC or perhaps in the future
  the Pacific Region
- international bodies

Each layer needs to be financed and makes expenditures which have
considerable impact on people and economies. Is there any way we can
allocate functions and taxes to each layer that will be optimum?

This chapter looks at some of the arguments for and against centralization and some implications that follow for a mixed system in a single
economy. It then examines different types of fiscal arrangement and
grant systems. Finally, it takes up the problems associated with equalization. In this chapter the emphasis is on central and local government
relations, although many of the arguments are valid for wider country
groupings which are taken up in the next chapter.

THE ECONOMIC ARGUMENTS FOR CENTRALIZATION

The allocative, distributive and stabilization objects of an area can
normally be more easily performed in a centralized economy. Problems
of the co-ordination of different plans of different areas are not likely to
be so acute. A highly decentralized society would find it extremely
difficult, for example, to maintain high employment and stable prices

since local areas are open economies and the multiplier effect of local action is likely to be quite small in the area initiating the action.

A serious problem in allocation is posed, as we have seen, for so-called public or social goods. Again, a more centralized system is likely to succeed rather better than a decentralized one in providing the right output levels, since in the case of goods with external benefits these are likely to be under-produced as the local areas are concerned primarily with the welfare of its own inhabitants. In a like manner goods that impose external costs are likely to be over-produced since a local area will tend to disregard that part of costs which falls on non-inhabitants of its area. Most expenditures have externalities to some extent. Pollution of the air, rivers and coastline have lately received a good deal of publicity. Much of the work of pollution control is carried out by local authorities but the benefits of less pollution are widely spread. Failure of an upstream authority to purify its waste before putting it in a river imposes greater cost on downstream authorities. Similar types of consideration apply to expenditures on education, justice, health and transport where the costs and benefits spill over to other areas.

THE ECONOMIC ARGUMENTS FOR DECENTRALIZATION

At first sight a highly centralized system has many advantages over a fragmented one. The problems of allocation, distribution and stabilization can be solved more easily at this level, and since the central authority takes the whole area into account, the difficulties associated with externalities are reduced. Likewise, the problems of managing the economy are easier.

The basic drawback of a highly centralized system is its insensitivity to different preferences among its communities. Central provision is likely to be a compromise, based on the decision of the majority, which may nevertheless leave large numbers dissatisfied. For goods with few externalities present, that is where the benefits and costs are largely confined to a local area, effective local government is likely to see a greater diversity according more with local preferences and needs. For example, in the public provision of recreation facilities a centrally decided package per thousand of population would be less likely to fulfil the needs of each area as the same amount of money allocated to recreation facilities as decided by each local area.

This argument is sometimes taken further. Given communities with local autonomy, we are likely to see diversity in the provision of public goods, and in turn individuals will tend to move to a community which satisfies their preferences. Tiebout (1961) and others have generally held that the result of such a process would be an improvement in consumer choice. The individual adapts through moving, in contrast to the collective adoption of the local government area to the wishes of its inhabitants. There is considerable doubt as to how far the tendencies listed should be encouraged. If left to themselves the rich would tend to cluster with the rich, and exclude the poor who might become a public burden to them. Similar ghettos built on religion, colour and age would not be unlikely. The result could well be a highly dangerous increase in tension and violence between these self-separated groups. The contrast of a balanced community composed of rich and poor, religious and agnostics, professional persons and artisans, old and young: in short, a heterogeneous community having a richness of diversity and culture can itself be held to be a public good in contrast to the mono-culture of self-selected groups.

Local variations may also increase innovation and efficiency. Local authorities have a substantial number of innovations to their credit. A far-sighted authority sees a need and tackles it and the process is adopted by others. It may be more efficient to deal with local matters on the spot than have to go through a central bureaucracy. A less tangible benefit is sometimes claimed – that a vigorous local government helps maintain an active interest in politics.

CENTRAL–LOCAL RELATIONS

The arguments which have just been briefly considered are reasons for preferring a system which lies at neither extreme but is counter-balanced with both a central and local structure. For an economic discussion of this issue in greater detail, see Oates (1968 and 1972).

There is one view that, if adopted, has considerable implications for the structure of each level of authority. There are those who argue that the central government should be confined to providing services whose benefits are felt by the whole nation, regional services provided for regionally and local services accounted for locally. Powerful support on these lines is provided by Musgrave and Musgrave (1989) and Oates (1968). While such a division may be of some use as a first approximation, it does not seem to be a useful criterion in actually allocating services. The Musgraves use the example of street-lighting as an example of a geographically limited benefit and therefore one that is ideally suited to local provision. The example seems particularly inept:

the light is of course shed locally but its use benefits anyone in the locality – especially, it might be argued, the stranger trying to find his way. Centrally financed lighting of trunk roads may be considered desirable to ensure some uniformity of standards, thereby helping to reduce road accidents.

The static viewpoint, that services can be divided into those with local benefits and those that benefit everybody, is in today's complex urban communities of little relevance. Almost all services have repercussions for good or ill outside a local area. Geographical mobility of the population, the national and international interests of many companies and the increasing interdependence among people everywhere are the stubborn facts that vitiate a good deal of thinking about local provision. The strike of dustmen in London, or New York, imposes not only a nuisance on inhabitants of that area but also a health hazard, since germs are no respecters of local boundaries, to the whole country. The box labelled 'services of purely local benefit' turns out to be empty. If this is so it raises the question to what extent it is justifiable to charge activities that local authorities undertake to local inhabitants? Or, to put the matter another way, to what extent do these services justify central grants?

One answer to this problem is to say that since the inhabitants of a country must live in a locality, then it is a simple case of 'gaining on the swings what is lost on the roundabouts'. In modern jargon, 'spill-outs balance spill-ins'. An inhabitant of, say, London will be paying for services that in part benefit people outside London, but in his turn he will benefit by payments made by 'outsiders'. There is a great deal to this contention, and if needs and resources between local areas ever become spread fairly evenly it would be possible, in principle, to rely on local sources of revenue for services run by a local area. However, this condition is not met, and given the fact that some localities are poorer than others, and the needs of areas may differ widely from each other, we would find serious under-provision of services in poorer localities if authorities had to rely solely on local finance. Some form of revenue pooling is needed.

Considering the other extreme, where the central government meets all local expenditures, there is the problem that local areas would have no constraint on keeping expenditures down. A local area may well choose to have a very high level of services – theatres, concert halls, swimming pools, large open spaces, and the like. Many of these services will be of most benefit to those living in the area with smallish externalities. Local autonomy means (at a minimum) that if this is the democratic choice of the community they should be allowed this level of services, but not out of the pockets of the general taxpayer.

To summarize, we find that because all services confer some benefit or detriment to a wider community, this does not by itself provide a sufficient reason not to have local taxation. Local taxation serves the purpose of limiting local expenditures. It has both a positive and a negative side. The positive side is that areas which want a high level of services can opt for them. The negative side is that too high a proportion of revenue which has to be met from local sources is likely to result in serious under-provision of resources in poor areas and areas of high need. If we arrange goods on a spectrum with those with few externalities on one side and those with large externalities on the other, we find that a local tax is needed so that goods with few externalities are not over-produced, and state support is needed so that goods with large externalities are not under-produced.

We thus reach an important conclusion that a mix of local and central finance is likely to result in a better community choice of services than either a purely local or a purely central system of finance.

There is no simple answer to the quantitative question of how much finance should come from each source. It depends on a number of factors, such as the extent of inequalities between regions, the form in which central finance is given and other factors which will be discussed.

The Layfield Committee in the UK gave consideration to these matters (*Local Government Finance* 1976), and the majority proposed either a system of responsibilities which frankly recognized the need for strong central intervention – the centralist approach – or that positive steps should be taken to increase the freedom of local authorities to manage their own affairs – the localist approach. A minority of the Committee rejected this polarization and suggested that the central government should set minimum standards which local authorities would be required to meet, leaving authorities free to provide higher standards if they wished. In the Green Paper the government rejected all these approaches:

> The central/local relationship is changing all the time because national economic and social priorities can alter substantially even within quite short periods. Any formal definition of central and local responsibilities would lack the advantages of flexibility and rapidity of response to new circumstances. It would be likely to break down under pressure of events. The Government's view is, therefore, that while clarification of responsibilities wherever practicable is

desirable, a fundamental redefinition is not necessary as a basis for solving the problems of local government finance. The disadvantages of both the centralist and localist approaches are clear, and the Government do not think there is a case for the adoption of either.

(Green Paper on the Future Shape of Local Government Finance 1977: para. 2.8)

The government sympathized with the minority view but saw it as too impractical since it would reduce the whole relationship between central and local government to a simply defined form of allocation of responsibilities.[1] Rather they envisaged central–local relationships as a form of partnership, with the balance of responsibilities varying over time. During the 1980s, while talk in the UK had been about strengthening local government, in practice they increasingly came under strong central direction and control.

Setting up minimum standards to which local authorities have to conform is similar to the suggestions for regional finance made in the UK by the Royal Commission on the Constitution (1973). This body suggested that there was no need to enforce standards so long as areas were provided with the means to maintain these standards, and they should be free to spend them as they wished. Unconditional grants to local authorities, outlined later in this chapter, adopt this latter approach, although the extent to which the government would allow a local authority to depart from national standards in an important service like education is subject to doubt.

THE IMPLICATIONS OF SOME CENTRAL FINANCING

The conclusion reached is that some mix of local and central finance is to be preferred to either a purely local or a purely central system. What are the implications of some financial provision to localities from central sources? Effects can be broken down into: (i) the effect on central taxes and expenditures; and (ii) the effect on local taxes and expenditure. The most likely situation under (i) above is the case where central taxes are increased to provide for the subvention to local revenues with the level of central government activity undiminished. It is, however, possible that the central government, by making finance available to local authorities, may be inhibited from raising so much revenue on its own account, and hence has to resort either to debt financing or to cutting its expenditures on goods, services, and/or transfer payments.

Under (ii) above is the possibility that central finance may form a substitute, or be a complement to, local revenue: if a substitute, the same level of local spending can take place but a bigger proportion will be financed from central sources; if a complement, then the level of local taxation can either be the same (with a higher level of services paid from central finance), or higher if central finance stimulates the level of services and therefore also the level of local taxation. In what follows it will be assumed that provision of revenue by the central government will not inhibit it from carrying out its own programmes and that local authorities will treat the revenue as a complement to their own resources. While these assumptions seem reasonable, the possibility of 'perverse' reactions should be borne in mind.

TYPES OF FISCAL ARRANGEMENT

The following types of fiscal arrangement will be briefly examined: rigid separation of central and local sources of revenue; tax-sharing systems; and grants.

Rigid separation

The rigid separation of central and local sources of revenue is at first sight an attractive proposition. It is simple administratively and it would appear that if a correct division of tax sources is arrived at, maximum freedom is given to all levels of authority.

There are two major problems. One is that such a system lacks flexibility to meet changes in expenditure needs and revenue over time. If the spending requirements of one level of authority increase more rapidly than the tax base, then either the tax mix is likely to be distorted or expenditures will be curtailed. The second problem is that for most of the taxes that have been put forward for local use, the tax base is spread very unevenly between areas.

Tax sharing

In dealing with tax-sharing systems a word will first of all be said on administration of the tax. The mere thought of having two levels of authority taxing the same tax base with both of them responsible for collecting their own share of revenue is sufficient to convince most people of the impracticability of the idea. Not, however, all: Hildersley and Nottage envisage a local income tax being collected by local

authorities on the basis of information supplied to them by the Inland
Revenue! They say:

> The relationship between the Inland Revenue and the local
> authorities for the personal income tax would thus be essentially the
> same as for the local property occupation tax. In both cases the
> Revenue would determine the 'valuation' or 'assessment' and the
> local authorities would decide the rates of tax to be levied and would
> collect the sums due.
>
> (Hildersley and Nottage 1968: 27)

What is omitted is the essential difference: that the property tax is drawn
on only by local authorities, whereas a local income tax would be
drawing on a tax base already used by the central government. In what
follows it will be assumed that there is no question of duplicate tax-
collecting machinery being allowed. If taxes are to be shared in some
way, then in principle any level of authority can act as agent for the
collection of the tax and so avoid the fatuous duplication in administration. Freedom does not reside in the accident of which body happens
to collect the revenue; it is in fact quite possible to imagine the whole of
revenue-gathering being farmed out to a public body responsible jointly
to central and local governments (or even a return to the days when tax
collecting was farmed out to private enterprise). In neither case would
this confer power on the tax-collecting body – a mere agent for the
transmission of the revenues to the appropriate government body or
bodies.

Various types of tax-sharing are possible: for example a split in some
proportion; areas free to vary rates; and a tax-credit system.

Tax splitting

The total proceeds of a tax are, let us say, split 50/50 between central and
local areas, with taxes allocated to areas according to the income
produced in that area. There is much to be said against such a system.
Besides being complicated to administer, it would tend to perpetuate
existing inequalities between regions. Alternatively, the tax share of
local areas could be allocated by some formula taking needs and costs
into account. This would be similar to a general grant from the central
government. With either type of sharing the setting of the tax rate by
central government would cause local fluctuations in revenue.
Alternatively, mutual consultation on the rate of the tax would be
possible.

Freedom to vary rates

Local areas are given freedom to levy their own rates, which are combined with the rate of the central government and collected by the appropriate authority and shared out accordingly.

The result of local areas having different tax rates may be the creation of a 'tax jungle' or the competitive erosion of the tax base. The dangers of not having co-operation has been called a 'tax jungle'. It refers to a situation where an individual or corporation is faced with very high taxes – cases of over 100 per cent of taxable income are not unknown. This can arise where a person has residences in several areas, or is resident in one area and works in another, or a company operates in several areas. If the areas operate different taxes, or both tax the same base with no regard to the taxpayers' other commitments, such inequities can occur. It is not enough to set up a local tax system and leave it at that. Machinery for co-ordination and periodic review are needed.

More common is competitive erosion of the tax base. Some areas, if they have freedom to levy taxes, may, for example, seek to attract industry by giving tax concessions to firms – the end-result can be a situation where local revenues are seriously depleted because each area feels forced to match the concessions given by others, and, of course, the end-result fails in its original purpose of redirecting industry. Areas may compete also in a negative sense of not putting up taxes, for fear of driving industry or people out of their areas. The result, if local areas are relying on local sources for the bulk of their revenue, can be a severe limitation on their ability to finance services they consider necessary. Variation in local tax rates may well be desirable and, if this is so, it points out the necessity of some permanent form of co-ordinating machinery. Local authorities, because of these difficulties, may find that their interests are better served if in fact they levy a common rate, to be decided by consultation among themselves. Under this type of tax arrangement it has to be faced that there may be a conflict in policy, with, for example, the central government reducing rates and the local authorities increasing theirs. If these differential changes take place in response to different expenditure trends between the two levels of government, no harm is done, but if the central government is reducing its share of the tax for demand-management purposes, the conflict is a real one.

There are, moreover, similar problems with this type of tax sharing to those outlined under the section on 'tax split' and equalization would probably be necessary between areas with both methods.

Tax credit system

It is possible for the central government to allow a tax credit, or tax deduction, for a locally paid tax against a centrally paid tax. Although systems of this kind are not uncommon in federal systems, they pose considerable administrative complications and problems in equity and stabilization. If the tax credit covers the whole of the tax paid locally, then there is little incentive for economy at the lower level. The tax credit benefits wealthier regions the most and equalization will probably be called for. This drawback could be an advantage if the tax credit were confined to development areas where it could boost the resources of those regions, but this implies that a development area and the tax area coincide. If local areas confine their tax to the amount of tax offset by the central government, and there would presumably be strong pressure from the electorate for them to do so, then the tax credit would do little to boost the resources of the localities. It is usually possible to achieve the same ends more simply under the 'tax split' or 'freedom to vary rates' schemes.

Grants

There is first of all a basic distinction between conditional and unconditional grants. The former type of grant is payable for the performance of specified things, while unconditional grants may be used for any legal purpose by the recipient. Grants can take on a variety of forms:

1 Grants that cover the whole cost, or almost all of the cost, of provision of a service.
2 Grants that match the revenue contributions of each area.
3 Grants that aim to compensate for differences in fiscal capacity of each area.
4 Grants, on the lines of 2 above, which, in addition, allow for differences in cost of services in each area.

Grants that cover the whole cost or almost all of the cost of provision of a public service are sometimes used to encourage authorities to undertake or extend the provision of a particular service. Later, the grant may be merged in a general grant.

General matching grants that mirror the total local revenue contributions of each area have little to be said in their favour. They ensure the perpetuation of inequalities between regions. In this context they do, however, serve the purpose of pointing out that equalization grants, in whatever form they take, will not be equitable between regions if local efforts to tax their own resources are not allowed for.

A specific grant for a particular service may cover the whole cost of the service, or it may require revenue matching by the locality. This usually takes the form of the central government meeting 75 per cent, or some other proportion of the total cost, with the locality meeting the rest. The latter may be required to provide the service, or it may be voluntary; in the latter case the higher the level of grant, the more likely is the widespread adoption of the service. Variations on straight percentage grants are possible whereby, for example, the state meets the whole of the cost of basic provision of the service and matches expenditure on the service over and above this by a matching grant of, say, 50 per cent.

Specific grants are an obvious way, but by no means obviously the best way, for a central government to stimulate the introduction of a particular service. Given a service with strong external benefits, a high specific grant is likely to see most areas adopt the service. The same aim could be achieved by requiring each area to provide some minimum level of the service and adjusting the unconditional grant upward to assist them to do so. There is probably some administrative gain to be had by keeping the number of specific grants to a minimum. This is likely to involve fewer central government departments in the financial arrangements of local areas and so cut down the amount of detail that needs to pass between them. Against this likely administrative gain must be set the element of compulsion if the alternative of requiring some minimum standard of service is adopted.

Equalization

It is difficult to better the definition of the purpose of equalization that is given in the Royal Commission on the Constitution's Research Paper 9 (1973a): 'Given that an objective of decentralisation is to permit diversity in public services, the objective of an equalisation grant is to eliminate relative poverty as a determinant of diversity.'

Equalization problems

It is known that local areas do have unequal resources and this section takes up some of the problems associated with attempts to equalize. Not only must the type of taxes and grants be decided on but some measure of local tax effort may be required and some measure of the costs of services in each area. These are contentious matters.

Tax effort has received little attention. Tax effort here means the extent to which a local areas makes use of its potential fiscal capacity.

If local areas are to have a substantial addition to sources of finance under their own control, then, in the absence of uniform rates (agreed among themselves), the problems of measuring tax effort takes on more importance. A local area should not receive a higher government grant merely by virtue of the fact that it taxes less than other local areas.

Uniform local rates of tax on a uniform tax base overcome the problems of tax effort by curtailing the right of local areas to change rates unilaterally. Against this must be set the advantage that the act of forcing local areas to get together among themselves, and presumably presenting a common case to the government on tax changes, might do much to foster the interests of local areas.

A theoretical measure of tax effort

The aim in measuring tax effort is twofold: to ensure, on the one hand, that as far as possible areas should not be penalized because they are poorer than others; and, on the other hand, that areas that choose a high level of services and a high level of local tax should not receive extra subsidies as a result. Consider the introduction of a local income tax collected by the Inland Revenue in which areas are free to vary rates, at least within limits.

Neither the level of tax rates, nor the yield from the tax per head, provides a good measure of tax effort. High tax rates could be the result of a very poor area having to set high rates in order to provide the bare minimum of services. On the other hand, it may be a reflection of local interests – collectively the citizens of that particular area prefer to pay more in taxes and receive more in benefit. Alternatively, low taxes may reflect an average level of services and a favourable tax base, i.e., a large number of wealthy citizens.

One obvious method is to make an adjustment for differences in local tax capacity – in the case in point an adjustment to take account of local differences in income. Indices can be used to express the national average personal income per head as 100. The index for local areas will be above or below the national average in proportion as the average income of their citizens are above or below the national average. In Figure 12.1 this information is plotted on the horizontal axis. On the vertical axis the actual tax revenue per head is plotted. Once again the national average is expressed as 100 and local areas arranged around this. The distance above or below the 45° line in a vertical direction

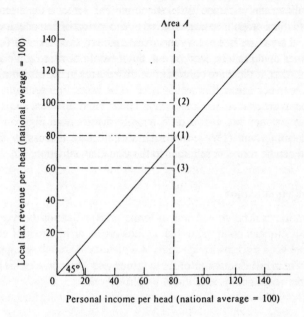

Figure 12.1   Adjustment for local differences in tax capacity

indicates the degree to which an area is making a higher or lower tax effort than average. The position of area A has been plotted, and has been found to have an average income per head which is 80 per cent of the national average. If area A is at position (1), where receipts are also 80 per cent of the national average, then the area is making an average tax effort. It should receive an equalization grant to supplement its below-average tax base. At position (3) less than average tax effort is being made – citizens of area A may have decided on less local tax and a lower level of local services, in which case its equalization grant should not compensate for the fact that they choose to tax themselves less but only for their taxable capacity being below the average. Considering position (2) a higher than average tax effort is being made. It has then to be decided whether this is due to the choice of the area to have a higher level of services (in which case no equalization is called for on these grounds), or whether it is due to increased costs of providing services in that region (in which case equalization is called for). Adjustment for differences in fiscal capacity have been made in the diagram. Local tax rates will differ between areas, therefore, but these differences will reflect differences in taxable capacity.

The above analysis traced out some important elements that need to be separated if tax effort is to be measured by the spread of personal income.

If local areas are free to levy more than one tax, then tax effort on the above lines could still be worked out, but it would be more complicated to do so. Also, if there are considerable differences in the distribution of income between areas, this would need to be taken into account, since the same average income in two areas could yield different sums from the same tax rate due to this difference in distribution. Figure 12.1 is adapted from Lynn (1964), in which an extensive discussion of this question can be found in relations to the Canadian situation.

Types of equalization

Equalization can be considered in terms of equalization between the groups of citizens comprising the various areas, or in terms of equalization between citizens irrespective of which local area they happen to live in. For a full discussion of these issues, see Musgrave (1961). The choice between them is essentially a political one.

Equalization between groups

Equalization between the groups of citizens comprising the various areas may be based on (1) equalization of fiscal performance; (2) equalization of fiscal capacity; or (3) equalization of fiscal potential. (See Royal Commission on the Constitution, Research Paper 10 (1973b), on which this section draws.) The differences between these measures can be brought out by a simple example in which we ignore differences in costs and needs between different areas. Let us suppose there are three areas, A, B and C, with A the richest and C the poorest authority. The yield per head from their respective local tax is given in Table 12.1. For example, area A has £60 per head from a tax of 8 per cent, £75 from a rate of 10 per cent and £90 from a rate of 12 per cent.

(1) Under equalization of fiscal performance the state aims to have equal amounts per head spent in each area and redistributes taxes from authorities whose tax yield exceeds the average to authorities whose tax yield falls short of the average. In order to get the authorities to apply local taxes, a minimum rate will have to be specified. Let us support the middle rate of 10 per cent and a desired expenditure of £60 per head: the figures in parentheses under heading (1) give the amount of grant, or if negative the amount of revenue the state collects. No area will in fact apply a rate in excess of 10 per cent since this will result in a direct loss

Table 12.1   Revenue (£ per head) and grants or payments after different equalization schemes

Tax rate (%)	Area A Yield	(1)	(2)	(3)	Area B Yield	(1)	(2)	(3)	Area C Yield	(1)	(2)	(3)
8	60	–	(–15)	(–10)	50	–	(0)	(0)	36	–	(18)	(14)
10	75	(–15)	(–15)	(–15)	60	(0)	(0)	(0)	42	(18)	(18)	(18)
12	90	(–30)	(–15)	(–20)	70	(0)	(0)	(0)	48	(12)	(18)	(22)

of grant or payment to the state. Thus at the rate of 10 per cent A pays £15 per head and C receives £18 per head. Here, as stated at the beginning of this chapter, no question of tax effort arises since uniform rates are applied and yields equalized by the grant system.

(2) Equalization of fiscal capacity is based on some decision on expenditure per head and level of tax which is common to all areas. If that level of tax applied to a local area fails to bring in the average revenue the area receives a grant, if more it pays the difference to the state. Local areas are free to tax as they wish, the amount of grant or state payment they have to make being, however, based on the standard rate of tax. If we again suppose the standard rate of tax to be 10 per cent and average yield £60 per head, we get the figures under (2) in the table. Looking across the table we find that a tax of 10 per cent yields £75 per head for A so it pays £15; B's yield is average and so is not affected, and C receives £18 per head since its yield is £18 below the average. These grants or payments are the same whatever rates the area chooses to apply. Again no tax-effort problem arises.

(3) With equalization of fiscal potential an area pays a tax or receives a subsidy equal to the difference between the yield obtained by applying its tax rate to the average tax base. Selecting area B as average as before, we get the figures under (3) in the table. Since B is average, the amount of grant or payment by the other areas is just sufficient to ensure that the net yield (i.e. yield less tax payment or plus the subsidy) from their taxes equals the yield from B's taxes. In terms of tax effort this case is more difficult to judge. The grant or payment made varies with the rate of tax levied and depends on the difference between yields in the area concerned and the average area. A very rich area would find most of its increased revenue from higher taxes payable to the central government, whereas a very poor area, by subjecting itself to rather higher local tax, would find itself in receipt of large grants. In between these extremes lies the whole range of possibilities.

Equalization of type (1) is unlikely in practice. In effect the local area has no discretion over its rate of tax.

With type (2) equalization, the grant is invariable with respect to the local tax rate, so that if areas tax at the same rate they have the same resources. However, different marginal tax effort is required if areas wish to raise additional finance. Thus the poor area C, by taxing at 10 per cent, has £60 per head (£42 tax and £18 grant); to raise £6 of additional revenue per head it would have to raise its tax rate to 12 per cent (£48 tax and the same £18 grant = £66), whereas for the same tax effort of 12 per cent area A has £75 (£90 tax less payment of £15).

With type (3) equalization any areas with the same tax get the same net revenue, and the grant or payment to the central government is proportional to the tax rate. Thus in the case considered in the last paragraph, area C, by taxing itself more than average, would receive a bigger grant.

The above illustration has assumed equalization in terms of the average, which involves redistribution from those above the average. It is possible to envisage levelling up to the wealthiest area, which would only entail redistribution from the state to localities. On grounds of cost to the central government, the former seems the most likely.

The example ignored, or assumed the similarity of, the costs and needs of local areas. In practice, both are likely to vary, and for many years grants to local authorities have attempted in rough and ready fashion to take some account of the most important differences by weighting according to proportion of children and old people, dispersion of the population, etc. To take account of these factors would complicate the example above but add nothing new, so we do not develop this point here. Similarly, we do not develop the example to include more than one tax being available to a local authority.

A unitary grant

This aims to equalize between groups of citizens living in different areas but differs from the models just set out in not redistributing revenue from areas with above-average taxable capacity.

The aim of a grant is to enable each local authority to meet its assessed spending needs by imposing the same tax burden. To achieve this, it uses the needs element to equalize spending needs per head and the resources element to equalize resources per head. If all authorities' needs and resources were the same, they could levy the same rate poundage to meet their assessed spending needs. It therefore approaches the equalization of fiscal capacity model that has just been set out, except that authorities with above-average resources are not required to redistribute revenue to below-average authorities.

Under a unitary-grant system compensation for differences in relative needs and taxable resources would still be given but by one grant element. The basic grant would be the difference between the cost to an authority of providing a standard level of service and the revenue it would raise from a standard tax. This is akin to the equalization of fiscal capacity model with redistribution since above-average authorities would receive a smaller grant by virtue of their higher revenue from a standard rate poundage.

A unitary-grant system means that two sets of figures are crucial: the assessment of the cost to each authority of providing a comparable overall level of services; and the corresponding standard local tax. Authorities would be free to spend more or less than the guide-lines provided by the standard level of service, but it is envisaged that additional expenditures would fall more heavily on the local ratepayer than the national taxpayer.

Equalization between persons

So far this chapter has been relating equalization to groups of citizens who live in a particular area. The philosophy behind this is that citizens of each area should collectively be placed in more or less equal positions. In the example used income was averaged for this purpose. But two areas may have the same average income but very different income patterns in each community, and the same point can be made whatever tax base is used for the comparison. There is a different idea of equalization which relates to individuals rather than to areas for further discussion of this issue, see Musgrave (1961) and Buchanan (1950). Musgrave says:

> Here, the idea is that the central fisc should neutralize the individual citizen of the federation against the fiscal operations of the particular state in which he resides. This requires direct transactions between the central fisc and the individual citizens of the federation. For this reason it seems more centralist in spirit, but this need not render it necessarily inferior or superior.
>
> (Musgrave 1961: 116–17)

If we start from the premise that local areas should be free to opt for better local services out of higher local taxes, then equalization between persons does not involve equalizing the proportion of income taken in tax from persons with the same income. Equalization requires that persons with the same income pay the same for the same services regardless of where they live, and it implies that citizens of local areas that opt for more or better local services will pay a higher proportion of tax than corresponding income groups in other areas that have not so opted. Buchanan (1950) develops this idea in terms of 'fiscal residuum'. This refers to the balance between the individual's taxes and the value of public services returned out of that taxation, so the residuum can be negative, meaning a net tax has been paid, or positive, meaning a net benefit has been received or zero, meaning tax and benefits balance. Buchanan formulates equality in terms of equalizing marginal benefits received from government services with marginal taxes paid. In Buchanan's words these and 'many other more technical problems make a precise application of the equity principle in the real world extremely difficult, but should not serve to prevent its use as a proximate standard for inter-governmental fiscal policy'.

A considerable amount of work has been done on a national scale in allocating taxes and benefits see 'The Incidence of Taxes and Benefits' in Chapter 7. A number of arbitrary assumptions have to be made about tax and benefit incidence and about how to allocate, or whether to leave out, certain social benefits such as defence expenditures. It is difficult to see this exercise being precise enough to make equalization between persons for purposes of local taxation anything more than an arbitrary exercise. Professor Buchanan does not explain how a principle difficult to apply can be used as a standard, and it would seem that at the present time equalization between groups in different areas is the only practical system.

Local equalization

The equalization schemes discussed above involve payment to the government by areas with above-average resources of money and this payment is allocated in a number of possible ways to authorities with below-average resources, or, alternatively, under a unitary-grant system, a smaller grant to richer authorities. It is possible to devise equalization schemes which local areas operate between themselves. In the UK the only scheme of general local equalization operates in London, which has had a scheme in some form or another for over 100 years.

Wider equalization schemes

The conurbation of London is seen as a special case because of its size and because of the disparity between the rateable resources of Westminster and the City and some of the poorer boroughs. But disparities in other conurbations and local areas are known to be far from negligible. There seems nothing in principle to stand in the way of applying equalization in this way, in practice, it may be more feasible for the central government to even out differences by judicious allocation of its grants.

Pooling

A limited amount of equalization takes place in the UK at the moment by adjustment to the amount of grant payable to an authority. Pooling takes place for teacher-training, advanced further education and pupils who are outside the responsibility of the local education authority. All authorities will benefit by teacher-training but not all authorities will need to set up training facilities. Costs for these services are therefore pooled and apportioned to all authorities on a formula basis.

SUMMARY

Some of the arguments for and against centralization have been detailed and the implications that follow for a system where part of the finance comes out of central resources and part is raised locally were examined.

Alternative types of fiscal arrangement were given: the separation of central and local sources, tax-sharing systems and grants. The dangers of a tax jungle and the competitive erosion of the tax base were explained.

The problems associated with equalization were looked at and the meaning of tax effort was detailed and the various types of equalization that can be attempted were outlined.

APPENDIX: THE COMMUNITY CHARGE AND COUNCIL TAX

Community charge is a much fairer charge . . . and a far fairer charge than the alternative roof tax.

(Margaret Thatcher, May 1990)

The poll tax was a grave error of judgement . . . it is the one big mistake this government has made.

(Nigel Lawson, November 1990)

The poll tax is dead: may it rest in peace. It has not been unique in the list of crass acts of British governments but it must rank high. It was introduced in defiance of all advice other than from sycophants, in defiance of common sense and public opinion. The tax was a monument to the arrogance lurking beneath the surface of Britain's over-centralized system of power.'

(Leader in *The Times*, 22 March 1991)

The discussion of tax principles in this chapter is far removed from the events that took place in local taxation in the UK. The Community Charge, or poll tax as it is universally known, was introduced in Scotland in 1989 and England and Wales in 1990. The then Prime Minister, Mrs Thatcher, had made an election commitment many years before to abolish domestic rates. She introduced the poll tax against the advice of many of her colleagues and advisers. Abolishing, or drastically modifying the poll tax, played a part in the leadership election which led to her replacement as Prime Minister by Mr Major in 1990. By March 1991 the announcement was made that the poll tax would be replaced in 1993 and details of this new tax were announced late in April 1991.

The old domestic rating system had faults partly inflicted by past governments, which had refused to revalue properties in England and Wales for many years. It was, however, a system which taxed very roughly in accordance with ability to pay, in that richer persons tended to live in larger properties with higher rates. There was a system of rate rebates for those on low incomes. The poll tax also had a rebate system but every taxpayer was expected to pay at least 20 per cent of the tax. A poor family of four adults could still find themselves paying more than a Lord living in a stately home. No amount of dissembling by politicians could convince the majority of voters that this sharply regressive tax was fairer than the rating system it replaced. The perceived gross inequity of this tax was sufficient to outweigh the fact that it was only a small part of total revenue. The usual argument against rates was that a single person living in a large property was subject to the same charge as several adults living in a similar property. Adults would, however, be contributing to general taxes and would therefore be contributing to local services in that way, since rates covered only a small proportion of local expenditure. It can also be questioned if it is sensible to encourage single people to live in large properties. If it is desirable to assist people in staying in their family home, there are other ways to assist than by the scrapping of an entire tax – for example, rolling up the tax so that it is due only when the person vacates the property, which might be at death, when the cumulative amount of tax would be a charge on the estate. The popular idea that the impact of rates was felt by only the people who paid rates is a misnomer which some politicians seem to have deliberately fostered. Rates were levied on the head of household so it seems reasonable to regard rates as a household tax. Rates could be, and were, passed on to tenants and payment for lodging would also reflect rates. The poll tax, by contrast, inflicts a tax on women who do not undertake paid work because they are bringing up small children, and a tax on families looking after elderly relatives who are just above the eligibility line for rebates.

One rationale given for the poll tax was that every adult should pay towards local services. It was also claimed that local authorities would be more accountable to local voters; increased expenditures would have to be met by increasing the poll tax and if unpopular the councillors could be changed at the next election. From the start, however, this argument was negated as central government capped high spending authorities to keep charges low. It is also the case that changes to government grant formulas can have a greater effect on local tax than local decisions.

Poll tax was set by local authorities and therefore varied between different places. The charge was made that government manipulated the grants paid to local authorities in order to favour selected councils. Wandsworth in London had the lowest rate in the country, with Lambeth next door the highest. The result when the government decided to reduce poll tax by an arbitrary £140 was that Wandsworth voters were paying nothing directly towards local services. In some other places the cost of collection of the local tax was also estimated to exceed the revenue obtained.

The cost of collection of the poll tax is about four to five times that of rates. Rates were a tax on immovable property and therefore difficult to avoid, the poll tax is on people who are very mobile. A year after the introduction many authorities were unable to collect more than 80–90 per cent of what was due and in some authorities the figure was much less than this. Part of the problem was changes to the tax introduced by the government itself, of which the most spectacular was the announcement in 1991 of a rebate of £140 to each person who was due to pay the full tax. This was announced just as the authorities had prepared demands for the next year and in some cases had actually sent them out. As well as the considerable cost in preparing new demands authorities faced a loss of revenue until they knew the new financial set up and many had to borrow and incur interest charges as a result. As Table 12.2 shows, this upheaval is to collect a forecast 11 per cent of local government revenue. The assault on local government by the central government which has been going for a decade is to continue. A commission to examine the scrapping of many county or district councils in favour of unitary authorities is being set up and a consultation paper on local government management is promised. Central government is taking over the responsibility for further education and sixth-form colleges and schools are being urged to opt out of local authority control.

The rebate on poll tax is to be paid for by an extra 2.5 per cent on VAT. VAT can be considered a slightly progressive tax but it still bears quite heavily on poor people.

In April 1991, the government announced the shape of a new 'Council Tax', due to come into force in 1993. It is a tax on residential property; rather than using the old rateable value as a proxy for the properties value this is to be based on the market value of the property. Details of the valuation were not given other than it was to be supervised by the Inland Revenue's valuation office. This is likely to be a very substantial and costly exercise. Assessing capital values could well be as controversial as the poll tax itself given that *valuation is inescapably an arbitrary act*. It is difficult to understand why the government didn't propose to take up an old idea, e.g. Othick (1973), himself a chartered

Table 12.2 Local authority revenues (1991–2 forecast)

Revenue source	£ bn	% of total
Poll tax*	7.3	11.0
Business rates	14.1	21.2
Current and capital grants from central government	38.3	57.4
Other sources	6.9	10.4
Total	66.5	100.0

Source: Financial Statement and Budget Report, 1991, HMSO.

* Net of all rebates and reliefs financed by central government.

surveyor, of a points system of valuation. This system is also arbitrary, as any valuation system is, but it can be applied *consistently* at a fraction of the cost of assessing capital values.

A points system would be based on such factors as type of dwelling (detached, semi-detached, terraced, flat), its location, floor space or number of rooms, whether it is connected to mains services, whether it has an inside toilet and whether it has a bathroom. The great merit of such a scheme is that the taxpayer, with the aid of standardized forms, would be able to work out his rateable value comparatively quickly and easily. Ratepayers' own returns could be used as a basis for preparing the valuation lists. For example, an additional page added to the Register of Electors form, which each household has to complete each year, would involve very little extra cost of administration, making annual revaluations possible or this could be done say every third year. Assessing the factors, and the weights to be attached to them, for a universal rating formula would be a controversial exercise, but it could be done very quickly and would not present great technical difficulties. Once the formula is agreed there should be little difficulty in applying the formula to individual properties as these characteristics are fairly easy to establish. In contrast capital values are likely to give rise to large numbers of disagreements and litigation.

The Council Tax proposed to assess property to one of seven bands with a 25 per cent discount for people living alone regardless of their income. The banding was increased to eight in July 1991. Students, student nurses and trainees will be entitled to discounts and those on income support are exempt. Those in the lowest band would pay less than the current poll tax, those in the highest band more but still less than under the old rating system.

Illustrative figures base the banding system on the assumption that the average property in England is worth £80,000, in Wales £60,000 and in Scotland £53,000. Table 12.3 gives the values of houses and the corresponding Band into which they fall for tax purposes.

People in the lowest band are expected to pay about two-thirds less than the middle band in their particular area, those on the top band about two-thirds more than the middle band. The head of household, on whom the formal incidence falls, of an H banded house will pay about three times as much as one in band A.

The government in announcing details of the scheme in April 1991 said that a couple living in a house in Band A and under a Council that spends in accordance with guidelines would pay £267, in Band D £400 and Band G £668. Whether these figures have much validity remains to

Table 12.3 Council Tax illustration of banding

Per cent of average value	Value of house in			Band
	England	Wales	Scotland	
Up to 50	Up to 40,000	30,000	27,000	A
50–65	40,000–52,000	39,000	35,000	B
65–85	52,000–68,000	51,000	45,000	C
85–110	68,000–88,000	66,000	58,000	D
110–150	88,000–120,000	90,000	80,000	E
150–200	120,000–160,000	120,000	106,000	F
200–400	160,000–320,000	240,000	212,000	G
over 400	320,000 +	240,000 +	212,000 +	H

be seen. When announcing the poll tax in 1987, the figure of £178 per head was given as the average charge, when it was introduced in England in 1990 its average level turned out to be £357, although transitional reliefs and income support reduced the actual level paid to £285. A combination of inflation and more importantly reduced government support for local authorities made nonsense of the original figures.

When the tax is operative the government proposes to announce for each band the amount of council tax necessary for a council to provide a reasonable level of service. If a council exceeds this level the extra expenditure must be shared equally across the seven bands so that all bills will increase by the same percentage. This proviso is meant to make the council tax relate to how much councils spend but the government proposes to continue with its policy of capping authorities who in its view spend too much. The idea that councils should be left to impose what level of charges they see fit on their residents and face the consequences at the polls has been ruled out in favour of the central government knowing what is best.

A consultative paper on the future of local government in England proposes the abolition of a number of existing two-tier county and district councils and their replacement by single-tier all purpose authorities. Further white papers are promised to deal with Wales and Scotland.

After the expenditure of billions of pounds the government has thus come back to a system of taxing residential property that could have been achieved at the outset by modifying the old rating system.

Chapter 13

Multi-level government

INTRODUCTION

In a grouping of nations such as the European Community (EC) there is a collective budget which has to be financed and expenditure objectives to be established. These will be examined in detail in Part Five. There is also the contentious question of how far it is necessary to harmonize the tax and spending plans of the separate countries which will be examined here.

We are told repeatedly that we now live in a global economy. Do we? If we look at money flows, financial and commodity transactions this is more or less true. In the fiscal area it is very far from the truth; we have a system of overlapping jurisdictions. The effects of fiscal actions may extend world-wide but each jurisdiction tends to jealously guard its fiscal rights. Taxes can influence labour flows between countries and, more importantly, affect the location of industry and commerce. On a wider scale the developed world heavily subsidizes its agricultural sector, to the considerable detriment of the developing world, which finds it difficult to compete with world prices depressed by the surpluses created by the developed world.

REASONS FOR HARMONIZATION

There are equity arguments for tax harmonization which will be touched on, but the more fundamental reason for harmonization is increasing the GNP of the region. By agreeing not to act in their own narrowly defined interests and instead to act for the common good, it is possible that all countries in the union can end up being better off, and provided this is not at the expense of countries outside the union, this is beneficial. This is the standard argument for free trade, and taxes may be one barrier to free trade. In the absence of distortions a good will be made in the areas with comparative advantage in that good. More goods can be made with the same resources and the gains shared between the trading partners. Tax differences may be by no means the most important barrier to trade but they gain in importance as other impediments are struck down. In this respect not all taxes are equal; some taxes are more distortionary than others. Different rates of VAT and excise duty are of less importance – since goods bear the tax of the country in which sold – than differences in corporation tax and taxes on labour, which can distort the investment and location pattern of firms. Without tax harmonization, countries, for fear of losing companies to another country, may engage in a competitive drift to the level of the lowest taxed country with no thought given to the 'best' tax system.

There are theoretical caveats to this reasoning. Although it may be established that free trade for the world is beneficial, the 'theory of second best' shows that it is not necessarily the case that achievement of free trade within a region produces this result. The theory of second best will not be established here: the interested reader is referred to a standard microeconomic text. The theory shows that if certain conditions have to be met to achieve a first best solution it cannot be assumed that achieving some of these conditions, but not others, is an improvement on the existing situation. It may, or it may not; this cannot be decided on theoretical grounds. A simple example can help to illustrate this point. If a person's ideal food is a hamburger, consisting of a roll, meat and mustard that person may well be satisfied, if he or she can't have all three, with a roll and meat. However the choice of roll and mustard may well leave that consumer very unsatisfied. The logic behind the second best argument can be illustrated by considering whether the creation of a trade region causes 'trade creation' or 'trade diversion'. Trade creation is the situation where expensive domestic production is replaced by cheaper imports from a partner, and the usual gains from trade argument prevail. Trade diversion is the situation where cheaper imports from the outside world are replaced by more expensive goods produced within the block. In this case the gains from trade are of the begger-my-neighbour kind; the bloc, if it benefits at all, does so only at the expense of the rest of the world. The bloc benefits, at the world's expense, to the extent that the diverted trade creates employment and growth in the protected sector, but against this has to be set the loss to other sectors of the economy both because of the diversion of consumer income on to the higher priced protected goods and loss of exports to countries who find themselves with less foreign currency to buy from the bloc. A number of commentators have expressed fears that the world will split up into trading blocs with detrimental effects on the levels of trade. The clear case where the EC acts against the interest of the rest of the world is agriculture and will be examined in more detail in Chapter 15. Briefly stated, the EC substitutes cheaper food from the outside world with food it grows only as a result of large subsidies, and this has detrimental effects both on the non-food sectors of the EC and the rest of the world.

The EC claims are that a single Euro market of 320 million consumers – with a GDP of over £3,500 billion in 1986 prices, where selling goods from Aberdeen to Athens is no more difficult than from Boston to Los Angeles – would mean greater competition and therefore cheaper prices, more output, employment and income. These would largely be of a trade-creating kind.

TRANSFER PRICING AND THIN CAPITALIZATION

As well as the gains to trade argument, states may choose to integrate or co-ordinate their tax systems for equity reasons such as to avoid undue taxation of income received from different countries, to facilitate their tax avoidance measures, to assist generally the flow of capital and simply to avoid a severe erosion of revenue.

The rise of the multinational company has made revenue erosion of particular relevance. The ability of these companies to 'source profits' to the country with the most favourable tax and to source costs to areas with the best reliefs and grants can cause a severe loss of revenue to a country. Recent rules though on *transfer pricing*'(the price at which different companies in the same group sell components and materials to each other) and *thin capitalization* (the extent to which different companies in the same group lend to each other) tends to limit this practice. Co-ordination can also avoid competitive bidding by countries for industry by way of tax relief and grants – a process that in aggregate leaves countries as a whole poorer and companies richer.

CIN AND CEN

Differences in tax systems impede the functioning of markets. Merged firms may, for example, pay more tax than the two entities separately. If tax rates differ companies will sometimes be tempted to invest in the low-tax country, even though it may cost more to produce there, i.e. an absence of *capital export neutrality (CEN)*. Also, an inefficient company may be able to sell its goods more cheaply than a rival even though its production costs are higher if a sufficient tax advantage is present, i.e. an absence of *capital import neutrality (CIN)*. CIN can be defined as the situation where the tax facing a company when investing is not dependent on its nationality. The aim of tax harmonization, as given in the Report of Fiscal and Financial Committee (1963) the Neumark Report, was:

> to encourage the interplay of competition in such a way that integration and economic growth may be achieved simultaneously and gradually.

The main losers of harmoniaztion will be those companies currently enjoying favourable treatment. Among these will be American, Japanese and other international companies, which, not unnaturally, currently 'do the rounds' of European countries seeking the maximum grants and tax breaks. These companies have large financial resources and political influence and can be expected to fight vigorously for their existing privileges.

REASONS AGAINST HARMONIZATION

One of the main arguments against harmonization is the political objection of removing the right of sovereign states to set their own tax regimes for a variety of ends. Any state may see an advantage in inducing firms to establish themselves in its area, balancing the loss of company revenue against higher employment and personal tax receipts. This argument, however, is of a beggar-my-neighbour type. Tax inducements are known to have a powerful effect in attracting firms to one area rather than another. There is, however, little evidence that the overall level of firms' activity is changed. In the absence of artificial tax advantages firms would settle in the area they saw as advantageous on other grounds.

A more subtle argument is the one that areas are merely seeking to 'level the playing field'. If they have disadvantages such as distance from a market they may see company tax incentives as a legitimate method of being able to compete with other areas. This argument, that some regions or areas may be depressed and need help, is a valid one that merits consideration but it is not clear that, if help is required, tax concessions to firms are the right way to go about it.

DOES THE LACK OF HARMONIZATION MATTER?

Theory shows that lack of fiscal harmonization can be important on equity and efficiency grounds. The equity argument is generally recognized by international tax agreements whereby nations agree not to tax earnings and dividends received by foreigners higher than those of their own nationals. In addition the country of the recipient of the earnings or dividends takes into account, in assessing its tax bill, the amount paid to a foreign government. The recipient therefore only pays tax at the rate applicable in the highest taxed country.

Are the arguments on efficiency grounds important in practice in the EC? The estimated increase of GNP of four to seven percentage points made by the Cecchini Report seems a goal well worth striving for and tax harmonization has a part to play in this. The Cecchini Report summarizes in 16 volumes a study for the Commission of the effects of The Single European Act – a summary version for the public will be found in Cecchini (1988). A more technical version is Emerson *et al.* (1988).

Tax does, in particular, influence the location and financial structure of firms. A recent substantial survey of British firms by Devereux and Pearson (1990) for the Institute for Fiscal Studies came to the following conclusions:

1 Tax does influence decisions about where to locate.
2 The financial structure of operations appears to be even more influenced by differential taxation, i.e. companies use branches and subsidiaries to optimize their international tax position. It affects decisions as to how to finance a project in which country to raise the money, whether and how the parent should fund its branch or subsidiary and whether borrowing or retained earnings should be used.
3 Corporate tax harmonization should be overwhelmingly supported.

Countries may differ by the tax base, rates of tax, the type of tax and the type of allowances against tax.

The equalization approach and the differentials approach

Two approaches vie for attention – the equalization approach and the differentials approach.

The equalization approach advocates uniformity of the tax base and the equalization of tax rates within the Community. It puts the Community above the goals of individual members. It is favoured by those who see it as enhancing competition on equal terms and as a way of moving forward with economic and political integration. While being favoured by many in the Community, the problems of implementation appear to be rather formidable. It may be more helpful to think in terms of particular taxes rather than all taxes; for example, the benefits of equalization in company taxation appear to be higher than in personal tax.

The differentials approach emphasizes the needs of the individual member countries. It sees the tax system of each country as an instrument of policy for attaining major economic objectives with the proviso that the adverse externalities of each country's tax systems on other countries should be minimized. Here the sum of the member countries' welfare is seen as adding up to the welfare of the Community: they coincide.

Tax harmonization can encompass both aspects, with unification of some taxes and a co-ordinated but differentials approach to others. It is clear that this process can have considerable effects on both a government's instruments of policy and the objectives of policy. So not only can there be resource and balance of payments impacts, but the stabilization, allocation and distributional roles of the budget can be affected.

The tax systems of the original six were very diversified, reflecting history and differences in their economic and social structures. The Treaty of Rome setting up the Community specifies that 'harmonisation of the legislation . . . concerning turnover taxes, excise duties and other forms of indirect taxation is a principal objective of the EC' (Article 99). In some respects progress has been slow and difficult, countries cling to their so-called tax sovereignty. Harmonization at a basic level is concerned with agreeing the *tax type*. Thus the Community has agreed on VAT rather than the cascade type of tax that was operated in Germany or purchase tax that was operated in the UK. Harmonization of the tax base is usually considered next and finally harmonization of tax rates. However, it is possible for the last two steps to proceed side by side. Chapter 3 gives details of the progress towards harmonization in various taxes. As with VAT, agreement may be sought on desirable tax bands within which goods shall be taxed even though harmonization of the base of the tax has not been achieved in practice.

FOREIGN SOURCE INCOME

Under a tax credit system the question arises as to what happens if a shareholder resides in a different country to the company paying the dividend? Should a Frenchman get a tax credit to offset his French income tax when the tax has been paid in the UK? In 1975 the EC wanted all shareholders in the Community to be given the same tax credit and proposed a clearing house to redistribute revenues from the country where corporate taxes were paid to where the tax credit was redeemed. This proposal has yet to be accepted in spite of the presence of withholding taxes being seen as a major distortion and their abolition as going a long way to achieving a fairer system. A witholding tax occurs when a country, in addition to taxing a foreign firm's profits as it would a domestic firm's, applies a withholding tax on profits of a foreign firm sent to another country.

Additional withholding taxes may be levied when profits are repatriated to residents of another country – the effect is to tax foreign owned companies more heavily than domestic ones a clear case of the violation of CIN.

Alternative treatment of foreign dividends to that proposed by the Commission would be to exempt all profits earned abroad from home tax. This is unlikely to be accepted by the treasuries of the home countries. Britain uses a credit system whereby tax abroad is compared with the tax that would have been paid in Britain if earned there. If less, then the shareholder pays the difference; otherwise no action is taken.

THE TAX BASE

Companies

In 1988 a 'preliminary draft' concerning the calculation of profits was produced. The Commission suggested that the depreciation rates applied for accounting purposes should be those used for tax calculations – the system used in several European countries. It would prevent, inter alia, accelerated depreciation. If adopted this would push harmonization back to consideration of the rules of depreciation. It differed from current practice within some member states in various ways, including the treatment of stocks and capital gains and losses. The most important changes were those relating to depreciation of assets for tax purposes.

Unitary or formula taxation

A possible tax base is a *unitary or formula apportionment*. Countries agree on a tax base and some formula for sharing profits. The formula usually uses the proportion of work-force, or property, or turnover in each country, or some weighted combination of these factors to share profits. This is used by many of the states in the United States. California wanted to adopt it on a world-wide basis for firms in California but this idea was dropped after foreign opposition. In Europe, a unitary base would mean that a company with a manufacturing base in only one country but sales in many would pay some taxes to all governments in which it traded.

A unitary tax is seen by many as a good way of taxing international companies but, perhaps because it stops the artificial transfer of profits from high- to low-tax areas, has always met some vigorous opposition from companies. If adopted, it would overcome the problem of transfer pricing and thin capitalization. There does not seem much difficulty in adopting it in Europe but it needs to be coupled with tax harmonization to achieve neutrality, otherwise the incentive to invest in a low tax country would remain. Another difficulty in setting up this system would be to get agreement among European countries on the formula to be used. Once this hurdle is overcome there should be substantial revenue gains for governments and this looks like an idea whose time has come.

Persons

Personal income tax and social security payments and benefits can influence labour flows on both the supply and demand side. In spite of this there is tacit agreement that, at the moment, these areas should remain under the jurisdiction of the individual countries. Harmonization of income tax, to be meaningful, would have to incorporate harmonization of social security and pension contributions and possible social security benefits.

WHAT CAN BE DONE?

There is clearly a clash, or at least a trade-off, between the achievement of economic neutrality and maintaining the right of member-states to set their own tax regimes. Short of going down the road of complete harmonization there are a number of alternatives.

1 Companies which are owned and operate in one country could be separated out for tax purposes. This is bureaucratic.
2 Corporation tax could be levied according to the residence of the parent company. This would achieve capital export neutrality – wherever a company invested in Europe it would pay the same rate

of tax. The country of residence taxes the Europe-wide profits, giving full credit for taxes paid in the source country and allocating tax proceeds according to some mutually agreed formula. It would avoid the need for provisions to deal with complex anti-tax avoidance devices. This could still put some companies in a poor tax position.

3 The abolition of withholding taxes would go a long way to achieve a more equitable system. Withholding taxes are levied when profits are repatriated to residents of another country, the effect is to discriminate against foreign-owned companies which pay more tax than domestic ones. An alternative is for companies to adapt the same level of withholding and the European Commission in 1989 proposed that this be 15 per cent.

4 Leave it to market forces but other motives of government may mean distortions remain.

If everything works out as planned, by 1993 the internal EC market should be a fact. The Community could then consider the further step of harmonizing direct taxation in Europe. This step, however, would be linked to an increase of the EC budget to permit expenditure policies that would compensate for the greater constraints caused by EC harmonization of direct taxation. Further reading on VAT and excise duties is found in Lee *et al.* (1988), Coopers and Lybrand (1988) and Cardarelli and Michele del Guidice (1988).

SUMMARY

Reasons for and against harmonization of taxation between countries were given. Failure to harmonize can result in companies setting up in the lowest-tax location rather than the lowest-cost location. Tax differences are large and do appear to affect company decisions. The abolition of withholding taxes is recommended by the EC. The conclusion reached was that the expected gain in the EC of achieving the single market is estimated at some four or more percentage points in GDP and worth striving for, and company tax harmonization in particular has a part to play in reaching in a single market. Treatment of foreign source income and company tax was examined. A unitary or formula tax system for the latter offers advantages.

Part V

The European Monetary System and European budget

Chapter 14

The European Monetary System

This chapter starts with a sector outlining some of the regional organizations to which European countries belong. The relevance of these to the EC will be brought out in this and the following chapter.

REGIONAL GROUPINGS

European countries belong to a number of regional organizations which themselves have evolved over time. Table 14.1 sets out the countries belonging to the European Community (EC), European Free Trade Association (EFTA), Organization for Economic Co-operation and Development (OECD), North Atlantic Treaty Organization and the proposed European Economic Area (EEA).

The EC forms our main concern: the countries in it (12 as at 1991) also belong to the wider grouping of counties that form NATO and the OECD. The role of defence in the EC and the place of NATO, as noted in the next chapter, is coming under review with the changes taking place in the Communist countries. At some stage in the future the EC might wish, if NATO survives, to negotiate in NATO as a bloc. The EC has the most complete aims of the blocs listed: free trade, monetary union and economic union. There is more uncertainty about eventual political union. EFTA and OECD are blocs of countries primarily set up to promote free trade, the former mainly with the EC and within their own bloc of countries. NATO, as its name implies, has the narrower aim of defence interests. The recently announced EEA proposes to extend the EC single market to the seven EFTA countries.

The EC is still adjusting to the Mediterranean-type economies of Spain and Portugal, which joined in 1986, and the unification of Germany in 1990. Further enlargement of the EC will bring additional problems and opportunities, but speculation about these will be avoided here.

Table 14.1　Some regional European country groupings

European Community (EC)

Original EC(6)

   Belgium
   France
   Italy
   Luxembourg
   Netherlands
   W.Germany

1st enlargement

   Denmark
   Ireland
   United Kingdom

2nd enlargement

   Greece

3rd enlargement

   Portugal
   Spain

European Free Trade Association (EFTA)

   Austria[1]
   Finland[2]
   Iceland
   Liechtenstein
   Norway
   Sweden[1]
   Switzerland[2]

Organization for Economic Co-operation and Development (OECD)

   Established in 1960 with 18 European countries, the United States and Canada, to stimulate economic progress and international trade. It now consists of 24 countries. It is coterminous with EC and EFTA countries, and also includes Australia, Japan, New Zealand and Turkey as well as the United States and Canada.

North Atlantic Treaty Organization (NATO)

   Established in 1949 consisting of 12 countries: Belgium, Canada, Denmark, France, Iceland, Italy, Luxembourg, the Netherlands, Norway, Portugal, the UK, and the United States. Since then France has withdrawn although it maintains close co-operation, and Greece, Turkey and West Germany have joined.

1　Have applied for EC membership

2　Expected to apply soon for EC membership

INTRODUCTION TO THE EUROPEAN MONETARY SYSTEM

The history of monetary co-operation in Europe pre-dates the formation of the EC. The Marshall Plan to aid war-torn Europe after 1945 was the start. The aid was given by the United States on condition that European countries agreed to a system of multilateral settlements among themselves, which they did.

The monetary history prior to 1939 is very different. It was characterized in much of the period between the two world wars by distrust, particularly by France of Governor Strong of the Federal Bank of New York and of Montagu Norman, Governor of the Bank of England. France and Germany, in particular, had experienced hyper-inflations which, not surprisingly, still colours some of their attitudes to monetary matters.

The EC, of which the European Monetary System (EMS) is a part, is an attempt to stop Europe dissolving again into war as it has done twice this century – 'that it would make war between member countries not only inconceivable but also materially impossible'.

In spite of the monetary co-operation referred to, the Treaty of Rome setting up the EC in 1973, probably wisely, laid down no firm policy in the monetary area. There was, and still is, a divergency between those who see monetary co-operation leading the Community into closer relationships and those who believe that domestic economic policies need to be co-ordinated and put on a converging course before much in the way of monetary stability can be achieved. The truth is probably in the middle, with progress on one front helping the other.

After 1945 most countries in the world adopted a system of fixed exchange rates, the so-called Bretton Woods System, named after the place in the United States where the conference initiating the system was held. It lasted a considerable time – until 1971, when some countries adopted a floating rate and others linked their currencies in some way to others.

With fixed exchange rates, countries need to take action if their currency threatens to get out of the agreed trading range. If the threat is a fall, this will mean loss of reserves and so force action to prevent this loss by some fiscal or monetary action such as putting up taxes, interest rates, or tightening monetary policy. Free exchange rates in theory offer more freedom. A fall will drive the exchange rates down but the government can ignore this and pursue whatever internal policy it wishes. In practice free exchange rates do have constraints; governments are not usually willing to see their exchange rates driven too high or too low in relation to others. In practice the difference between free and fixed rates is a matter of degree. Any fixed rate system must have some provision for currencies to realign if they get seriously out of line with each other – the case, for example, if two countries have very different rates of inflation. And no government is going to stand idly by in a free exchange rate system and see its currency buffeted by seasonal factors and speculators without attempting to smooth things out.

The European Community generally has a preference for fixed rates of exchange between member-states. The EC is the largest trading bloc in the world, about half of its members' exports are sold to each other. Currency stability should encourage trade, without the necessity, and cost, for mechanisms like forward currency hedging to offset the possibility of exchange-rate losses. It avoids the temptation for governments to try for competitive devaluation to gain an export advantage – a game that not everybody can win. Partly it is due to the past inflationary experience of a number of the member countries: they have a preference for a system that requires governments to take early action if currencies get misaligned rather than leaving matters solely to their discretion.

An early attempt to form a European monetary system, called the European Monetary Union (EMU), was started in 1971. The scheme was probably too ambitious at that stage of co-operation. It was subject to exceptional monetary strain as it was introduced at a time when the Bretton Woods fixed exchange rate system collapsed. A fresh start was needed and negotiations by Roy Jenkins, then President of the European Council, resulted in the EMS coming into force in 1979 with more modest aims. In spite of early sceptics the system has survived and met with considerable success.

AIMS OF THE EUROPEAN MONETARY SYSTEM

The President of the European Council set out the aims of the EMS as follows:

> The purpose of the EMS is to establish a greater measure of monetary stability in the Community. It should be seen as a fundamental component of a more comprehensive strategy aimed at lasting growth with stability, a progressive return to full employment, the harmonisation of living standards and the lessening of regional disparities in the Community. The EMS will facilitate the convergence of economic development and give fresh impetus to the process of European Union. The Council expects the EMS to have a stabilising effect on international economic and monetary relations.

(European Economy, July 1979)

The expectation was that greater exchange rate stability would contribut to higher growth and employment by:

1 allowing higher levels of demand;
2 preventing excessive appreciation of strong currencies and excessive depreciation of weak currencies; and
3 encouraging business confidence and investment. It was felt that firms were reluctant to go fully European because of exchange rate and inflation risks.

Sterling has from the start formed part of the ECU basket of currencies but it was not until 1990 that the UK opted to participate fully in the exchange rate and intervention mechanism.

Four aspects of the EMS are considered:

- the European Currency Unit (Ecu)
- credit facilities
- exchange rate and intervention mechanism
- projected European Monetary Fund (EMF)

THE EUROPEAN CURRENCY UNIT

The European Currency Unit (Ecu) is the weighted value of a basket of European currencies. It is calculated by taking a given amount of each participating country's currency and valuing each of the currencies in terms of one of them, or of some outside currency such as the US dollar or Yen. The resulting values are added up to form the value of one Ecu in terms of that other currency.

The amount of each currency in the currency basket is decided by the approximate relative importance of the GNPs and trade of the respective countries and is normally reviewed every five years. The value given the Ecu thus depends on the daily valuation of each of the participation countries portion of currency included in the basket. There is provision for a re-examination of the amounts of currency in the basket if any currency value changes by 25 per cent. Changes must be adopted unanimously by the EC Council of Ministers and must not affect the value of the Ecu at the moment of transition.

Table 14.2 gives the amounts of currency in the Ecu.

Table 14.2   Composition of the Ecu basket since 21 September 1989

Fixed currency	Amount
Danish Krone	0.1976
W. German Mark	0.6242
Greek Drachma*	1.44
Belgian Franc	3.301
French Franc	1.332
Netherlands Guilder	0.2198
Irish Punt	0.008552
Luxembourg Franc	0.13
Italy Lira	151.80
Portuguese escudo	1.393
Spanish peseta	6.885
UK Pound	0.08784

Notes: * Not in exchange rate mechanism.

The value of the Ecu-unit in each of the national currencies that make it up is easily calculated. For example, the amount of UK pounds in the Ecu is 0.08784, (almost 9 pence). This plus the sum of the other components of the basket converted into pounds at the current exchange rate of the pound against those currencies, provides the sterling value. In May 1991 this gave a value of around 0.69 pence to one Ecu. Likewise the value of the Ecu in terms of any currency not included in the basket, is simply the added value of each of the small amount of currency comprising the Ecu in terms of that outside currency.

USES OF THE ECU

The prime property that money needs is *general acceptability* within the community concerned. Money acts as a *medium of exchange*, a *store of value*, a *unit of account* and a *standard for deferred payments*. A *medium of exchange* is the obvious function of money: it allows goods and services to exchange for itself rather than having to seek sellers who require the goods and services you have to sell. It avoids the double coincidence of wants normally required in a barter situation. Money also acts in some degree as a *store of value*. If money were like a day-return ticket on a railway, valueless after the day has ended, nobody would keep it. It is because money is expected to have general acceptability and more or less the same purchasing power the day after, and the day after that, that money is held, and this function is termed a store of value. Money also acts a *unit of account* and as a *standard for deferred payments*. The unit of account refers to the fact that instead of valuing each and every article and service in terms of all others, it is valued in terms of a common denominator, the means of exchange. In a similar manner, contracts for the future payments are usually made in terms of the means of exchange, although they can be made in terms of the value of gold, a foreign currency, or a quantity of goods.

The Ecu acts in all of these ways. It was originally set up as a unit of account for official Community business, a reserve instrument and unit of settlement between member central banks, although it took some time to achieve much in this area. It also acts as the denominator (*numeraire*) for the Exchange Rate Mechanism, and the intervention and credit mechanisms, and forms the basis for the divergence indicator. It still performs these official roles. Official Ecus are only held by member central banks, international monetary institutions and central banks of non-Community countries which have been accorded the status of holders by the European Monetary Co-operation Fund (EMCF). Each Community member country swaps with the EMCF 20 per cent of its dollar and gold reserves for official Ecus. The reserves are revalued every three months. Central banks can then use these Ecus to settle official accounts with each other. They are not used directly in exchange rate intervention but can be changed for foreign currency if needed for this purpose.

In additional there is a private market for Ecus as a currency of denomination. There is no difference in the composition of official and private Ecus. The difference is that the creation and use of official Ecus is tightly controlled and remains within official circles. Private Ecus can be created by banks simply holding accounts in the currencies that make it up. It is most limited by lack of general acceptability, partly because European governments have been slow in granting it legal recognition within their borders. It is also limited because it does not exist as a note or coin, except as gold and silver coins for collectors. However, it is possible to open a bank account designated in Ecus and write cheques on the balances. Ecu traveller cheques are available and also, more importantly, a wide variety of financial instruments.

Given the existence of an official Ecu, private institutions and firms saw the advantages of a currency that was, since it was a weighted average of the component currencies, more stable than at least some of those currencies. Italian and French borrowers were keen because of the uncertainties of the Lira and Franc and raising funds in Ecus rather than in their home markets or in dollars gave lower interest costs. Over time a spot and futures market in Ecus has developed and a variety of financial instruments for borrowing and lending. So the Ecu can be used as an alternative to domestic currency borrowing and has been actively promoted in Italy and France. A *spot* market is one where the price is agreed today and exchange takes place. A *Future* market is one where the price is agreed today for future delivery of the commodity.

Given a demand it is easy for a bank to offer Ecu facilities. It merely has to hold accounts in the appropriate amounts of each of the currencies making up the Ecu to give itself protection against exchange rate changes. The market has grown from 7 billion Ecus in 1972 to 90 billion Ecus in 1988 (March). Ninety billion Ecus may seem a large sum of money but it is a relative small amount in relation to international assets, generally of some US$4,800 billion. Banks in France, the UK, Belgium, Italy and Luxembourg account for 90 per cent of all business.

Most of the lending, some 77 per cent, is interbank business, that is banks borrowing and lending among themselves. Use of the Ecu market was until recently affected by the official regulations of each country. Britain was whiter than white, Germany the most regulated. German restrictions were revoked in June 1987 and now most EC countries treat the Ecu on the same footing as other foreign currencies.

In 1985 the Bank for International Settlements (BIS) set up a clearing system for Ecus. The BIS was set up in Basle in 1983 and is concerned, as its name implies, with international settlements. It played a notable role in post-war European monetary arrangements. Its monthly meetings provide an occasion for governors of central banks to consult each other. Known as the Group of Ten, it in fact comprises 12 European countries and the United States, Canada and Japan. Meetings of wider group of countries also take place.

The BIS set up the Ecu Banking Association (EBA) to act as a clearing system for Ecus, to promote transactions in Ecus and to represent its members in all matters concerning the use of the Ecu in their relations with national and European authorities. It has 82 members with 33 selected banks from 10 countries providing a clearing system which is generally on a same-day basis. Net of interbank business, outstanding assets stood at 14 billion Ecus at the end of March 1988, double the level at the end of 1985. Since 1982 over 80 per cent of syndicated loans have been to Italian and French borrowers. The term *syndicated loans* describes the process whereby a number of banks co-ordinate their efforts to make a loan and each bank contributes to it.

In commercial transactions the Ecu's role is developing slowly. Some large Italian and French manufacturing companies invoice in Ecus, accounting for some 1 per cent of all their foreign trade. Some firms, notably Saint-Gobain in France, publish their accounts in Ecus. Some Middle Eastern and North African trade is now invoiced in Ecus rather than dollars.

In the bond market by 1987 the Ecu was accounting for some 4 per cent of the total of bond issues, compared with 9.5 per cent in Deutschmarks and 6.2 per cent in sterling. The largest borrowers in Ecus are The Euro Investment Bank and European Coal and Steel Community. But private borrowers also use it. London accounts for 22 per cent of total activity and is the second largest after Paris.

One currency for Europe?

The Ecu is not a genuine currency. For it to become legal tender as a parallel currency alongside national currencies, or as a replacement for these currencies, the internal legislation of member-states would have to be changed, and more importantly economic and monetary integration would have to be much closer. A fully fledged European currency cannot be based on a basket of currencies but would have to be issued and managed by a European monetary institution. In an opinion poll reported in *The ECU* (June 1987) carried out for the Commission in the six original member-states and the UK, 59 per cent of respondents were in favour of a currency that could be used freely in all the European countries alongside national currencies. Only 18 per cent were against, with 23 per cent not knowing or having no particular view on the matter. The majority saw the Ecu as a means of strengthening the European economy and as a symbol of European unification.

A single currency for Europe has much more to offer than a symbol: it is required if the EC is fully to meet its declared aim of achieving a financial common market. The Cecchini report (1988) and The European Financial Common Market (June 1989), in estimating a Community gain of 4.5 per cent of GDP by achieving a single market, broke the gains down as follows:

Customs barriers	0.40 %
Public procurement	0.50 %
Financial services and capital movements	1.50 %
Competition and economies of scale	2.10 %
Total	4.50 %

Thus benefits of breaking down financial barriers exceed the combined expected gains from removing customs barriers and achieving open public procurement policies. The Cecchini report, basing its figures on a survey conducted in banking and credit, insurance, and broking and securities, envisaged gains of 22 billion Ecus for eight Community countries: Belgium, France, Germany, Italy, Luxembourg, the Netherlands, Spain and the UK. It points to price differences of over 50 per cent in this sector, with margins at their widest in the prices charged for motor insurance, home loans, consumer credit and securities. Prices are, it seems, likely to fall furthest in Belgium, France, Italy and Spain, although substantial drops can be expected in the UK, German and Luxembourg markets.

EXCHANGE RATE AND INTERVENTION MECHANISM

Each central bank of full participating members of the the EMS is required to keep the market rate for its own currency against other participating currencies within 2.25 per cent of its cross parity, except for Spain and the UK, which are allowed a 6 per cent range. Italy moved to the lower band in January 1990. Further details will be found in the Bank of England Quarterly Bulletin (June 1979 and November 1988).

Cross parities are worked out by taking the market value of currencies against each other as they existed at the end of the previous week; this forms the central rate of one currency against the others and from this can be formed a parity grid. As an example, if 1 Ecu = 2.5 Deutschmarks (DM), 40 Belgian Francs (BF), and 6 French francs then by division the cross-parity between DM and BF is DM 1 = BF 16, or 1 BF = Dm 0.0625.

No currency, apart from Spain and the UK, should move more than 2.25 per cent from their central rate, so the movement of currencies against each other should be confined within the currency band or 'snake' of 4.5 per cent. In practice a divergence indicator is now built into the system and triggered when a currency is within ¾ of its maximum divergence from the average of all other currencies. If the divergence indicator is reached there is a presumption that the country concerned will take action such as interest rate changes. The trigger causes consultations in the appropriate Community bodies such as the Committee of Central Bank Governors, the Economic Policy Committee or the Council of Ministers.

A matrix of cross parities intervention rates can be set up using the illustrative figures above. The matrix is presented in Table 14.3.

In the example used in Table 14.3 the limits for the DM against the BF would be 15.6440 when the Belgium central bank would buy DM and the German bank would sell DM. The other limit would be 16.3640 when the Belgian bank would sell DM and the German bank would buy BF.

It is clear that keeping a currency within its permitted band can at times impose a severe strain on a country. There are a number of funds available within the EMS which a countries can use. *Very short term financing* of unlimited amounts applies for 45 days from the end of the month in which drawn which can be extended for a further three months. *Short term monetary support* is available for three months with an extension of another three months possible. The funds are made available from other central banks according to an agreed formula. The Council of Ministers can make conditional grants for a period of two to five years to any country with balance-of-payments difficulties. The sums available are considerable – about 20 per cent of the official monetary reserves of member-states. The European Commission is also empowered to borrow from capital markets to on-lend to member-states for balance-of-payments purposes.

PROPOSED EUROPEAN MONETARY FUND

The intention is to turn the European Monetary Co-operation Fund (EMCF) into the European Monetary Fund (EMF) with a more enhanced role, but this has yet to occur. The EMCF was created by the

Table 14.3 Grid to illustrate parities and intervention rates

Central bank		Belgian franc	DM	French franc
Belgium	buying		15.6440	6.5184
	parity	1	16	6.6667
	selling		16.3640	6.8184
Germany	buying	0.0611		0.4074
	parity	0.0625	1	0.4167
	selling	0.0639		0.4261
France	buying	0.1467	2.3466	
	parity	0.15	2.4	1
	selling	0.1534	2.4546	

Council of Ministers in April 1973 without any clear task but it has taken over the handling of Official Ecus and manages the currency arrangements and short-term monetary support. The original intention was to turn the EMCF into the EMF by 1981, but reluctance among a number of member countries to giving up some of their 'independence' has so far prevented this happening. The intention is that member countries will deposit their own national currencies to increase official Ecus by 20 per cent. This would be in addition to the 20 per cent of gold and foreign currency reserves they currently swap for Ecus. This could be seen as a stage in the process of turning the Ecu into an international reserve currency since one-half would be on a fiduciary basis.

HOW SUCCESSFUL IS THE EMS?

There is no single view of what people expect from the EMS. Motives for it at the inception were mixed. France was a strong supporter because it was seen as a way of disciplining countries in dealing with balance-of-payments and inflationary problems. Others saw it as a move to strengthen political union, which is generally considered anathema to France. Some hold that Europe will never be one until all its people carry the same money in their pockets or there is a system, like the Scottish and English, where a country's bank-notes circulate on a 1 for 1 basis with each other. Logically monetary integration would seem to lead to such a system but whether this is a political reality at present is conjecture.

The proclaimed objects of EMS are more modest than full integration. They were to reduce exchange rate fluctuations between member countries and to foster mutually helpful economic policies. Those who advocated free exchange rates seem to have been surprised by the swings in exchange rates that have taken place, which have been greater than was generally expected. The relaxation of controls over capital movements has probably contributed to these movements. The EMS does appear to have achieved its aim of damping down currency fluctuations compared, for example, to the UK where the exchange rate with the dollar during the 1980s has swung from bizarre extremes of $2.40 to the pound to $1.04. Europe also has had a better inflation record than the UK. It is impossible to know if the UK would have done better as a full member of the EMS but there is a considerable body of opinion that thinks so.

ECONOMIC AND MONETARY UNION

The 'Commission of the European Communities' (August 1990), on which this section draws, sees the Single European Act, which gives the measures desired for the creation of the internal market without frontiers by 1992, as one part of the process towards a more complete political union. For this to occur, agreement on the objectives of economic, social, foreign policy and security are required.

Monetary union

The stages envisaged by the European Commission are: firstly a convergence of economic performance and a single market. Secondly a move from co-ordination of independent monetary policy to formulation and implementation of a common monetary policy. Finally locked exchanged rates and ultimately a single Euro-currency.

Complete European Monetary Union (EMU) requires the indissoluble locking together of currencies so that they are complete substitutes; or the first best solution, their replacement by a common currency. The section above on 'One currency for Europe' gives some details. A single currency would have a symbolic character and would eliminate the exchange costs in moving from one currency to another. It would prevent the existence of separate capital markets and interest rate differentials between EC countries and be part of the process needed to establish a financial common market.

Locking currencies together, or a single currency, would require management by a new Community monetary institution. The European Commission is suggesting that in 1994 the committee of central bank governors would call itself a council and try and co-ordinate national monetary policies. This council would report, by the end of 1996, to a meeting of EC finance ministers (known as Ecofin). If successful the Ecu could replace national currencies in 1998. This would be followed by the creation of a European Central Bank. The name European System of Central Banks (ESCB), or Eurofed, has been suggested. Pooling of foreign exchange reserves as well as harmonization or unification of monetary policies would be required. To this end the Commission is urging countries now to draw up 'adaptation programmes' to try and achieve convergence of policies and submit these to Ecofin. It is envisaged that its ruling council of the new central bank would be independent of governments or EC institutions. It would include from five to seven full time-directors, and each country's central bank governor. The

Federal Reserve System of the United States is one possible model for the new management body, the German Bundesbank system another. The models differ chiefly in the sharing of responsibility for exchange rate and intervention policy. In the United States the executive is in charge while the German system gives more weight to the central bank.

Economic union

Economic union is less well defined than monetary union as there does not have to be a single economic policy for the Community as there does for monetary union. Within a country, economic policy is conducted at different levels of government and the Commission foresees that 'most economic policy functions would remain the preserve of Member States even in the final stage of economic and monetary union'. What is envisaged is agreement at the Community level on the principal objectives of economic policy and a harmonious development of economic activities to achieve these objectives.

The matters touched on in this section are necessarily tentative, the logic of the EC points towards a federated structure but logic does not always rule where nationalistic matters are concerned. Progress on economic and monetary union involves countries being willing to forgo the possibility of having independent monetary and exchange rate policies. Whether the political will is present to take this step is uncertain at the time this is written.

SUMMARY

The EMS continues the policy of monetary co-operation that has existed in Europe since the introduction of the Marshall Plan after the Second World War. There is a conflict of views between those who see its prime purpose as stabilizing currency fluctuations between members in order to promote trade and those who desire European integration or federation and see the EMS as a necessary step in this direction.

Europe's preference for fixed rather than floating rates is rational given that it is the largest trading bloc in the world with about half of its exports sold to other Community members. The experience of some of the Community members with hyper-inflation also predisposes them to prefer a fixed rate system which obliges member countries to take quick action when their currencies get out of line. It also stops countries trying competitive devaluations.

The declared purpose of the EMS was to achieve monetary stability, help the growth of economies, try and achieve full employment, reduce regional disparities and foster European integration. Inevitably the EMS has disappointed some but it seems to have a good record on currency stability and thus played a part towards the other objectives listed. Regional disparities and unemployment are both high but the EMS by itself is not going to solve these problems; it is unrealistic to judge the system on these criteria.

The mechanics of the Ecu were examined and the uses to which it has been put, both official and private, were given. Similarly the exchange rate and intervention mechanism were examined. The role of the proposed European Monetary Fund was outlined and an assessment made of the success of the EMS. A final section looked briefly at some of the issues if the EC is to achieve closer economic and monetary union.

Chapter 15

The European Community budget

INTRODUCTION

If we take a single country it is usual to find that some areas receive more benefit from government expenditure than they pay out in taxes, others less. Wealth and high-income earners are not evenly spread so tax receipts will differ, and needs will differ, in different areas of a country. As a rule this does not cause problems; individuals have largely come to expect some uniformity of public services and it follows from this that income and expenditures will not be balanced for each sub-region. Sometimes problems do arise: a region with a strong identity may complain about what it see as an injustice either on the tax or expenditure side, or claim that it should have a greater share of resources because of special needs.

When different countries get together for the purpose of harmonization, feelings of injustices about the common budget are likely to be high and not so easily solved as countries' internal budget problems. On the taxation side is the feeling that because of the nature of a tax some countries are paying more than is fair or that a poorer country is paying a disproportionately large amount. This is a difficult argument to judge. What is fair in a country context?

The fair or '*juste*' return is often used about the budget. Applied to the European Community (EC) it is obvious that this would undermine the whole concept of integration and convergence of economies, if it was interpreted to mean each country receiving as much in benefits as it pays in taxes. If it means that poorer countries should not be asked to pay for more than they benefit or that they should pay less it seems reasonable. The trouble with it is the not inconsiderable one of allocation of costs and benefits between nations.

The net contributions that a country pays to the EC or net receipts that it receives provide a measure of budgetary transfer within the Community, but they are subject to reservations. They should not be identified with the costs and benefits of membership in the Community without taking other factors into account. For example:

1 They do not take account of costs and benefits outside the budget. For example, the Cecchini Report (1988) and 'The Economics of 1992' (1988) on the completion of the market by 1992 envisage an increase spread over five years of some 4.50 per cent of the Community's overall national income as a result. Prices are estimated to fall by some 4 to 6 per cent with a gain in employment of 1.8–5 million. These are significant gains. These estimates have been criticized as optimistic but even gains of half this amount would be well worth having. These benefits are largely obtained outside the budget by altering rules, regulations and creating competition. To speed progress the emphasis on common standards for the whole Community has given ground to laws which favour mutual recognition of standards of other Community members. Also, unanimous voting rules have been relaxed so that a weighted majority of 75 per cent can pass some measures. To achieve these gains will require considerable effort and adjustment which may be quite painful in the short run but the benefits seem to clearly outweigh the disadvantages.

2 The attribution of customs duties and levies to a country whose ports pay them can be misleading where the trade is merely entrepot – passing on to another country.

If equalization between countries is an aim then this implies taxation according to ability to pay and a countries ability to pay needs to be judged. Similar considerations apply to expenditures from a common budget: equal expenditures in each country will not achieve much in the way of equalization.

This point can be made in a different way. If countries that are to combine are at roughly the same level of development with approximately similar levels of per capita income, and join in an association from the beginning, then the budgetary problems are not likely to be too severe. The original members of the EC, except Italy, did have reasonably similar structures. The major discrepancy was between highly industrialized West Germany and agricultural France and this was resolved by the Common Agricultural Policy, which has dominated the Community ever since. Italy was helped by loans. The UK opted out of the EC soon after its inception and only came into the system again after it had been established for some years and has had problems as a result.

That these were self-inflicted, by her opting out of the Community, does not help. Provisional arrangements were made for Britain and these have had to be extended which has resulted in some acrimony within the Community. The enlargement of the Community to include Spain, Portugal and Greece poses similar problems. These are Mediterranean countries with different cultures, agriculture and standards of living.

BACKGROUND

The EC makes up a market of about 323 million people – nearly a third more than the population of the United States, which has a land area four times as big. France has the biggest land area, Germany the largest population.

The three major components are the: European Coal and Steel Community (ECSC), set up in 1951; European Atomic Energy Commission (Euratom), set up in 1958; and the European Community, set up in 1973. The first two bodies are associations for a single purpose; the nations are coterminous with those of the EC but they still have some degree of independence, which will not be differentiated here. The EC is a general association not limited to any specific aim.

Defence might be expected to be a key linkage in the EC, both on the military and budget side. In fact it is not. Members of the EC are part of a wider grouping of nations, the North Atlantic Treaty Organization (NATO). It is a matter for conjecture if this will continue to be the case, or for how long this will continue to be the case. The possibility of 'Star Wars' defence systems that could mean the United States defending itself from its own territory, the re-integration of East and West Germany and the easing of the Cold War are causing a reappraisal of defence alliances. Defence is the most frequently quoted example of a public good – defence for one country in the EC means some protection for all members but at present each member spends very different amounts on defence. Past efforts to have common weapon procurement policies have been difficult to obtain. They could yield very substantial economies of scale but there are some very strong vested interests in each country to overcome before they are attainable.

AGRICULTURAL POLICY

Agricultural expenditures account for over 60 per cent of the Community budget, but little of the revenue. Although the cultivated area is only 2 per cent of the cultivated land in the world it produces 25 per cent of world production of milk, about half the world's wine, 16 per cent of beef and veal and 10 per cent of cereals. In evaluating the agricultural policy a difficulty is that individual countries in the Community were spending large sums on agricultural support before the EC started and would probably do so again if the Common Agricultural Policy (CAP) were abandoned. Farming is affected by forces outside the farmers' direct control, such as weather, pests and disease, which means that farmers' income can be subject to large random fluctuations. That is one of the main reasons why governments have long intervened in agricultural markets. Also, the income elasticity of demand for agricultural products is low i.e. as people's income rise they tend to spend a smaller proportion on agricultural products. So, other things being equal, agricultural incomes tend to fall below those in other sectors such as manufacturing and services where income elasticity is higher. By offering some protection to farm incomes governments hope to ensure a vigorous farm sector which will ensure a reasonable food supply. However, farm income can be maintained in ways that are less destructive than the CAP.

CAP has five main objectives as defined in Article 39 of the Treaty of Rome.

The first objective is to increase agricultural productivity by promoting technical progress and by ensuring the rational development of agricultural production and the optimum utilisation of all factors of production, in particular labour.

Agricultural productivity has certainly increased but this has been very uneven between small and large farming units. Three quarters of the producers supply only a quarter of the output. Oversupply of a number of products overshadows the aim of rational development. Labour employed in agriculture continues to decline but this is not necessarily in conflict with the aim of optimum utilization.

The second objective is to ensure thereby 'a fair standard of living of the agricultural community, in particular by increasing the individual earnings of persons engaged in agriculture'. Agricultural earnings have been improved although very unevenly and the gap with other groups of workers remains.

The third CAP objective is 'to stabilize markets'. The main methods adopted are intervention arrangements and price supports. Variable import levies stabilize EC farm prices above world market prices. Prices are guaranteed for any surplus, at the intervention price, although a few quotas have now been introduced to limit the open-ended nature of the farm commitment. The result of guaranteed prices for most of their output has resulted in increasing imbalances between supply and demand with 'wine lakes', 'beef mountains', etc. The intricacies of actual intervention, which varies product by product and includes price supports, 'green' currencies and monetary compensation amounts, are not our concern for an account see El-Agraa (1990 Chapter 9). Green currencies are the values at which support prices in Ecus are translated into national currencies; these may differ significantly from normal currency rates. Monetary compensation amounts are supposed to be a temporary measure, and describe a system of border taxes and subsidies designed to compensate for changing farm incomes when a country alters its exchange rate.

The Court of Auditors Report showed that in the early 1980s budgetary expenditure represented 40–60 per cent of the income of farmers producing tobacco, olive oil and oil seeds, and 10–20 per cent of those producing cereals and dairy products. While it is better to have surpluses, rather than the shortages experienced in the Communist world, these surpluses create additional cost in storage and final disposal and create serious distortions in world markets.

Fourthly, the CAP aims 'to provide certainty of supplies'. This has largely been achieved; the EC is self-sufficient in many food products with surpluses for export. However, much of this has been of a trade-diverting type: more expensive food grown in the Community has been substituted for cheaper imports of food from other parts of the world. Major exporters have been hit, such as Australia (butter and fruit), Canada (wheat), New Zealand (lamb) and Argentina (beef). But more importantly, exports from the EC of highly subsidized food depress world food prices, to the detriment of Third World countries which not only cannot sell their produce to the EC, but find that other markets are being eroded by subsidized EC exports. As a particular example the sugar industry of a number of countries, the Philippines, Brazil, Cuba, and the Dominican Republic, have been devastated by the loss of sales caused by subsidized sugar beet in the EC and the consequent depressed world prices. Other Mediterranean countries fear that with the accession of Spain and Portugal there will be another large trade division of the fruit and vegetables trade away from them. Details of trade diversion can be found in Roarty (1987).

One of the ironies of agriculture is that many Third World countries have followed opposite policies to developed countries. Agriculture has been neglected and prices held down to keep food prices for the growing number of urban dwellers low. The result have been a contributary cause of Third World famines. EC food surpluses have often been justified as providing famine relief for those countries in need. As shown above, there is a strong argument that far from providing relief from famine, the EC farm policy, by depressing world prices, is part of the problem. See for example Snowdon (1985) and Sen (1981).

The fifth CAP objective is 'to ensure supplies to consumers at reasonable prices'. At the start some CAP prices were below world market prices so the consumer was being subsidized; for many years CAP prices have been above world market prices, so the average household in the UK is paying an estimated £16 per week more for food. Another aspect of price support felt by the outside world is the increased instability of world food prices caused by the EC dumping its surpluses.

Additional objectives laid down in 1958 were:

1 to increase farm incomes not only through price support policy but by the encouragement of rural industrialization;
2 to contribute to economic growth by allowing specialization within the Community and eliminating market distortions; and
3 to preserve the family farm.

Listing the objectives of the EC farm policy highlights the incompatibility of many of the proposals and points to one of the reasons for the complexities that have grown up in support policy.

Budget changes in 1988 were, as will be shown, an attempt to limit agricultural spending. There were several reasons, probably the most powerful was that the Community was spending up to the limit of its resources – this is always a powerful prod towards change. Another motive was the concern about the imbalance in spending. If the integration of the market, with its expected substantial benefits, was to be attained by 1992, there was a need to spend more on innovation, research and development, and the energy and transport infrastructure. A further impetus to change came from the United States, which was alarmed at the amount of its agricultural support, so President Reagan announced a return to market prices within 10 years. This may not happen but US farm support has been curtailed even though this has led to many bankrupt farmers and to insolvency of many of the banks which had lent to farmers.

Potentially the most damaging aspect of EC farm subsidies was the part they played in the postponement of the Uraguay round of trade talks of the General Agreement on Tariffs and Trade (GATT), which had been going on for three years and was meant to be concluded at the end of 1990. One of the main reasons for the breakdown of the talks was the

EC refusal to make deep cuts in farm subsidies. The United States and the Cairns Group of 14 major agricultural-exporting countries (Argentina, Australia, Brazil, Canada, Chile, Colombia, Fiji, Hungary, Indonesia, Malaysia, New Zealand, the Philippines, Thailand and Uruguay) asked for a reduction of export subsidies by 90 per cent and a reduction by 75 per cent for other support measures over the next 10 years. The EC originally offered only 30 per cent reductions between 1986 and 1996; half of these had already been made, but has since offered a 30 per cent cut with 1999 as the base year. This still leaves a very large gap to be bridged.

Part of the concern as noted above is the devastation caused to agriculture in developing countries. They find themselves unable to compete with the heavily subsidized food from the developed world. Their agricultural exports face levies, quotas and other barriers in the EC and earn less as world prices are forced down by surpluses placed on the market by developing countries. The International Monetary Fund estimates that the complete elimination of all agricultural subsidies would raise the export earnings of developing countries by about $50 billion. That is about the same as the amount of development aid they received in 1989. Eastern European countries will also find it very hard to switch to free-market policies unless they have access to unfettered world markets for their goods. They need to be able to earn foreign currencies to allow them needed imports.

Developing countries had agreed to opening up their markets in services, if the OECD countries would reduce the annual $250 billion they are estimated to have spent on farm subsidies in 1989. The gains that would result from freer trade have been put by official United States estimates at $4 trillion ($4,000 billion) worldwide over the next 10 years. Failure to reach a compromise risks not only the loss of this substantial benefit but the possibility of mutually destructive trade wars of the kind not seen since the 1930s. A trenchant criticism of EC agricultural policy is to be found in Deutsche Bank Bulletin (March 1991).

A rather different aspect of CAP was brought out by a study by Breckling *et al.* (1987), employing a general equilibrium approach they come to the conclusion that the CAP 'has contributed significantly to the EC's relative economic malaise'. These conclusions were reached because of the adverse effects of agricultural protection on other economic sectors of the EC. Patterns of trade were distorted, terms of trade worsened, unemployment increased in relatively labour-intensive industries and too many resources were diverted to relative inefficient industries. The assumptions of this advanced study may be questioned but that adverse effects will be felt in the rest of the economy is unassailable.

Abrupt change is unlikely because subsidies have largely been *capitalized* in the value of farm land. That is, the price of farm land has risen by the value of the subsidies. It is not enough to point out the obvious absurdities of the CAP. People have made choices, bought farms and equipment etc., on the basis of existing policies; abrupt change, because it will benefit some but harm others, will be bitterly fought by those who see themselves as losers. Although farmers are a small and decreasing part of the labour force, the farm lobby is extremely powerful in most countries, whereas consumer interests are not so well represented. Politicians in Europe do not seem willing to contemplate the same adjustment to land farm prices which have been experienced in the United States. Fuller discussion of the CAP will be found in El-Agraa (1990).

THE COMMUNITY INSTITUTIONS

The Community is often a struggle for power and control of the budget is a way of exercising power. So the budget has often been, and is likely to continue to be, at the centre of many disputes. Disputes may be between member-states and the Community, between parts of the Community, such as the ECSC and the EC, or between major institutions of the Community, such as the Council and the Assembly. The EC is remarkable because whereas most international organizations are financed by contributions from member-states (indeed the Community started in this fashion), it now has its own direct revenue sources. Transfers from member governments are automatic, as agreed by the states, and are not given with the expectation of an exact return.

There are four major institutions intimately connected with budget-making: the Commission, the Council of Ministers, the Assembly and the Court of Auditors. A fifth institution, the Court of Justice, lacks budgetary powers but oversees the inter-relationship between Community decisions and their implementation in individual member-states.

The Commission

The Commission is the guardian of the Treaties, the initiator of policies, the executive organ and it acts as mediator of disputes. It is composed of 17 members, two each from Germany, France, Italy, UK and Spain, one each from the other seven countries. Members are expected to be completely independent of their own national interest in their duties.

The Council of Ministers

This is the legislative organ and has a member from each state, who is either the foreign minister, or in special cases some other such as the agricultural minister, finance minister or prime minister. The Council is the place for trying to reconcile the Community's interests with those of the states. Voting rules are important: some decisions require unanimous consent, others can be settled by either a majority vote or by a qualified majority on a weighted basis. It is the supreme decision-making body in the Community and budget problems have occupied much of its time.

The Assembly

This is the self-named European Parliament; it has a general consultative role. Members are elected by universal suffrage, with seats allocated approximately according to population. There are 518 members, of which the UK, France, Germany and Italy have 81 each.

The Court of Auditors

The Court of Auditors has 12 members, one from each state. Its function is to exercise control over the Community's expenditure and revenue. The Court tries to ensure that the Community gets value for money, and attempts to prevent fraud. The latter is no easy task and the annual reports of the Court of Auditors make fascinating reading and are often highly critical of the practices they find. For example, the Court of Auditors report on the 1987 budget concentrated on agricultural markets and made a special study of export refunds. It concentrated on the beefmeat sector and investigated four states, Britain, Ireland, France and Germany, which account for 80 per cent of the expenditure in this sector. It noted cases where claims were paid although the product was not exported at all, where the product exported was not beef, and where it was not exported to the destination intended.

The Court of Justice

The Court of Justice is not directly concerned with the budget but is an important EC body, as Community law takes precedence over national law. It consists of 13 judges, one from each member country plus one from the larger states on a rota basis, and six advocates-general. It deals with the interpretation, application and development of Community Law. It has jurisdiction between member-states on Community matters, between member-states and the Community institutions and in actions brought by individuals.

HOW THE BUDGET IS DETERMINED

Each of the Community institutions draws up estimates of its expenditures, which are consolidated in a preliminary draft budget by the Commission. The Commission adds its own views, which may include alternative estimates and places it before Council by 1 September of the year before the funds are to be spent.

The Council consults with the Commission and, as appropriate, the other institutions. It adopts the budget by qualified majority and this must be placed before Parliament by 31 October.

Parliament, acting by a majority of members and with two-thirds of the votes cast, can reject the whole budget and ask for a new one. This happened in 1979 and 1984. Otherwise Parliament has 45 days to adopt the budget, make *amendments* or propose *modifications*. Failure to give an opinion to the Council means the draft budget is adopted. If Parliament has proposed changes, the revised draft budget is sent back to the Council. Council has 15 days to prepare its second reading and thereafter Parliament has another 15 days to react. The process of to and fro can continue until agreement is reached.

In this process the Council was for many years the most important body. Parliament could only propose changes, which the Council did not have to accept. In 1970 the Treaty of Luxembourg gave more power to Parliament. In respect of expenditures the Community is obliged to incur under the Treaty or other acts, it is still the case that Parliament, by majority vote can only propose *modifications*. The Council decision, acting by qualified majority, is then binding although it has to notify Parliament of its decision.

In respect of other expenditures Parliament can propose *amendments*. The Council has power to reject amendments by qualified majority, accept them, or modify them. When modified it is returned to Parliament for a second reading when Parliament has the last word unless the subject is the adoption of a new rate. It is now the President of Parliament rather than the President of Council who declares that the budget has been finally adopted. The recent expansion of the budget with most of the increase being given for other than agriculture spending has also given more say to Parliament.

Parliament has also gained some power by what is called 'the Parliament's room for manoeuvre'. This refers to a sum that Parliament can assign as it wishes over and above the amounts put into the draft budget by the Council. This amount is announced by the Commission before the budgetary procedure starts and is calculated by formula.

Since the 1970s a procedure of 'budgetary conciliation' has taken place whereby the Council, before taking decisions on its first or second reading of the budget, receives a delegation from Parliament and likewise the President of the Council takes part in Parliament's work on the budget. These procedures and conciliation meetings have helped to smooth conflict but they have not stopped it completely as the rejection of the budget in 1979 showed. The Council and elected Assembly – Parliament – may often be at odds with each other, hard and fast lines are far from being drawn and the system is evolving with Parliament slowly obtaining a little more power from the Council.

RULES FOR DRAWING UP THE COMMUNITY BUDGETS

The EC has adapted traditional budgetary rules to form five basic principles: those of *unity*, *universality*, *annuality*, *specification* and *budgetary equilibrium*.

The rule of unity

Any official public body must bring together all financial transactions expenditures and income, in a single budget document.

There are two exceptions – the European Development Fund and certain capital operations. Parliament is strongly supporting the Commission in wishing to see these items incorporated, the Council refuses to agree. This formed part of the reason for Parliament's rejecting the budget in 1979.

The rule of universality

This has the same objective as the unity rule; it states that budgetary revenue may not be allocated to particular items of expenditure in advance and that no adjustments between revenue and expenditures may take place. That is netting off one against the other to make the budget seem smaller is not supposed to take place.

The rule of annuality

This is simply stating that the budget should cover a single year. In practice this is sometimes modified to allow carry-overs from one year to another particularly with the budget of the European Coal and Steel Community. The financial year in the Community is the same as the calendar year.

The rule of specification

This rule states that funds should only be spent in ways that have been allocated and not transferred to other headings.

The rule of equilibrium between revenue and expenditure

This rule perhaps surprisingly is enshrined in the EC Treaty. If strictly adhered to it would seem to rule out borrowing. The European Coal and Steel (ECSC) budget however allows balancing over several years.

The reason for the rule seems to be more political than economic: the wish to limit the powers of the Community *vis-à-vis* the member-states. In practice the ECSC had limited borrowing powers from the start to borrow for investment and other specified purposes. Euratom, the atomic energy agency of the Community since 1977, has also had borrowing powers. The EC was only authorized to borrow and lend in 1976. The original impetus came from the oil crises of that time and the wish to help member-states in balance-of-payments difficulties. In 1978 the EC was empowered to raise up to 1 billion Ecus to finance investment projects which contribute to greater convergence and integration of the economic policies of the member-states. These projects can be in energy, industry or infrastructure. The working procedure, both to obtain loan approval and to make loans, is complicated with interactions between the Council, the Commission and Parliament. The limit on borrowing was raised to 14 billion Ecus in 1988.

To sum up the borrowing powers of the EC, the original rule about equilibrium between revenue and expenditure has been breached in a number of ways. However, borrowing to balance the budget is not acceptable. Borrowing powers are laid down for specific purposes and a complicated procedure has to be gone through to establish that the borrowing will be used for the purposes laid down. Before the loan is made further safeguards are applied. Besides the funds available to members under the EMS, the bulk of lending is carried out by the European

Investment Bank (EIB). This was specifically set up to borrow and lend. It was created under the Treaty of Rome at the same time as the EC.

THE EUROPEAN INVESTMENT BANK

The role of the EIB is to grant loans and give guarantees which facilitate the financing of capital investment promoting the balanced development of the Community. Its capital is subscribed by member-states, but the bulk of resources comes from borrowing on capital markets outside the Community where it commands the finest credit ratings. It on-lends the proceeds on a non-profit-making basis. In 1987 the bulk of its 7.8 billion Ecus was for capital investment in the Community's less-favoured regions. This is equivalent to some 20 per cent of the Community budget. It includes lending for the improvement of communications between member-states, protection of the environment, energy policy objectives and the modernization or conversion of business enterprises. About 400 million Ecus is lent to countries outside the Community under the Lomé Conventions. These loans, mainly to former colonially dependent countries, include 12 Mediterranean countries and 66 African, Caribbean and Pacific countries.

EUROPEAN BANK FOR RECONSTRUCTION AND DEVELOPMENT

In April 1991 a new EC institution, the European Bank for Reconstruction and Development (EBRD), was opened in London to channel funds to aid Eastern Europe. While nobody doubts that massive amounts of aid are needed by Eastern Europe – the costs alone of bringing eastern Germany into line with West Germany have been put at £800 billion – doubts were expressed whether the new bank was the right institution to do this. The bank's total budget is 10 billion Ecus (£7 billion), of which 30 per cent will be initially available. Loans are expected to build up gradually over the years. These amounts are small in relation to the need, but the bank's policy is to finance only a small part of any project, so that the 'seed corn' of the bank should bring in several times the amount of its own lending from private sources.

THE COMMUNITY BUDGET

Table 15.1 sets out the Community budget forecasts from 1985 to 1989.
The budget, at 45.42 billion Ecus, looks a large sum but is only about 1 per cent of the GDP of member-states. National budgets are typically

Table 15.1   European Community budget forecasts, 1985–9

Appropriations for payments	1985 %	1986 %	1987 %	1988 %	1989 %
Support for agricultural markets	69	63	63	63	59
Agricultural structure	3	2	3	3	3
Fisheries	(0.5)	(0.5)	(0.6)	–	3
Regional and transport	6	7	7	7	11
Social	6	7	7	6	8
Research, energy, industry, technology etc.	3	2	3	5	4
Refunds to member-states and reserves	4	9	8	8	7
Development co-operation and non-member countries	4	3	3	3	3
Staff and administration	5	5	5	3	3
Other	–	2	1	2	2
Total	100	100	100	100	100
Amount (Ecus million)	28,103	35,174	36,407	43,376	45,425

Revenue	%	%	%	%	%
Agricultural and sugar levies	8	8	9	6	6
Customs duties	29	24	25	22	22
VAT (max. rate 1.4 per cent)	54	66	66	53	58
Financial Contributions	7	1	1	19	–
Available surpluses	–	–	–	–	4.5
Miscellaneous	2	3	–	–	–
GNP-based resource[1]	–	–	–	–	8.7
Total	100	100	100	100	100
Amount (Ecus million)	27,820	34,960	36,105	43,772	44,842

Source: *The Community Budget: The Facts and Figures* (1989) Paris.

Note: 1 The Fourth resource was brought in on 1 February 1989 with effect from 1 January 1988. It is calculated by applying a uniform rate to a base made up of the sum of member-states' GNP.

between 32 and 43 per cent. The top of the table gives expenditures from which it can be seen how unbalanced the Community budget is, with over 60 per cent going to agricultural support or structure. The increase in the size of the budget and apparent drop in agricultural spending in 1985–6 is due to the accession of Greece, Spain and Portugal to the Community, which distorts the continuity of the figures and led to large refunds to member-states. The increase in budget size in 1988 and drop in the share of agricultural spending in 1988–9 is, however, the result of policy change: its significance will be examined shortly. Even after this change agriculture spending, at 62 per cent of the total, takes the lion's share, with only 3 per cent of this devoted to changing agricultural structures and 59 per cent going in straight price supports. The Community spends more than five times on agriculture than it does on its regional and transport policies, which is its next biggest expenditure. Social spending accounts for 8 per cent of the total, refunds to member-states 7 per cent, the remaining headings between 2 and 4 per cent. Actual budget figures of the EC are given either as payment appropriations or commitment appropriations. The former covers expenditure to be actually incurred during the financial year in question which may be in settlement of previous commitments. Commitment appropriations define the ceiling on resources to be pledged in the current year. Figures given in this section are projections.

On the revenue side shown in the bottom half of Table 15.1, levies on agriculture account for only 6 per cent of the total. These are levies charged on agricultural imports from a non-member-state to offset differences in price. Some 58 per cent comes from VAT, 22 per cent from customs duties which arise from the application of the Common External Tariff and will vary according to the differences between world prices and higher EC prices. For the first time in 1989 nearly 9 per cent came from a GNP-based resource, which will be examined.

The EC sources of revenue leave a lot to be desired. Agricultural levies and customs duties are not designed and administered as revenue sources but to provide protection. The revenue is dependent, therefore, on several factors outside the control of the EC, such as world prices and decisions made by GATT. VAT is a less buoyant source of revenue than GDP because some items of expenditure are exempt from VAT.

The EC decided to harmonize on a system of VAT, details of which have been given in Chapter 3. The final incidence of the tax may of course be borne by the ultimate consumer, the producer, the employee or some combination between them.

The amount of VAT is now calculated by applying for all states a 1.4

per cent rate to a uniform VAT base which is estimated from National Income Accounts, with the proviso that the VAT base may not exceed 55 per cent of a country's GNP at market prices. The decision to harmonize indirect tax, not direct taxes such as income tax, was built into the Treaty of Rome (articles 95–9). It is not therefore imposed by the necessity to make VAT contributions to the EC but is a political objective of those whose object is a united Europe, although achievement would greatly simplify the movement of goods between member countries without the necessity to compensate for differing tax regimes. At the present time, as already indicated, all member-states have harmonized by having a VAT and some progress has been made on harmonization of the tax base – the goods subject to VAT – and some progress on the rates of tax but there is a considerable way to go to achieve uniformity. Whether complete harmonization should be the eventual aim is questioned by some who point, for example, to the United States, where local sales taxes are allowed at different rates which allows state prices to vary without serious trade distortions.

THE UK AND THE BUDGET

Paying taxes is always a bone of contention and the EC is no exception to this. There has long existed in the EC agreement on a 'financial mechanism' whereby a member-state would have a lower contribution if certain conditions were met. These conditions were, however, technical and complex which made them more or less inoperable.

In 1979 the UK protested that it had again become a net payer and asked for a review of the current budgetary system to secure an equitable burden. The UK case was that it was inequitable for a country with a GDP below the European average to be a net contributor. The UK case was recognized and a system of rebates operated which meant each budget became a debate over the size of the rebate. A more permanent solution was agreed at Fontainebleau in June 1984, which set the UK refund at 1 billion Ecus for 1984, and for subsequent years at 66 per cent of the difference between what it pays in VAT and what it receives from the Community budget. In return the UK agreed to the ceiling on VAT contributions being raised to 1.4 per cent. The agreement also allowed 'any member-state sustaining a budgetary burden which is excessive in relation to its relative prosperity may benefit from a correction at the appropriate time'.

In 1986 and subsequent years the VAT ceiling of 1.4 per cent was reached largely because the dollar value fell, thus appreciating the Ecu and increasing the cost of EC export subsidies. Exports also fell, increasing the cost of storage of surpluses and customs duties and agricultural levies were eroded as a result of international agreement reached through the GATT. These budget difficulties were temporarily hidden away by deferring certain payments until the following year.

These difficulties helped to provide the catalyst for more fundamental reforms covering the period 1988–92. The main reforms were:

1 The VAT base was adjusted to allow for the differences in the proportion of members' GNP accounted for by consumption. VAT, as stated, is applied to a uniform VAT base and now may not exceed 55 per cent of its GNP at market prices. This corrective is designed to be neutral to the UK, i.e. a continuation of the Fontainebleau system of rebate in a different form. The other states finance this in proportion to their GNP (not their VAT) with Germany as the richest having a one-third reduction, and Spain and Portugal receiving some transi- tional reduction. The 55 per cent rule should also benefit Ireland, Luxembourg and Portugal.
2 A fourth resource was introduced based on a member-state's GNP; taken as the most representative indicator of a country's economic activity. It thus helps align payment more closely to a country's ability to pay. This fourth resource is a balancing item calculated by applying to the base of members' GNP at market prices a rate to be determined during the budgetary procedure in the light of the yield of all other categories of expenditure.
3 Budget resources were enlarged and budget payments set at 1.2 per cent of total Community Gross National Product. This is equivalent to an increase in VAT from 1.4 to 1.9–2.0 per cent.

Table 15.2 shows this is an increase in budget of 16.5 per cent from 45.3 billion Ecus in 1988 to 52.8 billion Ecus by 1992. The 1987 figure had been 36.1 billion Ecus. However, agricultural spending is projected to increase only 7.6 per cent, and structural spending by 72.6 per cent. Compulsory expenditure, over which Parliament has less control, stays virtually the same over this period while non-compulsory expenditures, over which it does exercise most control, should increase by 67 per cent.

The agreement was thus reached that this enlarged budget should largely be spent on areas outside agriculture. The limit on the change in agricultural spending should not exceed 74 per cent of the annual growth of Community GNP. The hope is that a number of stabilizers, production ceilings, co-responsibility levies and a set aside of farm land will enable agricultural spending to stabilize. An early warning system

Table 15.2   EC budget projections to 1992: Ecu million (1988 prices)

	1988	*1992*	*% change*
Total	45,303	52,800	16.5
EAGGF	27,500	29,600	7.6
Structural	7,790	13,450	72.6
Compulsory	33,698	33,400	−0.1
Non-compulsory	11,605	19,400	67.0

Source: The Community Budget: The Facts and Figures 1989. Paris.

Notes: Total budget is up by 16.5 per cent in 1988 prices. Agriculture only increases by 7.6 whereas structural policy is up by 72.6 per cent. Non-compulsory expenditure is up by 67 per cent.

has been introduced. The Commission will if necessary present proposals to the Council to alter stabilizers within two months of the warning.

Stabilizers differ in detail from product to product but their intention is to end the unlimited financial guarantee for agricultural production. As an example, the guarantee threshold for wheat was set at 160 million tons per annum. If production exceeds this level, producers pay an extra co-responsibility levy. If this is not sufficient to keep expenditure within budgetary limits, the minimum guaranteed price is reduced by 3 per cent the following year.

As noted, the budget agreement covered the period up to 1992 and there will no doubt be extended discussion about the shape and content of the budget to follow this period. To this is added the developments in Eastern Europe which are already causing changes. The integration of East and West Germany will create considerable budgetary prob- lems. The single market and the debate about the level of agricultural subsidies already noted will add further to the difficulties of reaching satisfactory budgetary decisions.

SUMMARY

The introduction and background sections gave information to put the budget in context. The EC is, as yet, neither a federation nor a state; it does, however, have some sovereignty such as pre-eminence of European law over national law and in the financing of its budget. The name Community seems a good one to describe a unique grouping of countries. The EC is clearly in transition, its ultimate destination may be some form of federated system, but at the stage this cannot be said with certainty. The CAP was examined and some of its virtues and drawbacks outlined.

The Commission, the Council of Ministers and the Assembly or Parliament, and the Court of Auditors were outlined as a necessary part of understanding how the budget is determined. The role of the European Investment Bank was noted.

Tables were presented showing the budget and in particular the important budget changes implemented in 1988. Although the budget looms large in discussion of Community affairs, it represents spending of only about 1 per cent of the GDP of member-states. The budget is extremely unbalanced, with over 60 per cent of expenditure being allocated to agriculture but with agriculture contributing only 6 per cent of revenue.

With the completion of the single market proposed for 1992, acting as a catalyst, together with the budget ceiling being reached reform was initiated in 1988. It remains to be seen if the limit on farm spending can stick as this is subject to factors such as world prices, which are outside the control of the EC. The main source of revenue comes from VAT (58 per cent of the total) and customs and excise duties (22 per cent), but an important new source related to GNP was introduced in 1989. The position of the UK was outlined because this has played a part in the budgetary reforms. Budgetary agreement covered the period up to 1992 and extended discussion about the shape and content of the budget after this period is likely.

Notes

3 TAXATION

1 Tax avoidance is, not unexpectedly, still thriving. It was reported in the *Sunday Times* 21 October 1990, that because of a loophole in the UK Finance Act 1981 relating to capital gains the Treasury has been losing substantial amounts of revenue. The loophole involves setting up offshore trusts. A figure of losses up to £1 billion a year was mentioned. As an illustration the paper claimed that Richard Branson, who sold 25 per cent of his music business to a Japanese buyer in 1989, increased his family fortune by £46 million. By setting up Jersey-based trusts instead of having a tax bill of some £18 million (40 per cent of £46 million) he paid no tax.

Vic Washtell, a tax partner with Touche Ross, was quoted as saying: 'Yes, it's true there is one tax for the rich and another for the poor, what I do is beyond the realms of the man in the street.'

Serious concern was expressed in Parliament and an announcement by the Treasury was promised, but such a promise was also made in 1988 by Norman Lamont, the then secretary to the Treasury, and nothing has been heard of it since. The government has however devoted considerable resources to tracking down social security cheats who have defrauded the revenue of a few hundred million pounds.

2 Reported in the *Independent*, 17 October 1990.

4 NATIONAL DEBT AND THE PUBLIC SECTOR BORROWING REQUIREMENT

1 The reader interested in pursuing this topic to metaphysical heights is referred to a collection of writings (Ferguson 1964).

5 AIMS AND PRINCIPLES OF PUBLIC FINANCE

1 I am indebted to Professor A.B. Atkinson for this point.

8 WEALTH

1 Rights above ground can be important in a number of ways. For example, citizens in the United States were able to prevent Concorde flying supersonically over the country because they had rights above ground they owned. Airlines feared a large number of court actions from those disturbed by the sonic boom. Rights to sunlight, i.e. not to have sunlight blocked by adjacent buildings, can be important in countries where solar power is widespread.

2 He who held land as tenant of the royal lord could himself become lord by granting the land to another. The primary rung in the feudal tenurial ladder was the tenant in actual possession of the tenement, the tenant in dominico. The ultimate rung was the king, the one man in all the realm who was never tenant. Between the two extremes, the rungs were either an ascending series of lordships or a descending series of tenures, according to the view taken. There is no land unowned in all England. Land can be without a tenant, where he who is in possession is the king; but land without a lord there cannot be – *nulle terre sans seigneur* (see Denman 1958: 80).

10 INTRODUCTION TO POLICY CONSIDERATIONS

1 Differences may be small in two senses: firstly, the change makes no perceptible difference to behaviour; secondly, although the change makes a large difference, the numbers affected by the change are so small, or the amount of money involved is so small, as to make no significant change in overall saving, e.g. if only 1,000 people are affected by a change, then even though it is assumed they save the whole of the amount involved, this will have an insignificant effect on total savings. Any reactions of those who are not directly affected by the change must also be considered.

2 As Shackle writes:

> When we have no theory about economic affairs, no state of those affairs and no temporally succession of states seems inconceivable. A theory restricts the conceivable states and succession of states to those in which the relations between quantifiable things in the economy conform to some specified rules. Theories differ from each other in the list of quantifiable (not necessarily measurable) things to be considered, and in the precise character of the rules about their interrelation.
>
> (1961: 209)

12 THE MIX OF CENTRALIZED, LOCAL AND REGIONAL GOVERNMENT

1 On this crucial issue the Green Paper says: 'The Government will, therefore, as a matter of urgency, explore alternative methods with the local authority associations'. The suggestions made vary from 'common-sense (agreement) about the main factors which determine spending needs' to identifying the main client groups (e.g. schoolchildren, old people) and the national average

expenditure per person within each group. Finally, a longer-term approach is mentioned based on detailed analysis of the composition of expenditure on each of a large number of individual operations which go to make up each main service.

References

Alesina, A. (April 1989) 'Politics and Business Cycles in Industrial Democracies', *Economic Policy*, No.8.

Arrow, K.J. (1963) *Social Choice and Individual Values*, Yale University Press, New Haven.

Ashworth, M., Hills, J. and Morris, N. (1984) *Public Finances in Perspective*, Institute for Fiscal Studies, London.

Atkinson, A.B. (1989) *Poverty and Social Security*, Harvester Wheatsheaf, Brighton.

Atkinson, A.B. and Stiglitz, J.E. (1980) *Lectures on Public Economics* McGraw-Hill, New York.

Bank of England Quarterly Bulletins

—— (June 1977) 'Financial Forecasts in the United Kingdom', vol.17, no.2.

—— (June 1979) 'Intervention Arrangements in the European Monetary System', vol. 19, no.2.

—— (November 1988) 'Ecu Financial Activity' vol. 28, no.2.

—— (February 1991) 'The Exchange Rate Mechanism of the European Monetary System – A Review of the Literature'.

—— (February 1991) 'Housing Finance – An International Perspective'.

Bannock, G. (1990) *Taxation in the European Community: the small business perspective*. Paul Chapman London.

Barnett W.A. and Choi S.S. (eds) (1989) 'A comparison between the conventional econometric approach to structural inference and the nonparametric chaotic attractor approach', in *Economic Complexity Chaos, Sunspots, Bubbles and Nonlinearity*, Cambridge University Press, Cambridge.

Blinder, A.S., Solow, R.M., Break, G.F., Steiner, P.O., and Netzer, D. (1974) *The Economics of Public Finance*, The Brookings Institute, Washington, DC.

Boreham, A.J. and Semple, M. (1976), 'Future Developments of Work in the Government Statistical Service on the Distribution and Redistribution of Household Income', in A.B. Atkinson (ed.) *The Personal Distribution of Incomes*, Allen & Unwin, London.

Bracewell-Milnes, B. (1982) *Land and Heritage: The Public Interest in Personal Ownership*, Hobart Paper 93, Institute of Economic Affairs, London.

—— (1989a) *Capital Gains Tax: Reform Through Abolition*, IEA Inquiry, no.12, Institute of Economic Affairs, London.

—— (1989b) *The Wealth of Giving Every One in His Inheritance,* IEA Monograph no.43, Institute of Economic Affairs, London.

Breckling, J. *et al.* (1987) *Effects of EC Agricultural Policies: A general equilibrium approach,* Bureau of Agricultural Research, Canberra.

Bretton, A. (1974) *The Economic Theory of Representative Government,* Aldine, Chicago.

Bronfenbrenner, M. and Holzman, F.D. (1963) 'Survey of Inflation Theory', *American Economic Review,* vol. 53, no. 4.

Brown, C. (1988) 'Will the 1988 Income Tax Cuts either Increase Incentives or Raise More Revenue?' *Fiscal Studies,* vol. 9, no. 4.

Brown, C. and Sandford, C. (1991) 'Taxes and Incentives: the Effects of the 1988 Cuts', Institute for Public Policy Research, London.

Buchanan, J.M. (1950), 'Federalism and Fiscal Equity', *American Economic Review,* 583–600; reprinted in R.A. Musgrave and C. Shoup (eds) *Readings in the Economics of Taxation.*

—— (1977) *Democracy in Deficit: The Political Legacy of Lord Keynes,* Academic Press, New York and London.

Buchanan, J.M., Burton, J. and Wagner, R.E. (1978) *The Consequences of Mr. Keynes,* Hobart Paper 78, Institute of Economic Affairs, London.

Buchanan, J.M. and Tullock, G. (1962), *The Calculus of Consent,* University of Michigan Press, Ann Arbor.

Buiter, W.H. (1985) 'A guide to Public Sector Debt and Deficits', *Economic Policy,* November, no. 1.

Cardarelli, A. and Michele del Guidice, M. (1988) in Joseph A. Pechman (ed.) *World Tax Reform a Progress Report,* Brookings Institution, Washington.

Cecchini, P. (ed.) (1988) *The European Challenge,* Gower & Wildwood House, London.

Coles, J.L. and Hammond, P.J. (1986) 'Walrasian Equilibrium without Survival: Exis- tence, Efficiency and Remedial Policy' Stanford University Institute for Mathematical Studies in the Social Sciences, Economics Technical Report no.483; presented at the 5th World Congress of the Econometrics Society, Boston.

Commission of the European Communities (1989) *Program for Research and Actions on the Development of the Labour Market. Trends and Distribution of Incomes: An Overview,* Luxembourg.

—— (1990) *Economic and Monetary Union,* Luxembourg.

Committee for Economic Development (1972) *Taxes and the Budget: A Program for Prosperity in a Free Economy,* New York.

Committee of Inquiry on the Impact of Rates on Households (1965), *Report,* Cmnd 2582, HMSO, London.

Coopers and Lybrand *Tax Harmonisation and 1992 in the European Community.* Financial Times Business Information, 1988.

Dalton, H. (1959) *The Inequality of Incomes,* Routledge & Kegan Paul, London.

Denman, D.R. (1958) *Origins of Ownership,* Allen and Unwin, London.

Deutsche Bank Bulletin, (March 1991) 'The Uruguay Round Must Not Fail', Deutsche Bank AG, Frankfurt.

Devereux, M. and Pearson, M. (1989) 'Corporate Tax Harmonisation and Economic Efficiency', October, series no. 35, Institute for Fiscal Studies, London.

Devereux, M. and Pearson, M. (1990) '*Harmonising Corporate Taxes in Europe*', *Fiscal Studies*, vol. 1, February.

Dialogue no.3 (1989) US Information Agency, Washington.

Dilnot, A. and Kell, M. (1988) 'Top-rate Tax cuts and Incentives', *Fiscal Studies*, vol. 9, no. 4.

Dilnot, A. and Webb, S. (1988) 'The 1988 Social Security Reforms', *Fiscal Studies*, vol. 9, no. 3.

Dosser, D. (1961), 'Tax Incidence and Growth', *Economic Journal*, vol. 71, 572–91.

Dow, J.C.R. (1964) *The Management of the British Economy, 1945–60*, Cambridge University Press, Cambridge.

Downs, A. (1956) *An Economic Theory of Democracy*, Harper & Row, New York.

Downs, A. (1967) *Inside Bureaucracy*, Little, Brown & Co., Boston.

Drees, W., Jr. (1967) *Papers and Proceedings of the Twenty-Second Session of the International Institute of Public Finance*, International Institute of Public Finance, Washington.

Earl, P.E. (1990) 'Economics and Psychology: A Survey', *Economic Journal*, vol. 100, no. 402, 718–755.

Economic and Monetary Union (August 1990) Commission of the European Communities.

Economic Trends (May 1990) 'The effects of taxes and benefits on household income 1987', HMSO, London.

Economies in Transition Structural Adjustments in OECD Countries (1989), OECD, Paris.

ECSC-EEC-EAEC (1989) 'Comparative Tables of the Social Security Schemes in the member states of the European Communities' (15th edn), Luxembourg.

El-Agraa, A.M. (ed.) (1990) *Economics of the European Community*, Philip Allan.

Emerson, M., Aujean, M., Catinat, M., Gaybet, P., and Jacquemin, A. (1988) *The Economics of 1992*, Oxford University Press, London.

European Economy (July 1979).

Expert Committee on Compensation and Betterment (1942), Report, Cmnd 6386, HMSO, London.

Ferguson, J.M. (ed.)(1964) *Public Debt and Future Generations*, University of North Carolina Press, Chapel Hill.

Fleming M.C. and Nellis J.G. (1990) 'The Rise and Fall of House Prices: Causes, Consequences and Prospects' *National Westminster Bank Quarterly Review*, November, London.

Fry, V. and Pashardes, P. (1988) *Changing Patterns of Smoking: Are there economic causes?*, Institute of Fiscal Studies Report Series no. 30, London.

Friedman, M. (1957) '*A Theory of the Consumption Function*', University of Chicago Press, Chicago.

Friedman, M. (1959) 'A Monetary and Fiscal Framework for Economic Stability', in *Essays in Positive Economics*, University of Chicago Press, Chicago.

Friedman, M. (1976) 'The line we dare not cross, the fragility of freedom at 60%', *Encounter*, no.47.

Frey, B.S. (1978) *Modern Political Economy*, Martin Robertson, Oxford.

George, H. (1879) in (1954) *Progress and Poverty*, R. Schalkenbach Foundation, New York.

Gerelle, E. and Bernardi, L. (1988) in J. Peckman (ed.) *World Tax Reform a Progress Report*, Brookings Institute, Washington D.C.

Gillespie, W.I. (1966) 'The Incidence of Taxes and Public Expenditure in the Canadian Economy', study no.2 for the Canadian Royal Commission on Taxation, Queen's Printer, Ottawa, Canada.

Gleick, J. (1987) *Chaos: Making a New Science*, Viking Press, New York.

Goodwin, R.M. (1990) *Chaotic Economic Dynamics*, Clarendon Press, Oxford.

Gowland, D. and James, S. (1990) 'Macroeconomic Policy' in P. Curren (ed.) *Understanding the UK Economy*, Macmillan, London.

Green Paper on *The Future of Local Government Finance* (1977) Cmnd 6813, HMSO, London.

Grumbkow, J. and Warneryd, K.E. (1986) 'Does the tax system ruin motivation to seek advancement?' *Journal of Economic Psychology*, vol.7, 221–43.

Hammond, P.J. (1990) 'Theoretical Progress in Public Economics: A Provocative Assessment', *Oxford Economic Papers*, no. 1, vol. 42.

Harbury, C.D. and Hitchens, D.M.W.N. (1979) *Inheritance and Wealth Inequality in Britain*, George Allen and Unwin, London.

Heald, D.A. (1975) 'Financing Devolution', *National Westminster Bank Quarterly Review*, November, London.

Hibbs, D. (1977) 'Political Parties and Macroeconomic Policy' *The American Political Science Review*, no. 4, 4 December, 1467–87.

Hildersley, S.H.H. and Nottage, R. (1968), *Sources of Local Revenue*, Royal Institute of Public Administration, London. A paper of the same title appears in *Local Government Finance* (1973), Proceedings of a Conference, Institute for Fiscal Studies, London.

Hockley, G.C. and Harbour, G. (1982) 'People's Choice: public spending, taxation and local rates', *Public Money* vol. 1, no. 4. 11–14.

Hockley, G.C. and Harbour, G. (1983) 'Revealed Preferences Between Public Expenditures and Taxation Cuts: Public Sector Choice', *Journal of Public Economics*, 387–99.

Hockman, H.M. and Rodgers, J.D. (1969), 'Pareto Optimal Redistribution', *American Economic Review*, vol. 59, September.

Holtham, H. and Perrin, L. (1986), *Public Sector Accounting and Financial Control* (2nd ed) Van Nostrand Reinhold (UK).

Hopkin, W.A.B. and Godley, W.A.H. (1965) 'An Analysis of Tax Changes', *National Institute Economic Review*, no.32.

House of Commons Social Security Committee (1991), 'Low Income Statistics: Households Below Average Income 1988'; Social Security Committee, First Report, HMSO.

Inflation Accounting Committee (1975) (Sandilands Report), Cmnd 6225, HMSO, London.

Jackson, P.M. (1982) *The Political Economy of Bureaucracy*, Philip Allan, Oxford.

Jenkins, N.P. and Buchanan, J.M. (1951) *Journal of Political Economy*, August, 353–9.

Jenkins, S.P. (1991) 'Income Inequality and Living Standards: Changes in the 1970s and 1980s', *Fiscal Studies*, vol. 12, no. 1.

Johnson, H.G. (1967) *Essays in Monetary Economics*, Allen & Unwin, London.

Johnson, P. and Stark, G. (1989a) *Taxation and Social Security 1979–1989: The Impact on Household Incomes*, Institute of Fiscal Studies, London.

Johnson, P. and Stark, G. (1989b) 'Ten years of Mrs Thatcher: the distributional consequences', *Fiscal Studies*, vol. 10, no. 2.

Kaldor, N. (1955) *An Expenditure Tax*, Allen & Unwin, London.

Kay, J.A. (1985) 'Is Complexity in Taxation Inevitable', University College Cardiff Press.

Kay, J.A. (March 1990) 'Tax Policy: A Survey', *Economic Journal*, vol. 100, no. 399.

Keynes, J.M. (1926) 'The End of Laisser-Faire', in (1972) *The Collected Writings of John Maynard Keynes, Vol IX, Essays in Persuasion*, Macmillan, London.

Keynes, J.M. (1936) 'The General Theory of Employment, Interest and Money', in (1972) *The Collected Writings of John Maynard Keynes, Vol VII, Essays in Persuasion*, Macmillan, London.

Kogan, M. (1973) *Comment on Niskanen's 'Bureaucracy: Servant or Master?'*, Institute of Economic Affairs, London.

Kydland, F. and Prescott, E. (1977) 'The Inconsistency of Optimal Plans', *Journal of Political Economy*, vol. 85, no. 3.

Laidler, D. and Parkin, J.M. (1975), 'Inflation – A Survey', *Economic Journal* December.

Land Commission (1965), White Paper, Cmnd 2771, HMSO, London.

Leape J. (1990) 'The impossibility of perfect neutrality: fundamental isues in tax reform', *Fiscal Studies*, vol. 11, no. 2.

Lee, C., Pearson, M., and Smith, S. (1988) *Fiscal Harmonisation: an Analysis of the European Commission's Proposals*, The Institute of Fiscal Studies, London. Report Series no.28.

Levitt M.S. and Joyce, M.A.S. 'Public Expenditure: Trends and Prospects', with comment by Jackson, P.M., in M.S. Levitt (ed.) *New Priorities in Public Spending*, Gower Press, London.

Local Government Finance (The Layfield Report) (May 1976), Cmnd 6453, HMSO, London.

Lund, P.J. (1975), 'The Econometric Assessment of Investment Incentives', Department of Industry, Proceedings of a Conference, in *The Economics of Industrial Subsidies*, HMSO, London.

Lynn, J.H. (1964) *Studies of the Royal Commission on Taxation. No. 23: Federal-Provision Fiscal Relations*, Ottawa.

MacRae, D. (1977), 'A Political Model of the Business Cycle', *Journal of Political Economy*, vol. 85.

Meade, J.E. (1972), 'Poverty in the welfare state', *Oxford Economic Papers*, vol. 24, 289–326.

Meade, J.E. (1977) *Committee on Taxation*, Institute for Fiscal Studies, London.

Meade, J.E. (1978) *The Structure and Reform of Direct Taxation*, Institute of Fiscal Studies, London.

Mirrlees, J.A. (1977) 'Labour Supply Behaviour and Optimal Taxes' in *Fiscal Policy and Labour Supply*, Institute of Fiscal Studies, London.

Mooney, G. (1978) 'Human Life and Suffering' in D. Pearce (ed.) *The Valuation of Social Cost*, Allen and Unwin, London.

Musgrave, R.A. (1959) *The Theory of Public Finance*, McGraw-Hill, New York.

—— (1961) 'Fiscal Theory of Political Federalism', in *Public Finances: Needs, Sources and Utilization*, Conference Report of the National Bureau of Economic Research, Princeton University Press.

Musgrave, R.A. and Musgrave, P.B. (1989) *Public Finance in Theory and Practice* (5th Ed.) McGraw-Hill, New York.

Negative Income Tax, OECD, Paris 1974.

Nicholson, J.L. and Britton, A.J.C. (1976), 'The Redistribution of Income', in A.B. Atkinson (ed.) *The Personal Distribution of Incomes*, Allen & Unwin, London.

Niskanen, W. (1971) *Bureaucracy and Representative Government*, Aldine, Chicago.

Nordhaus, W.D. (1975) 'The Political Business Cycle,' *Review of Economic Studies*, vol.42.

Nozick, R. (1974) *Anarchy, State and Utopia*, Basil Blackwell, Oxford.

Oates, W.E. (1968) 'The Theory of Public Finances in a Federal System', *Canadian Journal of Economics*, vol.1.

—— (1972), *Fiscal Federalism*, Harcourt Brace Jovanovich, New York.

OECD (1984) 'Tax Expenditures: A Review of the Issues and Country Practices', OECD, Paris.

—— (1986) 'Personal Income Tax Systems under Changing Economic Conditions', Report by the Committee in Fiscal Affairs, OECD, Paris.

—— (1987) 'The Control and Management of Government Expenditure', OECD Paris.

—— (1988) *The Taxation on Fringe Benefits*, OECD, Paris.

Othick, F. (1973) 'Rating Valuation', paper in *Proceedings of a Conference on Local Government Finance*, Institute of Fiscal Studies Publication, No. 10, Institute of Fiscal Studies, London.

Parker, H. (1989) *Instead of the Dole*, Routledge, London.

Pashardes, P. (1988) 'Changing Patterns of Smoking: are there Economic Causes?', Institute of Fiscal Studies, Report Series no. 30, Institute of Fiscal Studies, London.

Peacock, A.T. (1974), 'The Treatment of Government Expenditure in Studies of Income Distribution', in W.L. Smith and J.M. Culbertson (eds) *Public Finance and Stabilization Policy: Essays in Honour of Richard Musgrave*, North-Holland, Amsterdam.

Peacock, A.T. and Shannon, R. (1968), 'The Welfare State and the Redistribution of Income', *Westminster Bank Review*, London.

Peacock, A. T. and Wiseman, J. (1961) *The Growth of Public Expenditures in the United Kingdom*, Oxford University Press, London.

Pearson, M. and Smith, S. (1988) 'Issues in Indirect Taxation', *Fiscal Studies*, vol. 9, no. 4.

Pechman, J.A. (1988) *World Tax Reform a Progress Report*, The Brookings Institution, Washington, D.C.

Platt, C.J. (1985), *Tax Systems of Western Europe: a guide for business and the professions*, (3rd edn), Gower, London.

Polinsky, A.M. (1973), 'A Note on the Measurement of Incidence', *Public Finance Quarterly*, vol. 1, 219–30.

Prest, A.R. (1968), 'The Budget and Interpersonal Distribution', *Public Finance*, vol.XXIII, nos 1–2.

Ramsey, J.B (1977) *Economic Forecasting, Models or Markets*, Hobart Paper 74, Institute of Economic Affairs, London.

Rawls, J. (1971) *A Theory of Justice*, Oxford University Press, London.

Report of the Canadian Royal Commission on Taxation (1966), Queen's Printer, Ottawa.

Report of Fiscal and Financial Committee (1963) Neumark Report, Commission of the European Communities, Eurostat, Luxembourg.

Report on Social Developments Year 1988 (1990) Commission of the European Communities, Eurostat, Luxembourg.

Roarty, M.J. (1987), 'The Impact of the Common Agricultural Policy on Agricultural Trade and Development', *National Westminster Bank Quarterly Review*, London.

Royal Commission on the Constitution 1969–73 (1973) *Report*, vols 1 and 2, Cmnd 5460 and 5460-1, HMSO, London.

—— (1973a), in D. Dawson *Research Paper 9*, HMSO, London.

—— (1973b), in D.N. King *Research Paper 10*, HMSO, London.

Royal Commission on the Distribution of Income and Wealth (1979) *Report no.8*, HMSO, London.

Royal Commission on the Taxation of Profits and Income (1955) *Final Report*, HMSO, London.

Sandford, C., Godwin, M., and Hardwick, P. (1989) *Administrative and Compliance Costs of Taxation*, Fiscal Publications, Bath.

Sen, A. (1981) *Poverty and Famines: An Essay on Entitlements and Deprivation*, Clavendon Press, Oxford.

Shackle, G.L.S. (1961), 'Recent Theories Concerning the Nature and Role of Interest', *Economic Journal*.

Shackleton, M. (1990), *Financing the European Community*, Royal Institute of Economic Affairs, London.

Shaw, G.K. (1984) *Rational Expectations: an Elementary Exposition.* Wheatsheaf, Brighton.

Smeeding T.M., O'Higgins, M. and Rainwater, L. (1990) *Poverty, Inequality and Income Distribution in Comparative Perspective.* The Luxembourg Income Study, Harvester/Wheatsheaf, Brighton.

Smith, Adam. (1976) *The Wealth of Nations*, Oxford University Press, Oxford, eds Campbell, Skinner and Todd. First published 1776.

Snowdon, B. (1985) 'The Political Economy of the Ethiopian Famine', *National Westminster Bank Review*, London.

Starrett, D.A. (1988) 'Effects of Taxes on Saving', in H.J. Aaron (ed.) *Uneasy Compromise Problems of a Hybrid Income-Consumption Tax*, The Brookings Institution, Washington.

Steiner, P.O. (1961) *Monopoly and Competition in TV: Some Policy Issues*, The Manchester School, Manchester.

Stern, N.H. (1976) 'On the Specification of Models of Optimum Income Taxation', *Journal of Public Economics*, 161–2.

Stewart, I. (1989) *Does God Play Dice: The New Mathematics of Chaos*, Basil Blackwell and Penguin, Oxford and Harmondsworth.

The Community Budget: The Facts and Figures 1989 (1990) Office for Official Publications of the European Communities, Luxembourg.

'The economics of 1992', *European Economy*, no 35 (March 1988). Office for Official Publications of the European Communities, Luxembourg.

The ECU (June 1987), European Documentation, Periodical 5, Luxembourg.

The European Financial Common Market (June 1989), European Documentation, Periodical 4, Luxembourg.

The Perception of Poverty in Europe in 1989. Poverty 3, March 1990. A survey Commission of the European Communities, Brussels.

The Treasury Department Report to the President (1984) *Tax Reform for Fairness, Simplicity and Economic Growth*, Office of the Secretary Department of the Treasury, Washington.

Tiebout, C.M. (1961) 'An Economic Theory of Fiscal Decentralization', in *Public Finances: Needs, Sources and Utilization*, National Bureau of Economic Research, Princeton University Press.

Townsend, P. (1974) 'Poverty as Relative Deprivation: Resources and Style of Living', in D. Wedderburn (ed.) *Poverty, Inequality and Class Structure*, Cambridge University Press.

Tullock, G. (1965) *The Politics of Bureaucracy*, Public Affairs Press, Washington.

—— (1976) *The Vote Motive*, Institute of Economic Affairs, London.

Uthwatt Committee (1942) *Expert Committee on Compensation and Betterment*, HMSO, London.

United Kingdom Green Paper 'Proposals for a Tax Credit System' Cmnd 5116, 1972, and the Reports and Evidence of the Select Committee on Tax Credit, 1973.

United Kingdom National Accounts (1989) HMSO, London.

Vickrey, W. (1974) *Agenda for Progressive Taxation*, Ronald Press, New York.

Wagner, A. (1890) *Finanzweissenschaft* 3rd edn, Leipzig.

Williams, Lady R. (1943) *Something to Look Forward To*, MacDonald, London.

Country index

Name index

Alesina, A. 38, 40, 169
Arrow, K.J. 37
Ashworth, M. 66
Atkinson, A.B. 84, 108, 137–8, 255
Aujean, M. 213

Bannock, G. 62
Barnett, W.A. 182
Bernardi, L. 261
Blinder, A.S. 158, 176
Boreham, A.J. 111
Bracewell-Milnes, B. 129
Break, G.F. 158, 176
Breckling, J. et al. 242
Bretton, A. 35
Britton, A.J.C. 111
Bronfenbrenner, M. 160
Brown, C. 165
Buchanan, J.M. 35, 37, 39, 201–2
Butter, W.H. 66, 72

Cardarelli, A. 217
Catinat, M. 260
Cecchini, P. 213
Choi, S.S. 182
Coles, J.L. 5
Coopers and Lybrand 217
Dalton, H. 18
Del Guidice, M. 217
Denman, D.R. 256
Devereux, M. 213
Dilnot, A. 137, 165
Dosser, D. 109
Dow, J.C.R. 153–4

Downs, A. 35
Drees, W, Jr. 15

Earl, P.E. 165
El-Agraa, A.M. 240, 243
Emerson, M. 213

Ferguson, J.M. 127, 255
Fleming, M.C. 127
Frey, B.S. 38
Friedman, M. 12, 153, 168, 176
Fry, V. 60

Gaybet, P. 213
George, H. 122
Gerelle, E. 261
Gillespie, W.I. 111
Gleick, J. 182
Goodwin, M. 63
Goodwin, R.M. 182
Gowland, D. 167
Grumbkow, J. 261

Hammond, P.J. 5
Harbour, G. 129
Harbury, C.D. 120
Hardwick, P. 63
Heald, D.A. 24
Hibbs, D. 261
Hildersley, S.H.H. 191–2
Hills, J. 66
Hitchens, D.M.W.N. 120
Hockley, G.C. 129
Hockman, H.M. 20

Subject index